BRIAN BLESSED

ABSOLUTE PANDEMONIUM

MY LOUDER THAN LIFE STORY

Visit www.panmacmillan.com to read more about all our books and to buy them. You will also find features, author interviews and news of any author events, and you can sign up for e-newsletters so that you're always first to hear about our new releases.

PAN BOOKS

First published 2015 by Sidgwick & Jackson

First published in paperback 2016 by Pan Books
an imprint of Pan Macmillan
20 New Wharf Road, London N1 9RR
Associated companies throughout the world
www.panmacmillan.com

ISBN 978-1-4472-9297-5

1 3 5 7 9 8 6 4 2

A CIP catalogue record for this book is available from the British Library.

Printed and bound by CPI Group (UK) Ltd, Croydon, CR0 4YY

This book is dedicated to my soulmate Misty,

a Jack Russell who sadly passed away a few months ago,

and left me feeling 'like a dog'

CONTENTS

INTRODUCTION

ANY OFFENCE IS UNINTENTIONAL

Have you ever tried going to the loo at 26,000 feet?

Well, take my advice, dear reader, and don't! I could write a book on this alone, you know. It's a nightmare! Nothing goes where it should.

In 1993 I was in that very position – about three-quarters of the way up Mount Everest on the Lhotse Face – when a member of our party, Ian Madron, decided he needed a shit. There were four of us in a two-man tent – perilous!

'What, NOW?' I said to him. 'But it's three o'clock in the morning. There's a four-mile drop directly outside and the weather's wilder than a randy bull elephant. You'll just have to go in your pants!'

He looked aghast.

'It'll turn to dust after half an hour,' I continued. 'Go on, man, it'll warm you up.'

I'm afraid that Ian didn't take kindly to this suggestion and, in hindsight, with us all being in such close proximity, I'm actually quite glad.

'Don't worry,' he said. 'I'll be fine.'

And so, with heavy hearts and nervous noses, we watched as Ian made his way across our bodies towards the zip.

'Don't forget to wash your hands,' I shouted after him. 'And make sure you tie up to a rope.'

What a time to want to go for a bloody crap, I thought to myself. Anyway, after a few nervous minutes the zip began to go again and in crawled Ian, followed by about half a ton of bloody snow.

'Success!' he shouted. Happy was the man.

Once Ian was safely back in his corner we decided to get up and try to make a brew. We were supposed to be going for the summit in just a few hours so there was no use trying to nod off again.

'Come on then you buggers,' I rallied. 'Let's try to warm some water up.'

After about five minutes another member of our party, Ian Frost, said, 'Do you know, there's a terrible smell of shit in here. It's absolutely awful. Can you smell it, Brian?'

'Yes, I can,' I replied. 'You're right, Ian. It's appalling!'

I looked nervously round the tent to try and find out where the pong was emanating from, and there, on Ian Madron's shoulder, was a turd.

He'd obviously done his business, the wind had caught it, there was a lull and it had 'flown home', so to speak. A homing turd! He was back outside double-quick.

Aaah, the glamour of Everest!

Mountaineers have a reputation for being both noble and heroic, which I applaud heartily. Nevertheless, I do remember an old climber reciting a poem to me one day:

> Mountaineers have furry ears and pee through leather
> britches
> They wipe their arse on broken glass, those hardy
> sons of bitches.

By the way, dear reader, a quick word of warning. If you ever do decide to climb Mount Everest take my advice and always camp above the French because, believe you me, when it comes to toilets, they will – and from a great height.

It is now over twenty-two years since I last wrote about anything other than mountaineering or exploring. Twenty-two years! I couldn't resist throwing in an Everest anecdote to start us off, but this book is going to take you from my childhood in Goldthorpe to *Z Cars*, *Flash Gordon*, *Star Wars* and much much more. There will be adversity overcome, punches thrown and even a love story. Yes, I am ready to burst forth once more and share with you some of my favourite stories and memories. Mark my words, though, this is no ordinary book, and is different to anything I've written before.

My previous five tomes, all of which I am tremendously proud, came from my head, if you see what I mean. I sat there for months on end and I thought and I wrote and I thought and I wrote. But this is something far more spontaneous. It is a conversation piece, if you will – which is why I must ask a favour of you. You must read the book with my voice in mind, as if I were there with you. This is *very* important.

You see, this is Brian Blessed speaking to you, not Stephen sexy gorgeous Fry! Try and imagine this, I beg of you: try and imagine I am sitting in a huge armchair and I am reading this to you and you only. I want to *leap* out of the pages at you! Not literally, of course. I mean, where on earth would you keep me? I'm quite a size.

The book does get a little bit racy at times, and you will find one or two naughty words along the way, but I promise you it's all there for a reason, alright? You see, when I *think*, I *don't* swear, which is why all my previous books are relatively clean; but when I *talk*, I do. It's just something that happens!

It was suggested that I might wish to remove some of the more colourful language . . . but then it would no longer be my book, would it? It'd be more Thora Hird than Brian Blessed, and that would never do. But mark my words, dear reader, I do not swear for the sake of swearing. Oh no. When

I swear, I BLOODY WELL MEAN TO SWEAR! (Did you imagine me shouting just then? You see, you're getting it.) Anyway, if you can get over the blue language, we'll get along just fine. Forewarned is forearmed and all that.

So, are you excited? I hope you are! This book is all about fun and adventure. It's a romp! There are some sombre moments, but I flatter myself that I can give even the saddest event a whimsical edge. I am an optimist, you see. A HUGE great bearded smiley optimist with a sunny disposition and 'can do' attitude, and that's what I try to get across in this book. Whatever you want to do in life, just go for it! Grab it by the scruff of the neck and shake the bugger until you're there.

Anyway, I think it's time we cracked on, don't you?

Remember, think Blessed!

1

ENTER THE PHANTOM

'Look at him! He's a monster!' were Mother's first words to me.

For the first week of my life I was known as the Toad. I was incredibly ugly! I didn't open my eyes a great deal at first and my mother was so horrified by my appearance that she couldn't even look at me, let alone nurse me.

It won't surprise you to know that I was a big baby; apparently they had to deliver me using a pneumatic drill. Actually, it was forceps, but by the time I eventually arrived on this planet my personage had been messed about with so much that I was quite badly disfigured. There were no 'coochee coochee coos' for Baby Blessed. Just: 'Look at him, he's a toad!'

Fortunately, the woman in the next bed, a Mrs Brindley, took pity on us both.

'Never mind, Mrs Blessed,' she said. 'Look, I'll nurse him while you recover.'

And so, for the first few days of my life, I had a foster mother – the wonderful Mrs Brindley!

Jumping ahead twenty-six years (I'll warn you now that I do this rather a lot, so you'll have to try and bear with me, OK?), I was filming an episode of *Z Cars* one day when all of a sudden an old lady approached me. She was playing one of the extras and was carrying a small dog.

'You won't remember me, Brian,' she said, 'but I'm Mrs

Brindley. I had to nurse you after you were born because you were so ugly.'

'Mrs Brindley!' I cried. 'Mother's told me all about you. Here, come and meet the rest of the cast.'

So I called all my colleagues over, Stratford Johns and Jimmy Ellis and all the stars, and introduced Mrs Brindley to them as my foster mother.

'This dear woman had to nurse me when I was a baby because my own mother couldn't bear to look at me!'

And do you know what? Nobody seemed that surprised.

Poor Mother, though. She really had been beside herself. She genuinely thought that she'd given birth to some kind of hideous amphibian.

'Don't worry,' said the nurses. 'Once he keeps his eyes open you'll see a different baby. He can't possibly stay like that forever. Anyway, most babies are ugly when they're born.'

Fortunately, when I did decide to keep my eyes open my appearance improved greatly, and I went from looking like an extremely ugly toad to a rather sweet human.

'There, you see,' said the nurses. 'Look at those lovely big eyes. He'll break a lot of hearts, Mrs Blessed, just you see.'

Mother wasn't convinced. She still thought I was more likely to turn stomachs than break hearts. She had cheered up a little bit, though, and so after about a week we were eventually released from hospital.

Now, I want you to prepare yourself for a shock. Oh yes, I'm afraid you must. You see, this may sound very strange to all of you, but I actually remember being born. I do: I genuinely remember making my way into this present life of mine. You don't believe me, do you? Well, this is all perfectly true. It is fact.

I felt very keenly at the beginning of my existence that I was surrounded by ice, and then, just prior to what was obviously the birth itself, I felt a tremendous pressure, as though an enormous rock was squashing me. Then, all of a sudden, I remember feeling free. I felt very, very free. I couldn't see anything up until this point by the way. The vast majority of this memory is based entirely around the sense of touch, but I knew as I experienced this overwhelming sense of freedom that I was actually being *born*. That this was my birth!

There we are: what a start, eh?

The memory ends with a flash of my parents' faces. This was 9 October 1936, and I remember seeing them both gazing down at me. You all think I'm absolutely bloody bonkers, don't you? Well, let me try and explain this a little further. You see, although this memory has been recurring prolifically in my mind for as long as I can remember, it was only when I began to learn about the birds and the bees that I was able to make any sense of it. So the more biologically aware I became, the more I was able to appreciate the significance of my recollection. And it's still there, as clear as day.

We lived at 30 Probert Avenue, Goldthorpe, which is halfway between Doncaster and Barnsley, about seven miles from both, and it was a lovely place to live. The houses on Probert Avenue were all relatively new when I was young and had been built specifically for coal-mining families. They were simple, but they were comfortable. Back then, Goldthorpe still had a thriving coal mine of course, which my father worked at, and I suppose it was a fairly standard South Yorkshire mining town. It had a couple of schools and a couple of cinemas. But, above all, it had a great sense of community. It was my kind of town!

Living next door to us on Probert Avenue was a wonderful lady called Mrs Dancy. Now, Mrs Dancy was a huge fat woman with enormous breasts. Great big tits! And she made bread for the entire street. What a magnificently warm, gorgeous woman she was. She had a *very* broad South Yorkshire accent, did Mrs Dancy, and inside her home sat two enormous ovens, in which she baked all her bread for the entire street. Her forearms were enormous: like Popeye on steroids!

When we arrived back home from the hospital after I was born, Mrs Dancy was on hand to offer Mother some much-needed support.

'Bring him in, Hilda love,' she said when we arrived home. 'Bring him in and let's have a look at him.'

Reluctantly, Mother agreed.

'Ah, you see, he's just a bit overcooked, Hilda love. He's just a bit overcooked. What was he, five days over? Ah yes, you mark my words, Hilda love, your new babby will turn out just nice.'

I remember the strangest things from that period of my life. I have this amazing memory, you see. For instance, I remember being put in a pram for the first time. It was a communal pram that was basically loaned out to anybody who'd had a baby on Probert Avenue, and was very old and rickety. It did have a wonderful little rattle in it though. I remember all this very vividly. I wasn't *told* there was a rattle in the pram; I actually remember playing with it. In fact, they once put another baby in the pram with me and he or she tried to wrestle the thing away from me. I must have been about a year old at the time and I remember this great battle ensuing, with each of us pulling to and fro, trying to gain control of the toy. What happened next was relayed to me by my mother some years later. As this horrible little bastard was trying to steal my rattle, I gradually became angrier and angrier, until I eventually cried out, 'BUGGER!'

Mother couldn't believe it. She was mortified!

'That was your first word, Brian,' she used to say when she recalled the story. 'Your first word was "bugger"! I didn't know where to look.'

Anyway, back to my homecoming.

Although I was no longer considered toad-like, I still had

a touch of the baboon's arse about me, and so when Mum and I went out for a walk or to the shops, she would go to great lengths to prevent her unsightly spawn from being seen. She never pushed me down the main thoroughfares. Instead we always took the side streets and alleyways, and if people tried to stop her for a look and a coo, she'd make an excuse and dash off.

Then, after about six months, I developed blond curly hair to go with my big brown eyes and became terribly pretty, like the child off the Pears Soap adverts, and so all of a sudden my mother was very proud of me. Down came the hood on the pram, out came the rattle and I was shown off to anyone who happened to be passing. No more back streets for me. I was now a bona fide bonny baby!

My mother and father adored me, you know. Apparently, I'd be put to bed at night and every fifteen minutes or so my mother would say to my father, 'Shall we go upstairs and have a quick look at him? Yes, come on, let's go and have a quick look.'

And then they'd nip upstairs and peep over my cot.

As well as being cute, pretty and tremendous, I was also a hardy little monkey. At the time there were all kinds of diseases going round, of which you had to be very, very wary. Or, at least, your parents did. The dreaded thing was pneumonia, which fortunately I didn't get. But I did get measles, mumps and then chickenpox, which, at the age of two, caused me all kinds of problems. My mother used to beg me not to scratch myself. She instilled a kind of fear into me, warning me that if I scratched the spots I would end up with great holes in my face and suchlike. I'm not quite sure that was the right way to go about things – after all, I was only two – but it worked.

All the other children on Probert Avenue would weep and cry whenever they caught these horrible diseases, but I never, ever did. You see, I've presented you with yet another

Blessed idiosyncrasy. I had the memory of an elephant, the face of a toad – and the lacrimal glands of a bloody crocodile. I simply could not cry. I was like Heathcliff in *Wuthering Heights*! I was sometimes in pain, of course, the same as any child, but instead of crying out I would just look at my mother with big open eyes, as if to say, 'It hurts a bit, Mum!' This, of course, drove the poor woman to despair.

'Why won't you cry, Brian?' she used to plead. 'Just cry, love. It's OK to cry.'

But for the life of me I couldn't. It was as if I'd somehow had the ability taken away from me. I would suffer in silence instead.

Once I got to about four or five years old, I began to blubber occasionally, but even then not a great deal.

I hope this isn't depressing you too much? Honestly, it's not as bad as it sounds. I couldn't really give two hoots, and despite my mother being affected by it all, most people were simply intrigued. She took me to the doctor's several times because of it, but because it never affected my actual health in any way, we were always sent home with a smile.

The worst thing I ever had as a child was yellow jaundice, and by God that was painful. I still can't give blood to this day because of that. I used to vomit, the pain was so excruciating, but no tears!

God willing, one always got over these kinds of diseases. It sounds very grim but it's no different to how things are today, really, except that the dreaded pneumonia is fortunately very rare these days, and the medical world seems to cope with it very well.

But that's enough about me for the time being. Let me tell you a bit about my parents, Hilda and Bill Blessed. They taught me honesty, truth, compassion, kindness and how to care for people. They encouraged me to take risks and to follow my

dreams. What makes me love them more is that they prac-
tised what they bloody well preached. My dad accompanied
me on many an adventure, one of which you'll read about
later, and died at the ripe old age of ninety-nine. Mum died
when she was eighty-seven, so we're a long-lived family.

My father worked as a coal hewer, which means he
removed coal for a living; around seventeen tonnes of it a
day, physically, by himself. Seventeen tonnes! That's the
equivalent of about five African bull elephants.

He used to hack the coal out using a pickaxe and then he
would shovel it all onto this huge conveyor belt, which had
lots of holes in it. The large pieces stayed on, and the small
bits fell through. And he would do this for over eight hours
a day with only a thirty-minute break for lunch. I'm telling
you, these men were as fit as butcher's dogs. They never saw
natural light, of course, and must have breathed in enough
dust every day to fill a tin bath. That was the life of a coal
hewer: the hardest job in a coal mine, bar none.

In many ways Mum was a typical 1930s Yorkshire house-
wife; hardworking, forthright, but ultimately very, very
loving. She spent most of her days as every woman did on
Probert Avenue; either cooking, cleaning or, when time
allowed, chatting to the next-door neighbours over the
garden fence. By Jove, my mum worked hard though. I don't
ever remember seeing her sit down for hours after my father
had returned home, and she'd been at it since the crack of
dawn. She did have her problems, bless her heart, which I'll
come on to a bit later, but she was a wonderful woman. Salt
of the earth!

So what was life like in the Blessed household? Well,
you'll pick up little bits throughout this book, but I always
remember ours being a very busy house. Each morning the
paper boy would arrive and once a week he would deliver a
copy of the *Beano* and the *Dandy*. For my mother he would
deliver a copy of *Woman's Weekly*, which came out every

Wednesday, and for my father a copy of the *Daily Worker*, which he always took on alternate weekdays. He was a big socialist, my father. In fact, before Stalin came to power he was actually a communist. Intermixed with comics, women's magazines and my father's red rags were occasional magazines on the art and science of coal mining. You see, to my father, being a coal hewer wasn't simply a job; it was indeed an art and a science.

The paper boy wasn't the only visitor to our home; there were always people popping in and out what seemed like every other minute. There were my father's brothers, for one thing. They hailed from Goldthorpe and even though they were siblings and all incredibly close, each one had a very unique build and personality. My Uncle Tom, who worked as a coal hewer and as a shotfirer, was incredibly tall – six foot three or six foot four – and he looked just like Henry Cooper. Not quite like a Blessed, somehow. Then there was my Uncle George, who was also a coal miner, but eventually became head of the insurance company, the Royal Liver Friendly Society. He was a very brilliant man, George, and very dramatic, and eventually became one of the Pitmen Painters. Have you heard of the Pitmen Painters? They were a group of Northumberland pitmen who painted as a means of self-discovery and in so doing produced an account of their community. It's a fascinating story and they've had all kinds of plays and books written about them.

I had an Uncle Alan, too, who became the manager at Darfield coal mine. He was also a very dramatic and powerful man, so perhaps you can see now where I get some of my drama from. Some of my immense power! (I thank God for my modesty!) Alan would go to places like Sheffield and Leeds to see all the big operas. He adored opera, especially German opera, and could speak the language almost fluently; in fact, he could recite every word of Richard Strauss's *Ariadne auf Naxos* from start to finish. Every single bloody line!

He also knew all of Hitler's speeches, and he could do the most marvellous impersonation of him. He used to say, 'He doesn't half sound powerful, Brian, that Adolf Hitler. What a pity he's such a horrible bastard!'

But, of all the Blessed brothers, my father was perhaps the most diverse in his thinking, and was a talented yet self-effacing man. Apart from his family, my father lived for his fellow miners. They were his second family and he would have done anything for any one of them. It didn't matter where you worked within a mine; whether it be in the offices or underground, if you had a grievance Bill Blessed would fight tooth and bloody nail for you. He worked with all the unions and would spend much of his spare time travelling up and down the country defending people. He even travelled overseas on a couple of occasions.

My father's childhood had been full of learning. His parents adored him and his brothers, and ensured that they all received a decent education. No mean feat in those days, I can tell you. It was a damn sight more than the majority of his colleagues ever received. Some of the men he worked with could hardly string two words together, and some hadn't been educated at all. This meant that there were an awful lot of people at those mines who were open to exploitation, and so it was up to people like my dad to ensure that they didn't get taken advantage of. He also gave up a very promising career to do this. You see, because he was a bright chap, and because he had always studied the art and in particular the science of coal mining, he was offered management and development positions left, right and centre; even as far away as Australia. Mr Godfrey, his boss, was forever trying to persuade him to come and work upstairs, but he never gave any one of these offers a second thought. To him, he would have been betraying not only his principles, but every single miner in the land.

So there was a great feeling of family and camaraderie; not

only at 30 Probert Avenue, but all over Goldthorpe. The place was full of wonderful, warm people. And I'll tell you something else about coal miners: it didn't matter how educated or uneducated they were, they could all spout Shakespeare like you wouldn't believe. Probert Avenue was awash with Hamlets and Othellos. They could do all that twice nightly! My Uncle George could recite 'To be or not to be' backwards, and my father would give us the whole of Cassius from *Julius Caesar*. They studied Shakespeare and they understood Shakespeare. They found what he said phenomenal!

These were just honest, working-class people, but they led amazing lives. My father, after he'd dug seventeen tonnes of coal every day, would come home and then go out and train with the Yorkshire Colts, Yorkshire Cricket Club's second team. He'd go and teach the likes of Fred Trueman how to bowl cutters and how to bowl against the seam, so that when Trueman eventually played against the Australians he could hit the buggers straight in the face.

'You can always apologize,' Dad used to say. '"Sorry about that! Did I get you in the face?"'

There was a terrific vibrancy about these people. They worked and worked and worked, yet they always made time for each other as well as for both learning and discovery. They didn't go anywhere, most of them, they couldn't afford it, so to compensate they read books and they watched films and they discussed things. They led full and interesting lives.

Now, I don't want to get too political for the simple reason that it bores the living daylights out of me, but back then there was always this great misconception about the working classes, and especially the miners. People assumed that they were all brown ale and bingo, 'eee by gum' and what have you. No! They were astute people. They were brilliant people. They were trailblazers who completely belied their schooling and social standing. They were a joyous and powerful contradiction!

Now, I want to tell you quickly about the first time I ever went to the cinema. I've appeared in squillions of films, of course, and so, in terms of this book, it is an event that I think should be marked.

I initially thought the film in question was going to be Walt Disney's *Bambi*. I think I was about six at the time, and Dad had agreed to take me after weeks of what I believe parents now call 'Pester Power'. (I love that phrase. How marvellous!)

Anyway, he said, 'I'll take you after swimming this Thursday, Brian, OK?'

My dad used to take me swimming every Thursday from about the age of five, and so as we left the swimming baths that night I took his hand and away we went. There were two cinemas in Goldthorpe, the Picture House and the Empire, and ever since I'd been old enough to play out I'd stalked these places like an animal stalks its prey: walking around and around them both, trying to stare inside. I was spellbound! There were posters everywhere, great colourful works of art, which offered you a glimpse of what awaited you through the gilded double doors. Even the usherettes fascinated me; their uniforms bright and elegant. Best of all, they had enormous trays full of ice cream looped around their shoulders. Ice cream *too*! This was my Eldorado in waiting. I remember once catching a glimpse of one of the auditoriums at the end of a matinee. The titles were still running, which meant that the whole place was still bathed in music and light from the big screen. They were theatres of dreams, these places, where adventure and reverie came to life!

And I was being taken to see *Bambi*, I assumed, as all that week my entire infant school had talked of nothing else. '*Bambi*'s on this week. We're going to see *Bambi*, we're going to see *Bambi*!' I was so excited! I'd read about the film in one of my comics and just couldn't wait to see it.

But, instead of turning left to go to the Empire after we'd been swimming, my dad stopped me and said, 'Brian, I don't think you'd like *Bambi*. I'm taking you to see something else.'

I was heartbroken. 'But Dad—' I protested.

'Trust me, lad,' he said. 'Just trust me. I promise you'll enjoy the film at the Picture House more.'

So my dad took me to the Picture House, where we saw Alexander Korda's production of *Jungle Book*. When the film opened on the tiger, Shere Khan, I almost fainted. Dad knew exactly what he was doing in taking me to see *Jungle Book*. I lapped it up; enjoyed every second! Have you seen it filmed in glorious Technicolor and starring the great Sabu as Mowgli? Well, I just lost myself in that film.

'Didn't I tell you, lad?' said Dad when we came out.

'You were right, Dad,' I enthused. 'It was wonderful!'

I remember the spirit of the trees welcoming Mowgli to the jungle.

'Enter little spirit, enter. Water and air, woods and trees welcome thee. Enter little spirit. What's your name?'

'M-M-M-Mowgli.'

'Mowgli? Little frog? We are of one body!'

The whole miraculous film took me over.

I didn't know it then, of course, but many years later I would actually visit Rudyard Kipling's home and sit in the chair and at the desk where he wrote his most famous poem, *If*. Remember some of the words?

> If you can fill the unforgiving minute
> With sixty seconds' worth of distance run,
> Yours is the Earth and everything that's in it,
> And – which is more – you'll be a Man, my son.

Oh my sainted aunt, WHAT GENIUS!

All the walls in Kipling's house were adorned with gigantic paintings of all his characters from all his greatest works: Akela, Mowgli, Bagheera, Baloo, Rikki-Tikki-Tavi, Shere Khan . . . It was honestly one of the most exciting days of my life.

As well as instilling in me a passion for cinema, that film also sparked what has since become a lifelong obsession with animals and their welfare. We still have quite a few pets at home, my wife Hildegard and I, but in our younger days we had hundreds. We had an animal sanctuary at home and employed six people to help us run it.

So there you go: my first ever trip to the cinema. What a marvellous recollection!

Now, I know you probably get this a lot in these kinds of books, but my father really was my hero. For starters, he was a good man – a very loving man – and he was a kind man; the kindest of them all. But what really cemented my father's position as my hero was his outstanding bravery. He risked life and limb time after time after time for his fellow miners, and treated death like an old friend. He wasn't afraid of dying because he'd actually become conditioned to it. It was an omnipresent threat – the ultimate tragedy.

The Duke of Edinburgh once visited my father's pit and lasted about ten minutes there. Dad worked at Hickleton Main Colliery, which was the largest in the area. You had Manvers and Barnborough and Darfield nearby, but Hickleton was the big one. Anyway, as I said, after about ten minutes underground poor Philip politely asked to be taken back to the surface. He didn't like it at all, according to Dad. But he's not the only one, of course. Apart from it being dark, dirty and dangerous in the pit, you can actually hear the roof moving over your head and, if you're not used to it, it can put the willies right up you! Apparently that had been the last straw for Phil, rendering him somewhat panic-stricken.

I used to hear story after story after story about my dad's heroism; but never once from him. He was a very humble man and if he ever heard such a tale being relayed to me, he would stop the conversation immediately.

'He doesn't need to know about all that. He's too young!'

Nevertheless, I did hear many accounts – usually from my uncles – and each one simply enhanced my admiration, pride and wonder. I remember my Uncle Alan telling me about the time they opened a new coal seam at Hickleton. My father went down there one day with a colleague of his named Colin Bennett. While they were there, my father began to sense gas. He didn't *smell* gas: he sensed it. He could sense it was on its way. You see, miners back in the day became so attuned to gas that their senses went beyond those of mere mortals. They could actually sense the killer's presence!

'Get back, Colin,' my father said. 'There's gas coming.'

Now this was right at the end of the day shift, when 300-plus miners were about to make their way towards the surface.

'If those men come this way, we could all be killed,' my father said. 'It's dangerous enough with you and me being here. Go and tell them to stay exactly where they are.'

You see, there's a peculiarity regarding the human body and carbon monoxide; the human body absolutely loves it. If it senses it in the air, the lungs move faster and will try to breathe it in. It means certain death, of course, but the body has an inbuilt yearning for the stuff.

Sure enough, about two minutes later, the flame on my dad's Davy lamp started burning blue, which is what happens when gases are present.

'Are the men still underground, Colin?' asked Dad.

'Yes, they're not moving.'

'Right, let's get it sealed and then get the men out.'

And so the famous Barnsley Bed was closed. I remember listening to this story, completely agog. Three hundred lives had been saved!

Another time, there'd been a huge fire down the mine,

and my father, who hadn't yet started his shift, picked up as many gas masks as he could carry and made his way down there. He wasn't supposed to, of course – the fire brigade were on their way – but his knowledge of the mine, every seam, could prove invaluable. He had to do something.

So round he went, handing out all these gas masks while they were trying to evacuate the men. Eventually, he came across a seam where the roof had fallen in and found three men who'd been crushed to death beneath it. Looking further into the seam, he then found another man who had also been crushed and was pinned by his legs. He was alive, but only just, and had boulders hanging over him that must have weighed at least twenty tonnes; that entire section of wall was about to fall in on him. My dad scrambled to the next seam as fast as he could and managed to find somebody with a crowbar, after which he raced back with the borrowed crowbar and began trying to lever the rocks out of the way. All the time these boulders were becoming ever more hazardous, and he and this chap were seconds from death. With only a moment to spare, my father managed to free this man and they both made it safely to the surface. The stricken miner had two broken legs, a broken hip and a fractured pelvis – but he lived. And he lived because of my father!

The coal miners at Hickleton absolutely adored my dad, and he them. He was their leader and he was their philosopher. He had knowledge in spades and enough kindness and love to fill a thousand Barbara Cartland novels. It was running through his veins. He was every single one of those men. A beautiful human being.

Although my father was a socialist, he was also a Christian, and you could see this element in him. I don't mean that metaphorically, by the way. My father was indeed a Christian and he believed in God, but he also believed in the well-being of his fellow man. That was his lifeblood. And, you see, his God didn't need praising every five minutes in church. He always said that if there is a God, He'd want us all to be out there doing good things in the world.

They used to sing a song down the mines every time they finished a shift. It was called 'Take Me Home'. You'll just have to imagine me singing this to you. If you're not familiar with the melody, make one up.

> I remember the face of my father,
> As we walked back home from the mine.
> He'd laugh and he'd say, 'That's one more day,
> And it's good to feel the sunshine.'
>
> I remember my mother was smiling,
> As I set out to make my own way.
> She seemed to know that I had to go,
> But I'd come back home one day.

There are one or two more verses, but isn't that wonderful?

Now, this next story is a teeny bit gruesome, but it's relevant – extremely relevant. You see, even by the mid- to late 1940s, I was already showing signs of becoming an actor. I'd actually begun by acting out an Abbott & Costello skit one day at school, which seemed to captivate both the teachers and my classmates in equal measure. I had no idea what I was doing, I was just acting out something I'd seen at the cinema, but the whole school thought it was absolutely hilarious. It seemed to have a kind of curative effect. Even my headmaster at the time, Mr Bedford, said, 'Blessed, you clearly have a talent for this sort of thing. Let's see if we can nurture it, shall we?'

But my father knew I'd become an actor, even before I did. When I told him what had happened at school that day, he didn't seem at all surprised.

'You mean one of those routines you do for us at home

every night of the week, our Brian? I was wondering when you were going to perform it at school.'

He knew, my old dad. He knew.

Fast-forward a few years to when I was in my teens and was involved with the local drama group. Dad came home one evening looking both dishevelled and completely despondent. He also had tears in his eyes.

'Brian, if you ever have to act out pain or death, don't ever give it any expression, lad.'

'What do you mean, Dad?' I asked.

'Well, lad, I watched a man die today. I was with him. He was twenty-one years of age and he died in front of me. Just slipped away.'

What had actually happened was, I'm afraid, far more eventful. As I've described, coal hewers worked alongside these enormous conveyor belts, onto which they would shovel the coal after they'd broken it out from the seam. Well, in the next cubicle to my father (for coal hewers worked alongside each other in cubicles of about ten metres), this young lad had got his foot caught in one of the holes while he was trying to shovel the coal onto the conveyor belt. So he hopped along, trying to pull it out, until his other foot got caught on one of the pit poles which held the roof up. Within seconds, the poor man had been ripped apart. He didn't die instantly, but lay there on the ground, surrounded by half his insides. My dad had screamed for the men to stop the conveyor belt, but it was too late.

'He was just lying there in a pool of blood and intestines,' my father said.

I remember his account as if it were yesterday: the most harrowing thing I'd ever heard.

'I'd done first aid,' my dad said, 'but I didn't know what to do. The poor lad was in a state of shock and so we wrapped him in our coats, gave him a cigarette and told him that everything was going to be alright.

'"Doctor's coming, lad, don't you worry," we said.

'"But it's my wife, Bill," said the lad. "We've got a young 'un at home and there's another on the way. You will tell her that I'm going to be alright, won't you, Bill? She'll be worried sick. You will tell her, Bill, won't you?"

'"Of course I will, lad."

'"I'm so worried about her, though, Bill. Tell her I'll make it up to her. Tell her I'm sorry."

'"Yes, lad. Everything's going to be alright."'

Dad said that he'd then smiled at the lad reassuringly and the lad had smiled back, and as he did so he just slipped away – dead.

'I've never seen anything so bloody cruel in all my life, our Brian.'

My dad was in floods of tears at this point. Totally inconsolable.

'What price coal, our Brian?' he wept. 'What price coal?'

Whenever you heard those sirens go off at the mine, in that moment you knew that there was a very good chance your father could be either seriously injured or dead. It was a sobering thought and one that cast an all-pervading shadow over Goldthorpe, as I'm sure it did every other mining town.

And so, when my dad came home – in the late evening, sometimes – there'd be this overwhelming sensation of relief. It engulfed the entire town – providing your loved one had been spared, of course. I remember my mother always used to do a little cry when she saw him coming home. Just a few tears.

'Your dad's home, Brian lad! Get his bath poured, come on!'

We had an enamel bath; just with no enamel on it! As a young boy I used to follow my father up to our tiny bathroom and help him bathe. What a bloody mess that was, though! Coal dust absolutely everywhere! It came from his hair, his ears, his nose, his arse. Anywhere coal dust could get, basically. It was my job to stand there and wash his back. It was like a mountain landscape, my father's back. You see, he often used to work half-naked and so throughout the day bits of the roof would fall onto his back. The roof is constantly falling in a mine – little bits here and there – and so his back was covered in these little calluses where the coal had hit him. The miners got used to it.

I remember seeing his wage packet each week, too. It was about fourteen pounds ten shillings and he always carried it in an envelope in his shirt pocket. Every note was covered in dust. Surface workers only got about eight quid, but the hewers were paid almost double that; the hardest job of all.

It is because of my dad that I have never, ever thrown money away. I'm generous to a tee, but I can't bear it when people waste money, because I've seen how hard it is for people to earn it. God, I was so proud of my old man! He pops up all over this book, so by the time we've finished you'll know him quite well.

Of course, he wasn't the only source of inspiration in my home at 30 Probert Avenue. I've always felt that the real strength behind mankind is its women, and my own dear mother, Hilda Blessed, is testimony to this. She had no education whatsoever and was also born illegitimate at a time when that wasn't simply frowned upon, it was considered almost a crime. The men always got away scot-free, of course. It was down to the women and the children to face the flak. Her mother, Emma, was twenty-eight when a man called Herbert Hill got her pregnant. Such was the shame and persecution Emma endured that she couldn't bring herself even to acknowledge my mother. She wouldn't even look at her. So my mother, would you believe it, was taken across the road just 200 yards to live with her grandmother. That did untold damage to my mother in later life. You see, until she was in her teens, my mother had no idea that her grandmother wasn't her mother. Nobody ever told her.

Years later, when she looked back on this, my mother used to say that whenever she saw Emma – whom she believed was her older sister, of course – walking down the road, a peculiar feeling came upon her. Not a pleasant feeling; in fact, she said it made her shiver somewhat. It was only when my great-grandmother was dying that she finally came clean and told my mother the truth. She was only thirteen at the time and it came as a great shock to her.

One initial upside to this was that she was finally acknowledged by her mother. But, alas, the reunion wasn't a happy one. Because there was nobody else to look after young Hilda, my grandmother Emma had no choice but to take my mother in. Yet instead of making her one of the family, she treated her like a skivvy, and my mother spent the rest of her teenage years looking after her mother, her husband Leonard and their two daughters Margaret and Lois. It was almost a carbon copy of the Cinderella story, except with far more realism and an extremely unfortunate legacy. For Hilda had no education and no social life whatsoever while she was there. She never experienced love or any kind of pleasure. There were no birthdays, no Christmases. She was effectively a slave. This, too, not surprisingly, left my mother with some serious issues in later life.

But, despite her difficult childhood, my mother always possessed a tremendous amount of common sense. She had a fine brain, and she put it to good use.

When she met and married my father, when she was in her mid-twenties and he towards the end of that same decade, she at last began to experience love, friendship and companionship in her life. My father absolutely adored her and he never, ever stopped telling her that. He knew all about her upbringing, of course, and I think he went out of his way to compensate for that. And he also helped her with her education. He tutored her at home every evening before I was born and it didn't take her long to catch up. So theirs was an unorthodox union to begin with, based more around friendship, perhaps, than courtship.

Socially, my mother was very forward; once again as a consequence of being locked away all her young life. She could have gone the other way and become a recluse, but happily she flowered and ended up blossoming into a bit of a social butterfly. My father, on the other hand, could be quite a shy person. Funnily enough, for a man who always considered himself a socialist, or indeed a communist, for much of his life, he was often quite conservative in nature. Regardless of these differences, my father helped my mother enormously and I'm happy to report that their marriage was a long and happy one. They had problems, of course – some absolutely gargantuan problems, a few of which I will allude to later – but they never, ever stopped loving each other, and, importantly, they never, ever stopped saying it!

To demonstrate the strength of my mother, I shall tell you a quick story that astounds me even to this day.

I was eight years old at the time and my mum had been told that her mother and her husband Leonard had been heard arguing, very badly indeed. This they did a lot, apparently. Both of them drank quite a bit and both had been unfaithful at some time during their marriage, so it had been tempestuous to say the least. Leonard was a revolting old bastard; a lecherous drunk with a big mouth. He once made an advance to my mother, and it took two of my uncles to stop my father going over there and killing him. And he would have killed him without a second thought. He was incensed, not surprisingly. Especially after what they'd put her through. My father hated both of them. We all did.

But, on hearing that they'd been rowing again, my mother told me to get my shoes on and together we walked over the bridge to their house. When we entered the kitchen, my grandmother's husband had a knife to her throat and was screaming into her face, something about her sleeping with another man. On seeing this, my mother said, 'Good! Good for you. I'll tell you what, cut her throat. Go on, cut her throat. And then, when you've cut her throat, cut your own throat, because you're as bad as she is!'

Leonard then burst into tears and fell to his knees. Mother said, 'Give me that knife,' and she snatched it away from him. And that was my mother. She didn't owe them anything. They'd kept her as a slave all through her teenage years. Yet it was still her who came to their aid and stopped them from killing each other.

She used to do similar things in the street. It was common practice in the streets around Probert Avenue for people to fight – and they did: morning, noon and bloody night. And for some reason it was always over children. You know the kind of thing: 'Your child's been bullying my child.' But my mother wouldn't tolerate this kind of nonsense. In fact, she used to go out with a frying pan and she'd hit the scrapping women on the elbows. It must have left them in bloody agony!

'Stop it!' she'd say. 'You couple of bloody idiots. You shouldn't fight over children. One minute they're friends, the next they're not.'

If a man had tried to stop them, it would have ended up escalating into a ginormous brawl. It had to be a woman. Different proposition altogether, you see.

Another quite surprising thing about my mother was her knowledge of acting and the movies and suchlike. It even surpassed my father's, and yet she only saw her first film at the age of twenty. She'd take me to the cinema on a Saturday night and then give me her opinions on all the actors and actresses. I lapped it all up. She was my Barry Norman!

'All the girls like Alan Ladd, Brian, but he's not much cop as an actor. He's very good at pausing, though. He pauses very well, and he's quite believable sometimes.'

'What about Gregory Peck, Mum?'

'Mmmm, I'd probably walk five miles to see Gregory Peck, but I'd walk twenty to see Spencer Tracy. He's five hundred per cent, Brian, Spencer Tracy. It's all gold with him.'

'How about James Mason?'

'Good actor, Brian. A very clever actor, James Mason, and very versatile. Doesn't matter if he's playing a romantic lead or a villain. He's quality, Brian. He's a Yorkshireman too. Did you know that?'

But while my mother may have loved the movies, as I've already said, her marriage wasn't always picture perfect. Though my parents' union was, in the main, a happy one, it did experience a certain amount of misfortune. Or perhaps I should say, the family as a whole did.

Now, you're not to worry, dear reader: I'm not about to get all *Bleak House* on you. We'll be back to the fun stuff soon enough. But here goes . . .

When I was about seven or eight years of age, my father was gassed. This happened at the mine, of course, and he was ill for quite some time. I remember him being brought home from the hospital. His head was rolling all over the place and his face was still purple. I was in floods of tears.

After that, he couldn't work for about two months and the sick pay back then was about fifteen shillings a week; a fraction of the normal wage. My dad always kept a bit by in case of emergencies but not enough to last more than a week or two, and so hardship soon set in and I remember Mother becoming very, very worried. My father was living in the box room upstairs and the doctors would come round twice a week to treat him. This was my hero, remember, and all of a sudden he was so very, very weak.

When things became desperate, my mother had to send me over to my grandmother's for help. This was a last resort, naturally, but needs must. I'd have to go and ask for sugar, butter, carbolic soap and suchlike; the essentials needed to run a house, basically. And I hated it. For you see, my mother's mother, in addition to being quite callous, was also an incredibly ugly woman; I was scared of her, in fact. She used to pull these revolting faces all of the time, and I used to have to go there and ask for help. I'd sooner have stuck pins in my bloody eyes, but her and her daughters – my mother's half-sisters – all worked at a local food factory, and so were able to get their hands on the odd tin here and there, as well as bits and pieces from the black market. Because there was a war on and rationing was in place, people weren't normally able to spare anything – if they had been able to, we'd have gone elsewhere, of course, to one of my dad's brothers or somewhere – so they were the only people we knew who usually had a surplus of groceries.

One day, after my father had been off work for about five weeks, my mother sent me on yet another aid mission to my grandmother's.

'I know you don't like doing it, Brian, but I'm desperate. I've got nothing in and no money. You've got to do it, Brian, you've got to!'

My own anxieties apropos being repulsed by my grandmother were a mere bagatelle compared with my mother's ongoing battle in trying to feed and clothe a family, so I did as I was told and went along.

After I knocked on my grandmother's back door, I began to hear voices emanating from the living room. She obviously had company. This wasn't a good sign, because the last time I'd turned up while she had friends round she'd gone bananas. I could only hope this time would be different.

'Oh Christ, not you again!' she shouted, when she saw it was me. 'Come in and stand in the corner so nobody can see you. Now, what do you want? I suppose you've been given a shopping list?'

'That's right,' I began. 'Mum's desperate. She's got no food and nothing to wash the clothes with. Dad's still not back at work, you see.'

Just then, she pulled one of her grotesque faces. 'I suppose I'll have to get you out of the mire – again!'

That was enough for me. I went absolutely off my little box!

'I'll tell you what, Granny [she hated being called Granny], you can bugger your sugar and you can bugger your butter. AND you can bugger your carbolic soap. You can stick the whole lot up your arse, you fat ugly pig! I'll never come back here again!'

With that, I gave her a V-sign (the opposite of Churchill's) and strode away with my nose in the air.

I thought, *You horrible old sod. You treat my mother like a skivvy for five years, then when she needs your help you act like this?* I was so distressed by what had just happened that instead of going home I did the unthinkable. I went to Aunt Toucha's.

Toucha Wall (I've no idea why she was called Aunt) was our version of Miss Havisham from *Great Expectations*. She was a spinster, very Victorian (probably born around 1870 or 1880), with lots of money that she'd inherited from a relative. She was quite eccentric – so much so that we were always told never to knock on her door. She used to wear ball-gowns all the time – even to clean and go to the shops – and slapped on enough make-up to put Danny La Rue to shame. Such behaviour probably wouldn't be considered too out of the ordinary these days, but in South Yorkshire circa 1943 it was tantamount to heresy! She wasn't considered to be evil or anything, and she always had plenty of friends, but having somebody so very different living in the area made people slightly nervous. As enlightened as mining families

invariably were when it came to things like culture and rec-
reation, I'm afraid that there was, nevertheless, still a fear of
the unknown. I didn't care, though. I'd always found Aunt
Toucha fascinating, like a walking piece of history, and had
it not been for the ban, I'd have been forever knocking on
her door. According to my mother, Aunt Toucha had met
Queen Victoria several times, and had also seen all the famous
Victorian actors and actresses; people like Lillie Langtry and
Gerald du Maurier. I had so many questions for her!

In a daze, I walked up to Aunt Toucha's house and
knocked on the door. It was much bigger than ours, and had
a whopping three bedrooms!

'Hello, Brian lad,' she said, greeting me with a big smile.
'How's your father getting on? Is he better? Is he back at
work yet?'

'Oh, Aunt Toucha! I don't know what to do. My mother
hasn't got anything in and we've no money. I went to my
grandmother's but she just pulled one of her faces and so I
called her a name and walked off . . .'

I must have gone on for at least five minutes. Eventually,
Aunt Toucha stopped me and told me to come in.

'Wait there, Brian lad. I shan't be long.'

I looked around and I remember seeing these great red
velvet curtains half covering the windows, and underneath
them an upholstered window seat. Apart from her two
black-and-white cats, there was nothing but Victorian furniture in the room; ornate wooden lamps with frilly shades
and suchlike. It was a period living room! *How wonderful*,
I thought.

When Aunt Toucha came back, the first thing she did was
wipe my face.

'Look at the state of you, Brian. You've got yourself all
upset, haven't you? Let's get you cleaned up before you go
back to your mother.'

Then she brought me a sandwich and a cup of tea.

I felt a hundred times better now, and in the excitement of being in Aunt Toucha's living room for the first time, I had totally forgotten about the sugar and whatnot.

'Here you are, Brian love,' she said, handing me a very large cloth bag full of shopping. 'You take that home and give it to your mother, and if she ever needs anything else, you come straight to see me, do you hear?'

'Yes, Aunt Toucha, thank you, Aunt Toucha!'

When I got halfway up the road and stopped to look in the bag, I couldn't believe my eyes. There wasn't just one slab of carbolic soap, there were four, and as opposed to her giving us half a pound of sugar, she'd given us at least five. It was a real Aladdin's Cave and the whole thing weighed an absolute bloody ton!

As I walked through our front door, I saw my mother sitting at the kitchen table. She had her head in her hands and was weeping uncontrollably.

'Mum, Mum, it's OK,' I shouted. 'I've got the lot, Mum!'

She saw the bag I was carrying and for a moment looked worried.

'Where did you get that, Brian? That's not from your grandmother.'

'No, Mum, I went to see Aunt Toucha instead. She cleaned me up and gave me a sandwich. Then she gave me this bag! She said if you ever needed anything else you've only to send me.'

The look on my mother's face was a mixture of vexation and relief. She was obviously annoyed that I'd gone against her wishes, but the fact that I'd managed to procure some groceries exonerated me immediately.

Good old Aunt Toucha. Do you know she lived on Prospect Road? Isn't that apt?

Unfortunately, all the weeks of worry and desperation had taken their toll on my mother and, around the time of me visiting Aunt Toucha, I began to notice signs of what would later develop into a full-blown nervous breakdown. You have no idea how much it saddens me thinking about this period, but I somehow feel comfortable writing about it. In fact, it's quite cleansing. It's good for the soul, I think!

Of course, my mother's spirit was damaged beyond belief when she was a child. If being born out of wedlock before being given away didn't eventually send you over the bloody edge, being reunited with a mother who showed you no love and treated you like a slave surely would. So the seeds of her troubles were always there, I think. The day-to-day worries were merely catalysts; a relentless series of cognitive detonations that dispersed a barrage of sadness and self-loathing.

Another product of her reprehensible upbringing was an almost constant need to be praised. If she cleaned the windows or dusted the furniture, I'd have to praise her; even when I was a child. You don't need to be a psychotherapist to understand why she needed this recognition, of course. Five-plus years of drudgery and scorn must do little for your confidence and self-esteem. This particular idiosyncrasy became worse as my mother got older, as did her propensity to become depressed occasionally.

Her first nervous breakdown occurred shortly after my shopping trip to Aunt Toucha's. As I said, I began to notice little changes in her behaviour. She'd all of a sudden start speaking in a different voice, as if she were acting out some kind of sketch to herself. And she was crying a lot more than usual. I remember being very worried about her.

My little brother Alan had been born about a year before my father was gassed, and towards the end of Dad's convalescence, Alan became ill with the dreaded pneumonia. Contracting pneumonia very often resulted in death back then, and Alan, who alas was never the strongest of children, was lying at death's door within days.

Before I go any further, I must tell you a bit about my

darling brother. As I said, he was never the strongest child, but he was full of fun and he absolutely worshipped me – and I him. He was always known in our house as the Milk Bottle Baby, on account of me being told by my mother that if I wanted a little brother or a sister I would have to start collecting milk bottle tops.

'If you start saving now, Brian,' said Mum, 'you never know what might happen!'

She was actually already pregnant at the time of me asking, so when the bump began to show, I thought it was entirely down to my hoard!

'It's worked, Mum!' I exclaimed. 'I must have saved up enough tops!'

Though Alan was often ill, his battle with pneumonia was particularly traumatic, especially for my mum. The treatment was archaic to say the least – hot poultices, which were warmed by the open fire before being applied to the chest – and so I'm afraid it was all a bit of a lottery. Mother was in a terrible state, of course. My dad was still suffering from the after-effects of being gassed, we had no money for food, and now her youngest son was on the brink of being taken from her.

Our neighbour Mrs Dancy helped out a lot with the poultices, I remember, as did my uncles. It was a twenty-four-hour job, you see, so they all took it in shifts. Eventually, the doctor declared that if Alan was going to die, it would be very soon.

'This is called the climax, Mrs Blessed,' he said. 'His breathing's bad, but if he gets through tonight, he'll live.'

As the evening progressed, Alan's breathing became so laboured that we were certain he was going to die. The doctor was called once again and I remember my mother screaming at him, pleading with him to do something. He couldn't. He was as helpless as we were. When the doctor left, Mrs Dancy took Mother in her arms and comforted her, while I sat by

Alan's crib and stared at his chest, praying for it to keep on moving.

At about eleven o'clock that same evening, I was shaken awake in my bed by my mother.

'Alan's started breathing better. He's getting stronger, Brian! Come and see!'

Sure enough, as I looked into his crib, my little brother's tiny chest was banging away like the privy door when the plague's in town.

I tell you, we had relief dripping off the walls that evening.

'He's going to live, Mum. Alan's going to live!'

My mother and I spent the rest of that night lying together on the sofa, watching her son – my little brother – live! She broke down periodically, and when she did I comforted her and stroked her hair.

'It's alright now, Mum. There's no need to cry any more. Alan's going to be alright.'

But, of course, there was every reason to cry, and despite Alan's recovery my mother's mental health deteriorated quite alarmingly. About five days after the drama with Alan, I was in the kitchen with my mother, Mrs Dancy and another neighbour of ours called Mrs Simmons. They were all having tea together while I was reading my comic, when all of a sudden my mother's voice changed. She started to speak in this awful kind of demonic cackle. I'd used something similar at school while we were acting out *Rumpelstiltskin*, which is probably why it alarmed me so much. It was as if she'd been possessed or something.

Straight away Mrs Dancy called the doctor, while Mrs Simmons tried to bring my mother round. She just got worse, though. And then she began swearing, which my mother rarely did.

The doctor, who lived close by, was there within a couple of minutes and I remember watching him slapping my mother around the face again and again, until eventually she returned to her old self. She had no idea what had gone on, and so the doctor had to try and explain what had happened. She was mortified, of course, but more than that she was absolutely terrified.

A few days later she went again, this time with a different voice, like that of a little girl. And then it happened again with yet another voice. She had voices within voices, as though she was rehearsing all the parts for some bizarre play. My dad later said that he thought she was acting out scenes from her younger life; the horrible demonic cackle being an impersonation of either her mother or her grandmother, with the voice of the little girl being her, of course. That always seemed like the most plausible explanation.

Treatment-wise, things weren't quite as archaic as they had been for Alan's pneumonia, but it was nonetheless basic in its approach. There were no talking therapies back then; no anti-psychotic drugs or anti-depressants. In those days, it was what they called electroconvulsive treatment, or electric shock treatment. It was like a cognitive equivalent of leeches, really, in the sense that it was all a little bit 'hit and hope'. It didn't matter what you had – psychosis, depression or a nervous disorder – if it was anything to do with the mind, they'd wire you up and shove a few hundred volts into you. Like something out of *Flash Gordon*!

I had to go with my mother to the hospital three times a month and sign for the treatment. I was only nine, although I looked more like twelve, but there was no other bugger around to do it. Watching her have the treatment was torture. I remember thinking, how can this be happening to my mother? I don't understand.

Eventually, after about six months, this treatment started to work. It didn't cure her; that – if it were even possible, which I doubt – would have taken years and years of therapy. But it did stop her going into those awful trances. We all remained quite nervous, though, for a long time after that. You see, not only did the doctors not know how electrotherapy worked, exactly, they also had no idea how long the benefit might last. Sometimes it could be weeks, and sometimes years. My father and I never really stopped keeping an eye on her. Even when she was in old age, I still remember worrying that she might one day have a relapse.

It's not a very happy story, is it? But, despite everything, Mother lived a long and happy life. She had problems, of course – but then, doesn't everybody? Mother's motto was that salient old adage, 'there's always somebody worse off than yourself', and she was absolutely right. Yet what really pulled her through, apart from the treatment and plenty of love, was an innate ability to laugh at herself. She used to say, 'Just because I've been off me chump for a while, doesn't mean I can't smile and enjoy myself. And if I go off me chump again, they'll pump more of that electricity into me. It does nowt for yer complexion, Brian!'

It was gallows humour, of course, but – my word – her ability to make fun of herself came in useful. Everybody in Goldthorpe knew what had happened to my mother and so, for a while, she became one of the main topics of conversation. The old gossips, of which there were many, had a bloody field day!

'Ooh, there she is, Gladys, that woman who went mad . . .'

That sort of thing didn't bother her, though. It was water off a duck's back to my mother. When people stared at her, she'd just say, 'Have you never seen a mad woman before? Have you never seen a woman who's off her chump? Well, now's yer big chance. Take a good look!' which of course made them all cower with embarrassment and fear.

I'm going to tell you a bit about my schooldays now. I started going to school during the war, which can be a very depress-

ing subject, of course, so let's start off with a song, shall we?
All together now:

> Hitler has only got one ball,
> Göring has two but very small,
> Himmler, has something sim'lar,
> But poor old Goebbels has none at all.
>
> *Daaa, de, da, de, da, da, da!*

Do you know we used to sing that in the playground at
school? In fact, there were four- and five-year-olds all over
the country singing songs about Nazi bollocks and suchlike.
It was all part of the war effort!

I went to Highgate mixed infants school in Goldthorpe,
and when the war started the teachers gave us all Mickey
Mouse gas masks, which we all had to wear in case Hitler
managed to drop his bombs on us. But it was all very exciting
for us kids. Very exciting! In the evening we'd listen to our
crystal radio sets, desperately trying to tune into the German
submarines, otherwise known as the Wolf Pack. Then back
at school the Home Guard would come in and then let off
little imitation incendiary bombs all over the yard.

'You see, boys and girls,' said the sergeant, 'if you get too
close to one of these things, you'll be killed.'

My first teacher there was a lady called Mrs Gummersall.
She was a lovely, bright, good-looking lady who I used to
have a bit of a crush on. I remember her talking about the
stars to us one day. It must have been in around 1943.

'You do know, children, that there are other worlds out
there?' she said. 'For instance, there's Mars, which is forty-
eight million miles away. You can see it sometimes at night;
it's known as the Red Planet.'

This was a revelation! This was life-changing! *Other
worlds?* I thought. *What on earth is she talking about?* But
of course she was right. Until then, whenever I'd asked my

parents about the stars in the sky, I'd always been given that 'Man in the Moon' mumbo jumbo. The stars in the sky were in fact planets – other worlds – and one of the planets was called Mars. What's more, it was red!

Imagine what that information would do to a six-year-old boy. It had a phenomenal effect on me. I just wanted to go there; to go into space and explore! I'd read about the sci-fi hero Buck Rogers and suchlike, but I had always assumed it was *all* completely made up. Much of it was, of course; but the planets weren't – and that was a revelation. The planets. Other worlds! I wanted to be in Buck Rogers' rocket, zooming past Venus, Mars and the Sun. I still do, for heaven's sake! After that, I started listening to Professor Fred Hoyle, the eminent astronomer, talking on the Third Programme about the planets and the universe. Did you know that I'm a fully trained cosmonaut? Perfectly true.

It wasn't just the stars that fascinated me. We had an Anderson air-raid shelter in our garden which was very rarely used – even less so once we started getting the better of the Germans – and so I turned it into an aquarium. I had lots of toads and newts and things, as well as green and yellow frogs. There were no such things as insecticides back then, you see, and so the fields were full of God's wonderful creatures. I remember walking across one of the fields at the back of Highgate school and it was absolutely teeming with young frogs. You could pick them up in handfuls! Anyone who was around at that time would be able to confirm this. So, when it came to curating my aquarium, I was spoilt for bloody choice. I had common toads and natterjack toads. I had great crested newts and smooth newts. I even had some palmate newts – *Lissotriton helveticus*! You can't beat a bit of Latin every now and then. I used to put all these wonderful animals in big five-pound jam jars and the glass would magnify them as they swam around. They're magnificent creatures, amphibians. I was one myself once, of course!

My parents used to find it hilarious watching their little boy creeping into his underground lair with a new batch of unfortunate victims! I didn't do anything nasty to them, I promise. I just studied them for a few days, then swapped them for a new batch.

I was also in charge of the aquarium at school, which leads me on to one of my favourite childhood stories. It involves me, some muddy feet and my head teacher Mrs Jarman's big fat arse.

Our story begins as I was taking a great crested newt that I'd found in the school grounds to the aquarium one day. In my excitement, I'd forgotten to wipe my feet. So, as I made my way eagerly to the science room, I left in my wake a trail of mud.

Now, she was quite a violent woman, Mrs Jarman. I suppose she must have seen (or been!) something nasty in the woodshed or something, because the way she reacted to my indiscretion – my word, you'd have thought I'd killed a thousand tiny orphans! After Assembly the next day, she pulled me up in front of the entire school.

'Look at this disgusting boy,' she exclaimed. 'He's put filth all the way down our corridors!'

And then she caned both my hands. The cane was slightly frayed at the end, so when it hit you, Jesus Christ you knew about it. I was almost paralysed by pain. I was only seven years old at the time and all I'd done was retrieve a miracle from a field – a beautiful great crested newt – which the other children would now be able to see.

'Disgusting boy!' she continued, after which she gave me a further four strokes on the back of my legs.

Mrs Jarman tried her best to make me cry, but she had no chance. For a start, I just didn't cry, but even if I had been able to I wouldn't have given her the satisfaction. I was the best fighter in school. I wasn't a bully, but I was already a good little boxer, and as she was hitting me I could see all the other kids looking at me, wondering if I'd break. When they realized I wasn't going to, you could actually sense the feeling of relief sweep across the hall. It gave my little friends strength!

You see, the school bully at Highgate mixed infants school was actually Mrs Jarman. She was the one who got a kick out of terrifying the weak and wielding power over the defenceless. I beat up a lot of bullies when I was at school, but she was by far the worst. I couldn't feel my hands or legs for a week afterwards, but I'd won! That big fat sadistic bully hadn't made me cry.

In fact, she'd made a big mistake in trying to humiliate me in front of the school: a big mistake.

Now, I've already referred to Mrs Jarman's big fat arse, haven't I? Well, it's time now to bring its considerable bulk into play. For you see, in addition to being what Mrs Jarman sat upon, her big fat arse now became an integral part of one of my favourite recreational pastimes – catapulting. It made the most marvellous moving target!

Nearby to where I lived in Probert Avenue, we had an old ammunitions dump. I talk about it more later on, in my *Flash Gordon* chapter, but this place was full of all kinds of wonderful stuff; thousands of pieces of metal of all shapes and sizes. Anyway, I went down there one day and I made myself what can only be described as an industrial catapult. It would have frightened the entire German Army, this thing. I could have won the bloody war with it! But I had my own battle to win. For I had declared war on Mrs Jarman's arse!

So I took this huge piece of metal from the ammunitions dump – it must have come off a bloody tank, probably – and then tied to it this long, thick piece of black plastic I'd found. It could take a stone about two or three inches thick quite comfortably, this thing. I was now armed, quite angry and very, very dangerous. Children have a tremendous gift for accuracy!

Mrs Jarman lived in a place called Swinton, which was about three miles away from Goldthorpe, and each day she would cycle to and from school on her bicycle. One afternoon, at about 3.40 p.m., I lay in wait behind a bush on the hill close to Manvers Main Colliery, just as it started to incline. She was a big woman, and I knew that as soon as she hit the hard bits, her arse would have to come up. So there I sat, teeming with adrenalin. I thought, *I'm going to have you, Jarman*. Children at the school even gave me a name, though they didn't know who I was. They called me – The Phantom!

Just before 4 p.m., I heard her coming up the hill, wheezing away like an obese asthmatic walrus. And, sure enough, the harder she pedalled, the loftier her arse became. When she was about five metres beyond me, I took aim and . . . WHAM! Right in the middle of the left cheek. A direct hit! I thought, *Take that, you bastard!* Somebody told me later on that she had a mark on her arse as big as a pancake. Success!

When I got to school the next morning, the police were there. I must admit I did feel a slight twinge of anxiety, but I thought, *They can't prove anything*. After Assembly, these two policemen joined Mrs Jarman on the hall stage.

'I was attacked on my way home last night,' she began. 'And I would like you all to know that I will not rest until I have found out who was responsible. When I do find out, that person will be prosecuted and will probably go to borstal. Do you all understand?'

There was only one person Mrs Jarman was looking at as she made her address – me! She hadn't seen me, but obviously had her suspicions. *Right*, I thought, *the only way to avert suspicion is to lead the investigation in apprehending this swine*. And so, as soon as the hall was cleared, I approached the injured party.

'Mrs Jarman,' I said. 'I want you to know that I will help you find whoever attacked you.'

God knows why, but this seemed to work. She seemed quite taken aback.

'Thank you, Blessed. That would be most appreciated.'

It was the least I could do! And so I became head of the 'Find the Phantom' squad and began reporting to Mrs Jarman daily.

'Do you know, we thought we had him earlier, Mrs Jarman. We'll keep trying though!'

'Thank you, Blessed. I'm very grateful.'

In this way, I became her champion as well as her assailant. Once again: success!

Time passed and Mrs Jarman thought she was out of danger. Big mistake!

Safely out of suspicion, I thought it was time to have another go, and so the following week I struck again, this time using a huge pointed stone. Up the hill she went, up went the arse and then . . . WHAM! Another direct hit, this time on the right cheek! The following day, she called me into her office.

'Blessed, we must find this hooligan!'

'Yes, Mrs Jarman. I heard he'd struck again. Are you alright? We've all been very worried.'

'Not really, Blessed. I'm in a great deal of pain. Anyway, we must catch him!'

'Yes, Mrs Jarman, I'll get about it right away. We'll find him, don't you worry!'

It was the perfect crime, really. Blissful! After, I think, about three more hits, I decided to grant the old ratbag a reprieve. Then about six months later, just before the end of term, I thought, *I'm going to give you a goodbye present, love*, and so I took up my original position once more, brandished the weapon, found the biggest, pointiest stone I could and

. . . WABOOOOOM! Right in the crack of her arse this time, and down the embankment she went. Game, set and match to the Phantom!

She must be long, long dead, Mrs Jarman, but just in case she is reading this somewhere in the fires of hell and damnation:

> *Up yours, you horrible old witch, and I hope*
> *your arse drops off!*
> *Much love,*
> *The Phantom*

Notwithstanding physical assaults on headmistresses' arses, I was in actual fact fairly well behaved at school. I got on with the majority of the teachers just fine and, when the occasion arose, would beat the living daylights out of bullies. Bright and brimming with enthusiasm, I was indeed just a younger version of the man I am today; with perhaps a bit less hair and not as many rude words.

My problem was concentration, or lack of it. I had the attention span of an under-achieving goldfish, which I'm afraid was considerably shorter than the majority of my lessons. I'd usually last about ten minutes, after which I'd be off; dreaming about Mars or newts or something. I always wanted to be anywhere other than the classroom!

And it was the same with exams. I remember taking my eleven-plus exam. Oh good heavens, what a balls-up I made of that! We'd moved to a little council house in Bolton-on-Dearne by then, which is a couple of miles away from Goldthorpe. My parents were keen for me to do well, of course, but I'm afraid that in my eyes success at school meant just one thing – time away from what I really wanted to do. So the eleven-plus and I never really stood a chance. In fact, after just one question – a ridiculous question, which I remember annoyed me somewhat – I walked out. It was not the last time I'd do such a thing, and I'll come back to this perplexing behaviour later, but for now let's just say that 'I wanted to be alone!'

So, although my actual ability was probably above average, my attention and application at school was such that after just a few weeks of being at Bolton-on-Dearne Secondary Modern I was placed – with about twenty-five other unfortunates – in what was referred to, by both the pupils and the teachers, as the Woodentops' class. I was a dunce! But, as opposed to giving us thickies a teacher who might be able to lead us out of duncehood, we were instead given somebody whom I believe to be the world's most dull and uninspiring man. To be fair to him, he'd been lumbered with some pretty dull and uninspiring pupils, but that was hardly our fault. Or was it?

After a few months of doing absolutely nothing, the headmaster, a Mr Brown, obviously realized that something was amiss and so decided to do something about it. One Monday morning, as opposed to being greeted by our usual teacher, we were met at the classroom door by Mr Brown himself. Once we were all sat down, he addressed us.

'Right then, children. I think I need to bring in a giant. Do any of you know what a giant is?'

For the first time since I'd been there, a hand went up. In fact, every hand went up!

'You, lad,' he said, pointing at the boy next to me. 'Tell us all what a giant is.'

'A giant is about two miles tall, sir, and it eats human beings.'

'Not quite, lad. You're thinking of *Jack and the Beanstalk*. Anyone else?'

'Me, sir,' I said, putting my hand back in the air.

'Go on, lad.'

'Well, there are lots of different kinds of giants,' I said. 'There's Goliath from the Bible, he was a giant. And there's Polyphemus, the great one-eyed giant.'

'That's right, lad. But I'm talking about a different kind of giant; a giant who, as of this afternoon, will become your new teacher!'

We were bewildered, to say the least. It didn't take a lot, admittedly, but by the time Mr Brown had finished speaking, the entire class was completely and utterly nonplussed. What did he mean? Were we in fact going to be taught by a giant? Speaking in metaphors to a class full of thickies probably wasn't the most judicious of decisions, so thank God we wouldn't have to wait long to meet our headmaster's new behemoth.

After lunch, we all nervously filed back into the classroom to await our fate. Then, a moment or two after we all sat down, the door opened and in came a woman I can only describe as a pixie. She was about four foot five inches tall, had small round spectacles on the end of her nose, a long black cardigan, thick woollen socks and small pointy shoes. *Jesus Christ*, I thought, *which mushroom has she come out from?* Mr Brown followed her in.

'Here you are,' he said. 'Here's your giant. This is my wife, Mrs Brown.'

With that, he turned and walked out. We all just stared at her, completely and utterly agog. Eventually, our giant broke the silence by writing on the blackboard. 'WOODEN-TOPS', she wrote, at which point somebody started giggling. Quick as a flash, she turned round and threw the board rubber straight at the offender's shoulder. Bang!

'Is that what you all want to be?' shouted our diminutive colossus. 'Is that what you want to be for the rest of your schooldays – the thick class?'

After that, she began going round us all one by one.

'You, how did Latin get into this country?' she asked.

'I don't know, Miss.'

Bang! A crack on the knuckles.

On to the next child.

'You, how did Latin get into this country?'

'I don't know, Miss.'

Bang! And so it went on.

Eventually, she got to me and as God is my witness I answered her, 'The Romans brought it, Miss.'

'YES!' she said. 'Tell the blockheads!' I repeated my answer. 'Right, this is the beginning of your education.'

And indeed it was. After a few weeks of being taught by Mrs Brown, we all ran to school! She instilled in us not only a thirst for knowledge, but also a work ethic. She had us quoting poetry and writing essays; she had us doing everything. Every day was a joy. An adventure!

I remember at the start of an English lesson one day she said, 'Put your books away, please. I'm going to read you a story.'

And then she read *The Hound of the Baskervilles* to us. We were all fascinated, of course. I mean it's one of *the* great murder mysteries, but at the same time we were stimulated and inspired.

Day after day, we never knew what to expect. One day we'd do drama and the next she took us out on a field walk. I'll tell you: she was a staggering woman, and because of her I passed every test they put in front of me. I actually *wanted* to learn. That was the big difference.

She even took me to see *Henry V* with Laurence Olivier at a cinema in Sheffield! If you excelled at something, she'd tutor you, and if you produced good work, she'd reward you, and because I seemed to do well at drama and had also written a good essay about my mother, she invited me to go and see *Henry V* with her and her husband. I sat in between them both and afterwards she gave me two oranges and two *Eagle* comics. That was my first introduction to Shakespeare on the stage.

After a few months with Mrs Brown, we were no longer known as the Woodentops. We were Class 1C, one of the best in the entire school. Mr Brown was right: she was indeed a giant!

Although I was only taught by Mrs Brown for a year, we got on so well together that we kept in touch long after I left school. In fact, if memory serves me correctly, she wrote to me way beyond *Z Cars*. She used to send me presents – and little bits of advice.

'I don't think you were terribly good in that last episode, Brian. Perhaps it's time you left *Z Cars* and moved on to something else?'

But I took it all in, you know. This pocket-sized Svengali knew exactly what she was talking about and over the years gave me a lot of very sage advice.

Thanks to her, the rest of my school life was hugely fulfilling and I excelled at just about everything. The only problem was that it finished a year or so early for me, which was a great, great shame. You'll read all about this in a later chapter, by the way, a chapter about death. Don't worry: it's quite humorous.

2

SHIT OR BUST WITH THE DEMON ACTOR

The Demon Actor I am referring to in the title of this chapter is Peter O'Toole, somebody I knew for over fifty years. Now, Pete O'Toole wasn't just *a* man of extremes; he was *the* man of extremes: Lord Byron with a knuckle-duster, love. He was indeed mad and bad, but most of all he was dangerous to know.

As a friend and fellow actor, he could be supportive, generous, thoughtful and entertaining. One of the best! That was only on alternate days, however, or when he didn't have his head either up his arse or inside a bottle. Otherwise, he'd just be moronic, bumptious, insulting and violent: a complete pain in the arse. And it was the same professionally. When Peter was good he was, in my opinion, the best there ever was. Better than all the great actors. But if he messed up, and he did sometimes – most famously in a play he persuaded me to appear in – he did so majestically. There was no middle ground with Pete. As he himself used to say, 'It was shit or bust, love.' Incidentally, I use the word 'love' because of O'Toole, although not quite as frequently as he did. He originally began using it simply to mock the theatrical establishment, having heard so many of his teachers and colleagues use it, which I found hilarious; so I suppose it just stuck. Very O'Toole!

From a personal point of view – and carrying on the 'extremes' analogy for a bit – I both loved and loathed Peter O'Toole. Not in equal measure, of course. If I'd loathed him more than I loved him, I wouldn't be wasting half a chapter of my new book on the bastard. Good heavens, no. He'd be assigned to the 'Where the bloody hell are they now?' file. No, I adored the old swine. He was just astonishingly infuriating and at times about as hazardous as me in full voice atop a large snowy mountain.

One question I think you might have been asking yourself while reading this book is: 'How did good old Brian get into acting?' Well, that's a very good question and one that I have decided to answer in this very chapter. It's relevant to O'Toole as I actually met him at drama school – the Bristol Old Vic, to be exact – so they fit together quite nicely. What's more, I do enjoy hopping back and forth a bit. Makes it all a bit more interesting, don't you think? Mixes it up a bit. There's nothing worse than these chronological autobiographies. In the words of O'Toole, they're about as boring as the Pope's balls!

Anyway, shall we begin?

My training for drama school came about in two stages, really. Stage one took place at my secondary modern school and stage two in amateur theatre; and let me tell you now that the people involved in both were nothing less than titans! Amateurs in name only.

When I was a boy, South Yorkshire was festooned with wonderful drama departments and amateur dramatic societies. They were everywhere and, what's more, they were brilliant. They put on operas, they put on musicals and they put on Shakespeare. The school teachers in particular used to put on the most marvellous productions, but none of them ever took it up professionally. Had they done so, they'd have been great successes. They'd have gone to the top! The Grey-friars of Doncaster were compared to the best professional companies in Britain, as was the Mexborough Theatre Guild. They were the crème de la crème of the area. The professional theatres would *complain* about the power of amateur theatre in South Yorkshire. Valentine Dyall, the actor who appeared most famously in radio's *The Man in Black*, actually protested about the expertise of these organizations. He thought they should have been made to disappear!

At my secondary modern school in Bolton-on-Dearne – where, you'll remember, I'd flowered under the wonderful Mrs Brown – there was a brilliant man named Steve Jones: my first titan. Steve Jones was a cross between David Niven and James Mason, and I don't mean aesthetically. He really was that good as an actor, and he became my first teacher. He spotted a modicum of talent in me and, for as long as I was there, he made it his business to nurture it. Then there was the wonderful Mr Donaldson, the art teacher. He would act you *Othello* three times a bloody week! He was brilliant. Dark eyes and a strange voice, like Donald Wolfit, the famous Shakespearean actor. These people were responsible for introducing children like me to theatre, and helping us realize our potential, and they took their roles very, very seriously.

Not all children began their secondary education with an interest in theatre, of course, and so they had to go looking for the actors and actresses of tomorrow. And once they'd found you, that was it: you'd be hooked. One week you'd be in *Toad of Toad Hall* and the next in *Rumpelstiltskin*. Then you'd start learning *Henry V* or *Hamlet*. Year after year after year, they brought together and nurtured as best they could these astonishing mini-societies of talent and enthusiasm. And these were all working-class boys and girls; the children of miners and plumbers and electricians. As I said, the major-ity couldn't even spell the word 'theatre' when they first

arrived at the school – let alone have any interest in or aptitude for it – which makes the achievements of the Mr Joneses
and the Mr Donaldsons even more astonishing.

You can tell I'm enjoying this, can't you? You see, that was
such an extraordinary time for me, especially after such an
inauspicious start. Steve Jones and Mr Donaldson took me
to Sheffield Rep and they took me to Doncaster Greyfriars;
they took me everywhere! I lived in a world of constant
engagement and inspiration. They even took me to see Wolfit
play his celebrated King Lear. How about that? Sir Donald
Wolfit, the GREATEST Lear of all time! But this wasn't simply
entertainment. These experiences were presented to me as
opportunities.

'This is what you could become, Blessed,' they said. 'You
can do this!'

At first, their words were alien to me. After all, I was just
a teenager. How could a coal hewer's son from C-Class possibly become an actor?

'Rubbish, you've got a future, Blessed, just go for it! This
could be your key to a better life. The best life!'

And that's where my first rule for living came from. Just
go for it! Whenever I'm signing an autograph, I nearly always
write that before my name. 'Go for it!' But these people drove
it into me, you see. They drove me on! Failure to try and to
give myself the best possible chance simply wasn't an option.

'Not everyone's destined for a life down the mines, lad,'
they said. 'You have a talent. You should use it!'

To be honest, I think my father was a bit puzzled by it all
at first, but he could see that I had this strange flair within
me. My mother was far more excited because she enjoyed
watching people like Spencer Tracy, and so the prospect of
her son trying his hand in the profession evoked all kinds of
wonderful dreams.

Nevertheless, I still found it difficult to accept what they
were saying. After all, they were adults. The teachers were

adults and the actors on the screen and on the stage were adults, yet I was just a child. I went to school and, like all children do, I lived pretty much in the moment, so seeing beyond my schooling was a struggle. It impeded my confidence somewhat. In fact, trying to share in their enthusiasm was like trying to comprehend infinity. I just couldn't get my fat little head round it!

Then, at the age of fourteen, something very, very strange happened to me.

'Something strange happened to old Brian?' I hear you say. 'That makes a change!'

Well, the only way I can describe this particular episode is that I in fact EXPLODED as a human being. I did. Something inside me burst free and I suddenly felt awake. I felt joyous! A great birth took place inside me that had me literally shuddering with possibility: the possibility of LIFE! Exploring new horizons and frontiers. The shackles had been removed! I no longer recognized any differences between myself and the adults. I could act, I could be in films, I could take the lead role in a Shakespeare play, I could cross deserts and I could climb mountains! Every single dream or aspiration I'd ever had in my life all of a sudden became a possibility. Even going to Mars! This wasn't a road-to-Damascus moment; it was a bloody ten-lane motorway! I could do what Mallory did; I could do what Captain Scott did; *and* I could do what Olivier and Wolfit did. Every time I have a good idea (I have a lot of ideas, not all of them good), this feeling is what comes over me. Why? Because I don't see obstacles! Anything is possible. *Just go for it!* I write my own script for life!

Now, without wanting to put a downer on such excitable proceedings, my awakening brought with it an almost indescribable yearning to be alone. I was already prone to seeking periods of solitude at inopportune moments – remember my eleven-plus! – but this feeling was now far stronger, and resulted in me walking out of rehearsals and all manner of important events. I got into all kinds of trouble with people. I wasn't what you'd call anti-social; I had dozens of friends and played out most evenings. But I also loved nothing more than disappearing into the Anderson shelter for hours on end and building aquariums and suchlike. I have always enjoyed being alone or in the company of animals. I love silence and I love stillness. The things that interest me most in life are still and silent. Space is silent. Mountains, on the whole, are silent. (It's the weather that makes a racket.) You see, despite us perhaps feeling lonely on occasion, we are never, ever, truly alone. Yes, I could be as gregarious as the next boy, but given a choice I was always happiest sitting by a pond or strolling through a field. Just alone with nature.

So there we are. At last, in an explosion of possibility, I had become a man. An occasionally quiet man, but a man nonetheless. But if you think the above was a bit strange, wait until you read *this*.

About the same time as me emerging into the Brian you know today, I began having these episodes where I would fall unconscious for a time. Stranger still, when I awoke I would actually be able to read people's thoughts. Now, I know you think I'm probably taking the mickey, but this is all perfectly true and if you'll just bear with me, I'll do my best to make sense of it all.

It happened at about 9.15 a.m. every morning in the school assembly hall. First of all I'd collapse, and then the teachers would sit me on a chair and wait for me to come round. This could take up to half an hour sometimes. Mr Jones always said he thought I'd gone into some kind of coma, but I hadn't. You see, despite appearing like I was gone to the world, I was in fact perfectly conscious. The moment these episodes came upon me, I started to experience what I can only describe as pure bliss. I transcended the universe: sailed past planets and galaxies, almost as if I'd penetrated

some kind of bubble and was at last free to explore. I suppose
it was almost a cognitive version of what had happened to me
when I'd EXPLODED as a human being – this was a cognitive
awakening.

When I came round, the first person I always saw was Mr
Jones, this warm and quite brilliant teacher, and then as I
became more aware of my surroundings I began to see clouds
around people's heads, and within these clouds were both
pictures and words which were constantly changing. I could
see what they were thinking! It was then that I noticed that
people lied in silence. I could actually see them lying.

I was later told by a mystic in India that these were the
clouds of ignorance: the clouds of ignorance that keep us
asleep.

But these experiences also had a knock-on effect. My
senses were suddenly heightened to such a degree that when
I listened to things like classical music I could listen to each
instrument individually. I could separate them out, so to
speak. My sight was also affected drastically. I could see
molecular structure in leaves and so forth. It was the most
extraordinary thing!

My parents became very concerned as this would also
happen in the early evening, again for about half an hour. I
didn't suffer at all, and I wasn't in any pain. I would just drift
away for thirty minutes and basically travel the universe.
They too thought I was in some kind of a coma, but in fact
what was actually happening to me was a kind of accidental
transcendental meditation.

I spent hours trying to explain this to my parents and
teachers – and to lots of doctors, incidentally – but of course
nobody could quite get their head around it. This was the
late 1940s and early 1950s, remember, and so transcendental
meditation hadn't quite penetrated South Yorkshire. What
was happening in my mind was almost *beyond* words, though,
and certainly not within the lexicon of a fourteen-year-old.

Everyone simply looked at me as if to say, 'Bye 'eck, tha's one sandwich short of a bloody picnic, Brian.'

Now, I'm about to make sense of all this for you. Or at least I'm going to try. Some of you will get it and some of you won't. Anyway, during every single one of these meditations I kept on hearing a word being spoken, a word that was pronounced 'Raam' but that I later found out is actually spelt 'Ram'. I remember asking my parents and Mr Jones about this.

'Are you sure, Brian?' they said.

'Yes,' I replied. 'It sounds like the name of a sheep.'

Anyway, eventually the teachers decided that the only way to deal with this was to stop me going into this state in the first place, and so when 9.15 a.m. came round, they were ready. They pinched me, tickled me, gently slapped my face and talked to me.

'Don't go into it, Brian. Stay here. Stay where you are!'

It was a fight, but gradually they stopped me going into these meditations. This to me was a mistake, however, as when I went into them I not only experienced feelings of bliss, I also garnered a great deal of knowledge and perception. They improved my brain.

Thirteen years later, when I was twenty-seven, I received meditation from the Shankaracharya of northern India, who was a fully realized man. It was a great relief for me and has brought me untold happiness. I'm pleased to say that since that meeting I've never looked back. I meditate twice a day for half an hour and I'm attached to a study group in London called The Study Society.

Anyway, back to Bolton-on-Dearne Secondary Modern.

In addition to having the help of Mr Jones and all these other wonderful teachers, I was also sent on drama courses: dozens of them, all over the county. They were weekend courses mainly, attended by dozens of hopefuls, and each one had a professional present. It was so exciting! The chap who ran these drama courses was another theatrical titan named Johnny Adams, who reminded me of David Garrick: a small man of incredible power! He could terrify audiences. Johnny could have made a fortune in professional theatre but, like Mr Jones, he decided to stay where he was and help young people. He ran youth theatres, youth productions and drama courses. You name it, he organized it. An astounding man! So you see, I actually had this ensemble of astoundingly talented good Samaritans everywhere. Wonderful, wonderful people!

One day, Mr Adams told me that he had decided to hold a course at Bolton-on-Dearne Secondary Modern. Joy of joys! An entire weekend of professionally taught drama just a stone's throw from home. *It doesn't get any better than this*, I thought. The professional on the course was a director called David Giles from the Bradford Civic Theatre. He had black hair, a very deep voice and actually went on to direct me in a television play many years later called *The Recruiting Officer*, alongside people like Ian McKellen and Jane Asher.

Any old how, all weekend David delivered lectures, answered questions and directed scenes from various plays. He even cast me as Macbeth. I'll never forget it: he had all the witches coming down ropes in the gymnasium. It blew my mind. I was now working with professionals. Getting closer to my dream!

About this time, the Northern Children's Theatre, which was attached to the Bradford Civic Theatre, put on a production of *The Smugglers' Cave* at the Welfare Hall in Bolton-on-Dearne. These days, the Welfare Hall is known as the Dearne Playhouse, but whatever the name, it always was and still is an extremely good theatre. Packed with talent! I remember watching them do what's called the 'get in' for the show, where they bring in all the sets and equipment and so on. I'd never seen anything like it in my life. There were trucks of stuff and it all looked so professional. Anyway, the

richest people in the area at the time were a family called
Hunter. They owned the coach company and whatnot. I got
along famously with them generally, but I remember speaking to Mrs Hunter after a performance of *The Smugglers' Cave*
one evening. She'd asked me how I was and so I'd told her all
about my ambitions to join an amateur theatre group and
eventually make it to drama school. But, do you know, she
absolutely shot me down in flames. Or at least she tried to.

'You're getting ideas above your station, young man,' she
said. 'Folk round here don't go waltzing off to drama school.
Join the amateur theatre by all means, but you concentrate
on getting yourself a decent job. Drama school indeed . . .
You have a frightful accent.'

She wasn't a bad woman, Mrs Hunter. She was just a bit
of a parochial snob. She didn't believe that working-class
people could become actors or artists. Anyway, as she walked
away – obviously confident that she'd knocked every last
drop of theatrical ambition out of me – I just smiled to
myself. I didn't need galvanizing, but her words certainly
put a shine on my determination. I thought, *I'll show you, you
old hag!*

The way I go on, it sounds like success was already in the
bag for me, doesn't it? All these wonderful teachers and
drama courses . . . Well, believe you me, that was not the case.
In fact, there was one thing in particular that stood between
me and success – and that was my bloody accent! (Mrs Hunter
was right about that, if not about anything else.) It was so
strong that even the old boys down at the working men's club
couldn't understand me sometimes. Geoffrey Boycott sounded
like Brian bloody Sewell compared to me. It was very colourful in tone, my accent, and very, very thick. People used to
say to my mother, 'Could you ask your Brian to slow down
when he speaks? I can't understand a bloody word!'

In the end, Mr Jones asked me to work with a speech
therapist; something I was dead against. I felt like I'd lose my

identity if my voice changed. Become a different person. In fact, if I'm totally honest, it scared me a little.

'Look, Brian,' said Mr Jones, 'all he's going to do is take the edge off your accent, which will enable you to perform the classics. It will be done slowly and carefully, and you'll be in complete control. If we don't work on it, not only will you remain incomprehensible to some, but you'll be limited as an actor.'

Fortunately, my desire to succeed completely outstripped my fear of changing personality and sounding like a whoop-sie, and so straight after I'd agreed, Mr Jones set about arranging speech lessons with a wonderful man named Frank Cooper of Rotherham. He had a warm, caring personality.

'Brian,' he said, 'you will gradually lose your Yorkshire accent, but *not* your Yorkshire expression. You will always be able to use your Yorkshire accent for work, whenever you please. You will never become artificial.'

The results of his labours are what I'm left with today, of course. The voice I hope is helping to bring to life these very words!

Anyway, it's about time we got on to stage two of my training, which took place at the Mexborough Theatre Guild. I'm sixteen in our story now, which means I need to introduce you to the man who sits at the very top of my list of collaborators and mentors. Even above the wonderful Mr Jones! He was a theatrical colossus named Harry Dobson, and he was the house director and head of Mexborough. And what a director he was. Revered throughout the industry and urged to go professional. Had he done so, he'd have sailed past the likes of Trevor Nunn and Peter Hall. Would have made mincemeat out of them!

For an aspiring actor from Goldthorpe, getting into Mexborough really was akin to getting into the Bristol Old Vic. The place had such a good reputation that if you managed to be accepted, you knew you'd be that bit closer to making it.

I had all this planned out, you see, and Mexborough was at stage two of my plan. It went: school, Mexborough Theatre Guild, Bristol Old Vic, the Old Vic, films. Hardly any TV then, of course.

But getting into Mexborough wasn't easy. Just like the Bristol Old Vic and every other drama school, there was an audition process, and you also had to be interviewed. It didn't matter if you were the best actor in the world with the most pleasing personality, if you had an off day and buggered it up, that would be it. Come back next year!

Harry Dobson was a huge man with great sausage fingers and I remember every single word he said to me at my audition. My first *ever* audition as an actor. Allow me to recall his address for you:

'It's all about giving,' he insisted. 'The more you give in life, the more you get out of it. I can see that you're passionately determined. That's fine, Brian, but be careful. Your very determination can blunt you and create extreme tension.

'Balance and grace, Brian, you must learn balance and grace. You simply have to trust me to help you approach the task with both. Remember, the maximum effect with the minimal of effort – that is grace.

'The basis of all is love. You say you eventually want to enter the professional theatre? This is, of course, a fine ambition, but it has its problems. The commercial theatre is tremendously competitive and in that atmosphere you can at times lose your way and forget yourself. In a nutshell, you can bury your conscience. You will always have to remind yourself to constantly love and honour your fellow actors.

'Honour talent wherever you go, and don't be afraid to make a fool of yourself. Everyone should be allowed to do that. Progress is like a stairway: when you take one step there will always be a slight interval as it flattens out, but don't lock yourself in a cupboard when this happens. Have the courage to keep your heart open so that you may share with your fellow artists. You will come to understand how much you need other people. You can't do it all on your own.'

Those words have served me well these past sixty-two years; not simply on the stage, but throughout my life.

'Well, lad,' he then said, 'I've said a bellyful. Let's hear you read the part of Robert in *The Silver Cord*. Don't look so nervous. I won't bite you.'

Gradually, I relaxed and managed to read with some conviction.

'Not bad, lad,' nodded Harry. 'Not bad at all. You've a hell of a lot to learn, mind, but you've a naturally good voice and it sounds like you know how to use it. Those speech lessons you told me about paid off, didn't they? Right then, you big ape, I'm going to give you your first part. You're going to play Robert in *The Silver Cord*, the part you've just read. My God you've got to work, though, lad!'

I was in! Words cannot describe how I felt. I took Harry's right hand with both of mine and I shook it vigorously.

'Thank you Mr Dobson! I'll not let you down.'

'I'm sure you won't, lad. I'll see you at the first rehearsal. And make sure you know your lines!'

So here I am, at sixteen years of age – this Woodentop from C-Class whom nobody could understand – and I'm actually part of the Mexborough Guild; surrounded by doyens! There was no guarantee of success, of course, but I was in bloody good hands.

The weekend drama courses continued, except now I was surrounded by grammar school boys. This could have been a problem as yours truly had had to leave school a year or so early.

When I was fifteen my father was involved in another terrible accident down the mine. His injuries were so severe that he was unable to work for well over a year, leaving but one potential breadwinner in the Blessed household – me.

It sounds rather more tragic than it actually was, as in the evenings my teachers would come round to my house and tutor me, but at first I was devastated. I was the happiest and most enthusiastic pupil in the entire school, so to have all that taken away from me suddenly was pretty hard to bear. Anyway, as the saying goes, what doesn't kill you makes you stronger. And it certainly did make me stronger! But all this is for a later chapter. Let's keep on ploughing towards Bristol, shall we?

Luckily, I didn't find these grammar school boys nearly as intimidating as I'd first thought; in fact, it turned out that I was way ahead of them with regard to theatrical knowledge and expertise, which meant I actually ended up leading all these posh buggers. Also, if I was ever quizzed about what qualifications I had, I would say:

'Oh yes, I left with eight O levels. I'll probably just do the four A levels before drama school. How about you?'

Harry Dobson thought this was hilarious, but it annoyed him slightly too. 'You shouldn't feel like you have to lie to them, Brian. Just because you left school at fifteen and don't have any qualifications doesn't mean they're better than you. You know more about life.'

Do you know, the first time I ever encountered anyone from the Bristol Old Vic was at one of these drama courses. Bristol Old Vic's movement teacher, a German fellow named Rudi Shelly, had been invited to attend one as a professional. When he was introduced to us, I couldn't believe it. Surely it was fate! *I've got to get to this place*, I thought. *Harry Dobson says it's the best there is!*

Rudi Shelly appears in dozens of these kinds of books – for the simple reason that he was one of the most influential drama teachers this country has ever known. Here are a few names for you: Anthony Hopkins, Patrick Stewart, Daniel Day-Lewis, Jeremy Irons, Pete Postlethwaite, BRIAN BLESSED, Miranda Richardson; each indebted beyond measure to this superman. Meeting him at the course inspired me more than ever to follow my dreams.

Now, the very last piece of advice Harry Dobson had given me at my audition was a few words on the benefits of having patience.

'There's no use jumping the gun, lad. If you move too soon and make a mess of things, you may never get another chance. Timing's as important off the stage as it is on it. You have to be patient.'

Sage words indeed – although I have to admit patience is not something I've been known to practise a great deal. I flatter myself that my timing both on the stage and in front of a camera lies just north of average, but I'm afraid that in real life it is somewhat lacking. In fact, let's not beat about the bush, I just can't do it. I am impatient with a capital IMP!

So, as soon as the auditions for the new term at Bristol Old Vic came around, as opposed to sitting tight and learning my trade, I was away on a train quicker than you can say Jack Robinson.

My endeavours were flawed, of course. You couldn't go to drama school until you'd done your national service, and you couldn't do your national service until you were eighteen years of age. I had just turned sixteen and so was four whole years away from being eligible. *Bollocks to that*, I thought. *Four years is an age! No, no, no, I must enrol now.* And so, as I said, after absolutely no thought whatsoever, I contacted Bristol Old Vic, booked an audition, borrowed some money and away I went. I was flying like a kite!

I had my story all worked out. I was twenty years of age, had just completed my national service with the RAF and was a senior member of the Mexborough Theatre Guild. In actual fact, not even that last bit was true; I was merely a junior member. That didn't bother me, of course. I had my story and I was sticking to it.

On the day of my audition I was up at the crack! I got the

6 a.m. train from Bolton-on-Dearne to Rotherham and then caught the next train to Sheffield. From there, I jumped on the 7.30 a.m. train to Bristol Temple Meads. I had my speeches, my ten shillings and sixpence for the audition, and an air of confidence that would have put Peter O'Toole himself to shame. Surely it was just a question of what colour I wanted my codpiece?

I arrived in Bristol literally dripping with adrenalin and confidence. That feeling I'd first had at fourteen was back with me in spades. I'd played Robert in *The Silver Cord* and was about to play Branwell in *The Brontës of Haworth Parsonage*. I could recite every word Shakespeare had ever written for Christ's sake! Surely the audition would be a formality and then – THEN – I would become a real actor. A star was about to be born, ladies and gentlemen. Behold the future king of British theatre!

Boy was I excited. I sang a fanfare as I stepped off the train.

'DA – DA DA DA DA – DA DAAAAAAAAAAAAAAAAA!'

I am here, people of Bristol, I am here!

I'd read as much about the Bristol Old Vic as I had about Everest. They were the two places in the world that I dreamt about going.

When I eventually arrived at the Theatre Royal, the place was littered with fellow hopefuls, except they all looked slightly different to me – or I to them. They were all tall, far taller than me, and they had a confidence and tone to their voices that felt ever so slightly beyond me. Not alien to me, just not quite within my grasp. They were all twenty, of course. The required minimum age!

After I paid my audition money, I sat down and waited to be called. All the other aspirants stared, but that didn't bother me. I simply stared back. I may have lacked a little confidence in my voice, but in my mind I was still the best in the room. Cock of the bloody North, love!

Eventually, I was called.

'Mr Brian Blessed? Would you step this way please?'

As I entered the auditorium, I was greeted by the principal of the school, a Mr Edward Stanley.

'Mr Blessed, I'm Mr Stanley. My word, you do look terribly young for your age!'

'Yes,' I lied, 'people often tell me that.'

Just then, I saw a familiar face.

Oh Jesus Christ, I thought. *It's Rudi Shelly!*

It hadn't occurred to me that I might bump into him. Even though there had been quite a few people on the course he'd attended, I'd been at the front for every lecture and had bombarded him with literally hundreds of questions. There was no way in the world he'd have forgotten me. I'd even played the Angel Gabriel for him at the Calder drama course. And there he was, holding a cigarette and looking very, very suspicious.

'Mr Blessed, isn't it?' he said, with a knowing smile. 'We've met before, I think. I'm looking forward to hearing you.'

I may have been uber-confident and naive, but I wasn't stupid. I'd been well and truly rumbled. He didn't say anything, though. *Perhaps he's going to give me a chance?* I thought. After all, if you're good enough, you're old enough.

'Have you done your national service, Mr Blessed?' asked Mr Stanley.

'Yes, of course. I was with the RAF.'

'And what are you doing now?'

'Well, I'm hoping to become a full-time student,' I quipped.

'A very good answer. Now, what are you going to recite for us?'

'The dagger speech from *Macbeth*.'

'Really? How very interesting, Mr Blessed. That's quite different to what we're used to. Off you go then.'

With that, he beckoned me towards the stage. I looked at him as if to say, 'You want *me* to go up *there*?' I couldn't believe it. It was actually happening.

As I walked slowly up the steps, I stared at the stage before me. Edmund Kean, Laurence Olivier, John Gielgud, Eric Porter. They and countless others had trodden these boards. I didn't feel nervous, just reverent. When I at last reached centre stage and turned to face the auditorium, the circle, dress circle and ceiling were painted in greens and golds, the most beautiful sight ever.

'Whenever you're ready, Mr Blessed.'

Now, just try and imagine for a moment a sixteen-year-old Brian Blessed. There I am, standing centre stage in a large theatre, and I'm about to act the dagger speech.

Is this a dagger which I see before me,
The handle toward my hand? Come, let me clutch thee . . .

At last, it was over. Actually, what am I saying? I didn't want it to end!

'Good heavens, is that really your voice, Mr Blessed?' asked Mr Stanley. 'Are you sure you didn't pinch that from somebody? Really, that was splendid. Come and sit down with us for a moment, would you?'

As I made my way down from the stage, I heard a faint round of applause coming from the assembled panel. I wasn't sure if this was out of sympathy or admiration, but quite frankly I didn't care. I'd just delivered a Shakespearean speech on the stage of the Bristol Theatre Royal. Nothing else mattered.

'Now then, Mr Blessed, how old are you?'

'I'm twenty, sir.'

'You obviously have talent, but I'm sure it doesn't stretch as far as ageing yourself prematurely. Now, how old are you really, Master Blessed?'

I was in a kind of daze at this point. I knew they knew,

but that didn't matter any more. I was just very, very happy to be there.

'I'm only sixteen,' I admitted. 'I didn't want to wait four years so I thought I'd give it a go. I'm sorry. I'm desperate to come here, you see, and I think I can get a scholarship.'

'Well, we're very glad to hear it, Mr Blessed, but please, you must do your national service. There can be no exceptions. Not even for such an amazing voice as yours!'

'I understand. Thank you, though. I've had a marvellous time.'

As I walked back towards the foyer, I suddenly heard the voice of Mr Shelly.

'Stop a minute, would you, my boy? Now look, my colleagues and I were all very impressed by what we saw and heard today, and I remember you from the course. You asked a lot of very pertinent questions. You have talent and you have a good brain. Work hard and we'll see you back here soon. OK?'

If I'm honest, that was just what I needed as I began the long journey back to Yorkshire. I suppose my confidence had been bruised slightly, and the four years still in front of me didn't seem any less like a life sentence. No, Mr Shelly's words were a tonic alright, and I was going to need them once Harry Dobson had finished with me.

When I arrived at rehearsals the following week, Harry was indeed waiting for me. He looked amused but nevertheless vexed.

'Come here, lad,' he said, before taking me by the scruff of the neck and parading me round the rehearsal room.

'Are you listening, everyone? Look at this great ape. If any of you ever become impatient for something, take a look at this fool. Went waltzing off down to Bristol and got himself an audition at the Old Vic Theatre School. Not a word to anyone! Well, he's still here, isn't he? You see, ladies and gentlemen: patience, patience, patience, *patience*!'

Fortunately, that was the extent of my punishment and Harry still allowed me to play Branwell in *The Brontës of Haworth Parsonage*. At the time it was unheard of for a sixteen-year-old to play such a large role and it generated a lot of interest in the area. My father, who was still not convinced about me becoming an actor, uncontrollably wept at my death as Branwell. My final line was something like: 'What have I done with my life? I can't hold on, I can't hold on.'

Bolton-on-Dearne was a sea of tears after that, love. A town full of emotional wrecks! It was all pretty dramatic stuff.

After the first performance, my father came backstage.

'Take it up, lad,' he said. 'Take it up. I think you'll be terrific.'

To top it all, I won Best Actor of the season. Oh, ecstasy of ecstasies!

Anyway, to cut a perilously long story short, I did my national service, won my scholarship and then made my way down to Bristol for a second time. I actually joined the Parachute Regiment for my national service and made forty-six jumps. It was fun, but Bristol was never far away from my thoughts.

I still had to pass my audition though. There was a new principal in place by then, an extremely popular fellow named Duncan Ross, and fortunately, after I'd read my speeches, I was offered a place on the spot. I didn't say anything to my parents when I returned and instead waited for the letter to arrive. Once again, there were tears galore everywhere. From my mum, my dad – even me! I thought, *Why not? Let's all have a good blub*. My parents were so happy, and so proud. Actually, the entire town was proud. It was big news, you see: a coal hewer's son going off to drama school. Not an everyday occurrence, I can assure you. I wonder what Mrs Hunter thought?

*

So, eventually I arrived in Bristol, completely laden down with gear. I had leotards, jockstraps, plays, shorts . . . all kinds of paraphernalia. There were trunks and trunks of the stuff! The school curriculum covered everything: speech, fencing, judo, gymnastics, theatre history, the lot.

People often ask me why I never wanted to attend a drama school in London – and that's quite an easy question for me to answer. You see, I was always told that RADA was under the influence of the West End and that the West End could be a distraction. Whether that's true or not I'm not sure, but the Bristol Old Vic was always sold to me by Harry Dobson as the best there ever was, and there were no distractions down there. You had Bristol Old Vic, Bristol Old Vic Theatre School and Bristol University, and because the drama department at the university was attached to the Old Vic Theatre School, I could get help on the academic side. I could 'fill in the holes', as Harry Dobson used to say: the holes in my education. And that's exactly what I did; I educated myself with the help of one or two teachers. They told me what I needed to read and I went ahead and bloody well read everything!

But the most exhilarating part of being a student at Bristol was being able to watch the Bristol Old Vic theatre company. We were allowed to watch one or two of the rehearsals and then we'd go either to one of the previews or to the opening night. Watching a professional company at work though; oh my God! The shows were a joy to behold, but the rehearsals? They were a revelation!

Our teachers at the school included Rudi Shelly, of course, who taught movement; Mrs Manvel, who taught speech; and Daphne Heard, who taught drama. Daphne was a great actress and played Peter Bowles's mother in *To the Manor Born*. And what a wonderful character she was. Full of spunk! I used to call her Daphers and I flirted with her all the time. We had the most marvellous conversations.

'Why have you cast me as the Bastard in *King John*, Daphers?' I said one day, locking her in a bear hug.

'Are you making a pass at me, Mr Blessed? And you shouldn't call me Daphers!'

'Yes, I am making a pass at you, Daphers, and I don't care what you say, I'm going to ravish you. Do you hear me, woman? RAVISH YOU!'

'Well, I can tell you now that I cast you as the Bastard because I can't think of a bigger bastard to play him. Now kindly put me down.'

So it was all that kind of stuff. Tremendous fun. Wonderful woman!

Now, I'm afraid that Mr Shelly's movement lessons were anathema to me. I have about as much grace and poise as a heavily sedated brontosaurus and back then I simply hated dancing. Think about it for a moment, will you? Can you imagine me doing high kicks? If you can, you must have a pretty twisted mind. It's ridiculous. Anyway, because of this I always attempted to hide during his classes – boys who were 'good with colours' to the front, and fat gorillas like me at the back. But, after a few weeks, Mr Shelly got wise to what I was doing and decided to put an end to it.

'Brian, I can see you hiding again. Come to the front, please.'

Oh no! I thought.

'Whenever you enter a room, Mr Blessed, you always look like you're here to deliver a piano. Well, no more. Today you will learn how to walk. Walk for me, Brian: walk to the door and back.'

I had to do as I was told, and so wearing a bright red tracksuit I walked as fast as I could to the door and back.

'Oh no, no, no, *no*, Mr Blessed. I asked you to walk to the door. That was more of an amble, really. Almost a trot. Anyway, now I want you to become a tulip.'

'A what?'

'A tulip. You know what a tulip is, don't you?'

'Well, yes, of course I do. But I don't know how to become one.'

'Think about it for a minute, Mr Blessed, and then become a tulip for me.'

And so, in front of all these people and wearing a lovely red tracksuit, I had to pretend to be a tulip.

'That was beautiful, Brian, beautiful. Now, no creeping off to the back again. You stay here. OK, I want you to become a stick insect now.'

'A what?'

'A stick insect.'

'But I'm sixteen stone.'

It used to go on like that all the time. I'd begin the lesson at the back of the room and always end up at the front making a complete arse of myself.

The last teacher I must tell you about is the wonderful Mrs Moody, our singing teacher. Now, as with movement, I was to singing what Peter O'Toole was to divinity – or at least that's what I thought. I'd tried a bit of warbling on stage over the years but it had always sounded so bloody horrible that in the end I just gave up. It wasn't fair on those around me. When it came to a lesson with Mrs Moody, I decided to sit at the back and just pretend. She, though, like Mr Shelly, had other ideas.

'Can you sing, Mr Blessed?'

'I'm afraid not, Mrs Moody.'

'With your voice, I find that very difficult to believe. Come to the front, please, Mr Blessed.'

As it happened, Mrs Moody coached singers at the Welsh Opera at the time and her husband, John Moody, was in charge of the Bristol Old Vic Company. They were quite a formidable partnership and very, very well respected.

'Alright, Mr Blessed, I'd like you to imagine you're a farmer and somebody has stolen some of your sheep. I'm going to play you a note on this piano a few times, and when you're ready, I'd like you to call after them in that note. Do you understand?'

'Perfectly, Mrs Moody.'

'Alright, Mr Blessed, here's your note.'

With that, she began playing a note on the piano and I began trying to imitate it.

'OI,' I sang. Not shouted, sang! 'OI, OI, OI, OI, OI!'

'You're singing, Mr Blessed. Can you hear that? You're singing.'

I promise you that within five weeks I was singing Wagnerian tenor. Nobody believed it, least of all me. I sang everywhere! I sang when I got up and when I went to bed. I might even have sung when I was asleep. Mrs Moody said I was a tenor with a dark quality, whatever that means!

Two weeks later, the greatest soprano in the world at the time, Birgit Nilsson, was playing at the Bristol Hippodrome and she had with her the great Nicolai Gedda from La Scala, Milan, the most recorded tenor in history. Mrs Moody invited me to go and see these two legends and I was absolutely blown away by them. They made the most beautiful sounds.

It turned out that Mrs Moody knew both Nilsson and Gedda, and had invited them up to the school the morning after the performance.

'Nilsson and Gedda are coming here?' I asked in disbelief.

'That's right. You must come and meet them. They're both expecting you.'

'I'd love to!'

It was all a set-up, of course. Mrs Moody had a feeling that I might actually make a better singer than I would an actor, but she wanted a professional opinion.

And so, after some gentle persuasion, I actually sang with these two legends of the opera world. I sang 'The Pearl Fishers' Duet' with Gedda, from Bizet's opera of the same name, and with Nilsson I sang a duet from Wagner's *Siegfried*. It was a truly mesmeric experience. I was new to opera but already had a profound respect for these two artists. They were opera's *haut monde*!

When I'd finished my duet with Birgit, Nicolai, who is still alive and now ninety years of age, asked us all to sit down.

'Mr Blessed,' he said. 'I must insist that you leave drama school and you come with me to La Scala. Mrs Moody is correct; you are a dramatic tenor with a dark quality. Caruso had a dark quality. You have gold in your voice, Brian. In two years you will be a leading tenor at La Scala, Milan. This I guarantee.'

Shocked wasn't the word. Even Mrs Moody looked flummoxed.

'I'll need some time to think about it,' I said. 'I've only just started my course.'

'You must believe me, Brian: singing is your future. Come with me, Brian, come to Milan.'

Over the next two days, I spent hours and hours talking things through with Mrs Moody. All she'd sought was a professional opinion – and now this.

'I think you ought to think very seriously about this, Brian. After all, La Scala is the greatest opera company in the world – bar none.'

I loved opera, but that simply wasn't enough. Acting was a *must*. Good, bad or indifferent, I must do it. I also wasn't sure I wanted to sing and act with people while not actually being able to look at them. Everything's far less fluid in opera, and to me that felt stifling. And what about all those great big tits! Too weighty for me, I fancy. No, I was afraid, for Nicolai's sake, that I was happy where I was.

Despite not taking it up professionally, I carried on singing opera and still do a bit to this day. If you see me in the street, stop me and ask me to give you a few notes. I'll gladly oblige. Not only has it helped me in certain roles I've played, such as Old Deuteronomy in *Cats*, but I've found it does wonders for my speaking voice, especially with regard to building stamina. Actors suffer dreadfully with this, even to this day, and I'm in no doubt that a few days' training in opera would work wonders. It is the finest training for the voice.

Anyway, time to introduce our second protagonist. You'll find the language rather colourful here, but it's just as it was and I can't see the point in changing it. Do you really want 'Blessed Lite'? Well, of course you don't. Here we go, then.

As I think I've already intimated, by far the most exhilarating aspect of life at the Bristol Old Vic was having almost constant access to a professional theatre company. This was akin to having a perpetual masterclass playing in just the next room. We weren't supposed to mix with the company socially, but we were allowed to watch them at work – from the very first rehearsal through to the opening night. This was not only a great privilege, of course; it was an educational experience. It was indeed a masterclass!

I remember watching them rehearse for the first time. This was repertory theatre, remember, and so the output was prolific. Show after show after show. The atmosphere was frenetic but somehow quite controlled. It was organized chaos, really.

When they were stuck for a line, they'd shout over to the prompt corner.

'Give me the line, would you, give me the line!'

Then they'd carry on, without losing any character or shape. And it would happen again and again and again until they knew it all by heart. No time to take the script away and learn it. You could only become word perfect on the job, so to speak. To a young actor this was mesmerizing stuff! This was how professionals worked.

The company at the time was sheer class. You may not have heard of some of these actors and actresses, but mark my words you'll definitely know their faces. They were stalwarts of British television and theatre for decades. People like Wendy Williams, David King, Wendy Hutchinson, Robert Lang, Joseph O'Connor, Peter Jeffrey, Alan Dobie, Edward Hardwicke and Emrys James. Great professionals! They also had the marvellous Rachel Roberts in the company, who, despite suffering a sorry end to her life (she committed suicide in LA at the age of fifty-three), went on from Bristol to become a big star, and was a truly inspirational actress.

I remember seeing Rachel in a play at the Bristol Old Vic called *The Queen and the Rebels*. This was in September 1956. She played a prostitute called Argia who gets mistaken for the queen and is subsequently bumped off. She allows the rebels to shoot her in order to protect the queen. Anyway, Rachel's performance had the press and all the students in raptures, and rightly so, but it was another member of the cast who caught my eye that evening. He played a guard and only had one line, but I'll tell you what, when he spoke, you sat up and bloody well listened. I think his line was something like: 'She's confessed to Biante, she's confessed! She is the Queen!'

I remember thinking to myself, *Who the hell's that?* It was O'Toole, of course. The way he said the word 'confessed' was almost hypnotic. Now, you've got to *think* O'Toole here. Bring to mind that marvellous voice of his.

'She's *confessed* to Biante, she's *confessed*! She is the Queen!'

Stunning! Just the one line, but I couldn't take my eyes or my ears off the actor.

From then on, each time I went to see an Old Vic production I always looked out for O'Toole, but regardless of which play they were producing, he always had the smallest of roles. I think he understudied, too, but he never had more than a few lines. *I* found this frustrating, so God knows what it must have been doing to him. Anyway, a few months down the line there was a ruckus within the company and a lot of the leading actors and actresses left. I forget what it was about – politics, most likely – but it left the company more than a little depleted. O'Toole, sensing an opportunity, duly announced to John Moody that he too was about to leave!

'I've had enough, love. Sorry, but I'm joining the exodus.'

'But you can't go, Peter. We need you!' said Moody.

'Well, I could stay, I suppose. All depends on the roles, though, love. All depends on the roles.'

He had them over a barrel, of course, and so when it came to the new season, he had all the best parts! They knew he was an immense talent and would probably have ended up offering him more lead roles eventually. It just happened a little sooner this way.

After this, as opposed to going to watch the odd rehearsal and one of the previews, as one normally did, I turned up to every rehearsal and *all* of the previews, and all because of O'Toole. I was desperate to see him in a lead role and desperate to watch him rehearse. He had thick, wavy black hair, sapphire blue eyes and a nose that was twisted somewhat. That said, it was a very noble-looking nose. But the two qualities that set Peter O'Toole apart from other mere mortals – besides natural talent and good looks – were self-belief and presence, the former begetting the latter. I have never in all my life met anybody as confident as O'Toole. This was when he was sober, of course. When he was pissed, the confidence came from alcohol and that was a very different Peter O'Toole, as you'll find out during this very chapter. Then he was just a pissed-up idiot who got on people's nerves. When he was sober, though, nobody fazed him.

I watched him go from strength to strength – from one lead to another. First he was the General in *Romanoff and*

Juliet by Peter Ustinov and then Mr Jaggers in *Great Expect-ations.* 'I should think not, Mr Pip.' I can actually see and hear him now. A wonderful performance!

After this, he did *Waiting for Godot* with Peter Jeffrey and they were both quite devastating. They said in O'Toole's obituaries that he realized an ambition by doing *Waiting for Godot* at the Royal Court. No, no, no, no! He did *Waiting for Godot* at the Bristol Old Vic, and I saw him! And it was better!

I remember watching him rehearse *Waiting for Godot*. He and the other actors weren't quite sure of their lines but as opposed to sitting there trying to get to grips with them in the rehearsal room, he dragged them all off to the cafe round the corner. A man named Denis Carey was the director and I remember his face when he announced their departure.

'We're just going round the corner, alright Denis, love? Can't think of a fucking line at the moment; none of us can. Need a change of scene, I think. It'll do us all good. We'll be about an hour and a half, alright, love? We'll be back, love, we'll be back.'

I watched this, thinking, *Who the bloody hell's in charge here?* But O'Toole was in charge. This tall, twenty-five-year-old, half-Irish, half-Scottish Yorkshireman. And do you know what? They all came back word perfect.

So, how did I finally get to meet O'Toole? Well, that happened in stages, really. First he spoke to me at a party, although I didn't reply, and then he stared at me during a lecture. My first actual conversation with him took place after I'd appeared in a play. Anyway, all will be revealed . . .

The only way you ever really came into contact with members of the Bristol Old Vic company is if you met them at a party. You weren't supposed to meet them at parties, of course, but occasionally they'd gatecrash if the students had something big on. Actually, what I meant to say was that *O'Toole* would gatecrash. The other company members would quietly follow. O'Toole, however, could smell a piss-up at a thousand paces and didn't care with whom he drank. No, he'd be there like a bloody shot.

'Room for one more, love? You don't mind if I pop in for a while? I've got a bottle.'

So the first time I ever came into contact with O'Toole was at one of these very gatherings. I remember it well because I'd just punched Harold Pinter down a flight of stairs. Oh yes, I'm afraid so. No long dramatic pauses this time, Harold; he got one right on the side of the jaw. Wham!

Some of the students had given a party to celebrate the opening night of Pinter's first play, *The Room*, which premiered in the Drama Studio at Bristol University. Incidentally, I directed *The Room* at Stratford-upon-Avon a few years ago. It got marvellous reviews. The toast of the season! But, anyway, as we all know, Pinter did have a little bit of a temper on him. He was unknown in those days and when in an 'advanced state of refreshment' could be an extremely rough customer. I didn't know this at the time, of course, but when he started wandering round threatening the other students, something had to be done. All throughout the evening, I had student after student coming up to me.

'Somebody's got to do something, Brian. He's going round threatening to hit everybody.'

The other students knew I'd boxed and looked to me for protection.

Eventually, Pinter saw me standing at the top of some stairs and confronted me.

'You must be the hard man all the students have been talking about. One of them said you were going to knock my block off.'

'If you don't stop bullying them, then yes, I will knock your block off.'

Shouting? Swearing? Threats? Menacing looks? I know what you're thinking: it sounds just like a Harold Pinter play!

With that, he ran to where I was standing and threw a punch.

Now, Harold Pinter was without doubt a great dramatist – the heaviest of them all – but I'm afraid there was nothing Pinteresque about his punches. In fact, they were more Gilbert & Sullivan, really. Once I'd dodged him a couple of times, I let go a quick left hook, which sent him tumbling backwards.

O'Toole was first on the scene and after giving me a 'Did you do that?' kind of look, he examined Harold, helped him to his feet and led him away.

I did feel slightly guilty for a time, but what else could I have done?

The next time I saw O'Toole was at a make-up lecture a few days after this at the Bristol Old Vic School. He looked at me as one might look at a rival before a boxing match or a race – except there was definitely a hint of mischief in his gaze.

O'Toole was absolutely appalling with make-up and so he had decided to come to our lecture to see if he could learn something.

'I'm awful, love, awful. Don't know the first thing about make-up. Beards are my nemesis. They never hold because I sweat so much. Do you know what I use to keep 'em on, love? Do you know what I use? Liquid cement. Wonderful stuff! I'd recommend it.'

The students found this hilarious.

'Ruins the bloody beard after one performance, but it stays on, love.'

More laughter from the students.

'These lectures are meant for the students, Mr O'Toole!'

O'Toole then wet his hair, parted it in the middle, took a pair of glasses from somebody and put them on.

'There you go, my lovelies, how's that? Now I look like a student. Who said I couldn't do make-up?'

Conversely, I remember once he had to give a speech to the school about acting, and at the end of his address the principal, Mr Ross, asked him if he had any last pieces of advice.

'Yes, love,' he said. 'If ever you're on board one of Her Majesty's ships and you hear a twine wire play "Auld Lang Syne", RUN LIKE FUCK!'

It was a piece of advice he'd been given as a signalman in the Royal Navy. God knows what it meant. I'm not sure even he knew. We all howled, though, save for the teacher.

As I said right at the beginning of this chapter, O'Toole could be tremendously generous to his fellow actors. Even in the late 1950s, when he himself was only twenty-five or -six, he would turn up to student productions and leave notes for people. He didn't have to do this, of course, and there was no hidden agenda. I think he just enjoyed watching people improve. He was also regarded as the new Scofield – Paul Scofield was a tremendous actor – and so his advice was always accepted with a great deal of gratitude.

It was after one of these productions that I had my very first conversation with O'Toole. The play was Peter Ustinov's *House of Regrets*, which I believe was his first play and semi-autobiographical, and it was staged, as with *The Room*, in the Drama Studio at Bristol University. I forget the exact synopsis of the play but I remember playing a very old Russian Admiral, with a great big white beard. The moment the curtain came down on the first performance, O'Toole rushed straight over to me.

'It's Brian, isn't it?' he said. 'I'm Peter. You work from power, Brian, don't you? Your stance is power. I work from fragility. I can't do power. I have to come from underneath. Tonight, though; tonight you came from fragility. That wasn't natural for you, but it was fantastic. Well done.'

This was a truly astonishing insight. I had indeed found the role unnatural and it had been very, very difficult to master. I was dumbstruck. After that, the conversation nose-dived somewhat.

'Yorkshireman I hear?' he continued.

'That's right,' I replied. 'South Yorkshire.'

'I'm West. Hunslet in Leeds. National service?'

'Yes, Parachute Regiment.'

'Violent bastards, the Paras. I fucking hate them. Kicked the shit out of the Irish, didn't they?'

'I didn't touch the Irish. Where were you?'

'Royal Navy, love. Do you have a problem with that?'

It was a very strange encounter. He went from praising me to picking a fight with me in probably a little under thirty seconds. He was weighing me up, of course. Was I an enemy of his career? Was I a competitor? Was I physically stronger than he was?

'We're going to be at the gymnasium later on, Brian, just doing a few strength tests. Why don't you come along?'

'I'd be delighted,' I said. 'What time?'

'About 6 p.m. Make sure you bring a towel. You're going to sweat a bit.'

'I'll be there.'

'You scared?'

'Not of you, no!'

By this time, we were almost eyeball to eyeball. Testosterone was seeping through our pores! Even so, his parting shot was just astonishing.

'I think people who work from strength as actors are about as boring as the Pope's balls, Mr Blessed. See you at the gym.'

So that was my first conversation with Peter O'Toole. Not quite what I was expecting, but at least it was original. Anyway, as promised, I joined him and his cronies later on at the gym.

He always had a gang with him, O'Toole. He always had cronies; big hard men who would cause mayhem. At Bristol, these were the Fulbright students from America. They were only there for about eight months and so the 'Them & Us' rules between actors and students didn't really apply. The one I remember most was a man named Phil Bruns, who went on to appear in quite a few films and television programmes. He was about six foot three and made of steel. A perfect O'Toole foil, really. Oliver Reed was exactly the same, of course, and I know this from first-hand experience. Usually pissed, but always surrounded by hard men.

When I arrived at the gym there was, not surprisingly I suppose, a rather unwholesome atmosphere. O'Toole had obviously notified his cronies about this new kid on the block and they were all ready for me. Fully clothed, O'Toole looked like he wouldn't even be able to take off his hat if a convoy of bloody hearses drove past, but believe me he was very, very powerful, and actually reminded me a bit of Henry Cooper. Henry used to be quite slight for a heavy-weight, but by Christ could he punch. You ask Muhammad Ali! And it was the same with O'Toole. The moment he stripped off to his vest, you could see that he was all muscle, but in addition to this he also had the biggest veins I have ever seen on a human body in my entire life. The ones on his forearms must have been over half an inch thick.

His social capers – as a pub fighter, and would-be strong-man – were wholly at odds with how he was as an actor. There was a definite yin and yang in action. He'd already admitted that as an actor his stance was fragility, and I believe that bothered him somewhat. Drinking, fighting and challenging people helped redress the balance. I found him utterly fascinating and inspirational.

Anyway, after I'd slaughtered Peter and his cronies at bench-pressing, pull-ups and abdominal crunches, the stupid bastard then challenged me to a bout of catch wrestling; something I'd been proficient at since I was quite young. I did try and warn him about this, but he'd already challenged me in front of his heavies and so was in no position to change his mind. About two minutes in, I got him in a chokehold and he submitted.

'I can't breathe!' he gasped.

'That's the idea, Pete!' It was the first time I'd ever called him Pete. 'There you go, one to me. Want to go again?'

'No fucking way, love! No way. My God, you're a rough bastard.'

O'Toole's attitude towards me changed slightly after that – for a time, at least. He could sense that I wasn't scared of him and he also knew I didn't drink, which meant I was probably a bit of an anomaly to him, and I think this drew us together. The reason I don't drink, by the way, is quite simple. If I ever have more than two pints I become violent. It really has the most terrible effect on me. It's just not my cup of tea! Anyway, from then on O'Toole and I were friends. Companions, even. It was as though I'd passed some kind of initiation ceremony. I certainly wasn't going to become one of his bloody cronies, though. I had a little bit more about me than that.

The physical challenges continued, which was fine by me. The most exciting of these came in the form of a running race around Clifton Woods and over Clifton Suspension Bridge. We went for miles and miles and miles, and by God could he run. He was built like a gazelle! He might even have got the better of me – had he not smoked a pack and a half of cigarettes every day.

So there we were, at about two o'clock in the morning, racing towards Clifton Suspension Bridge, when all of a sudden we almost collided with Professor Josephs and Professor Murray from the school. They'd been to Bath to see *Ages of Man* with John Gielgud, his now legendary solo show, and were obviously quite overcome by what they'd seen. In fact, they were in tears.

'Never, *never* have we seen acting like it; such a phenomenal grasp of the script. It was sheer poetry.'

They actually wept in our arms!

'We'll see you tomorrow, boys, but you must go and see
him. Tell everyone you know!'

With that, they walked off.

O'Toole then turned and looked at me and said, 'God,
Gielgud must have had a hell of an effect on them. It's not
dawned on 'em, has it, Brian, that you and I are stark bollock
naked?'

We were indeed both stark bollock naked! At first, it was
only going to be a race, but then O'Toole had the bright idea
of doing it starkers. Typical O'Toole. How on earth could I
refuse?

Although the women at the Bristol Old Vic were all crazy
about O'Toole, I'm not sure he ever really knew how to
handle them. I was no expert, by the way. I kept away from
women as much as possible when I first went to drama school
(although that changed in my second year), for the simple
reason that I felt privileged to be there and didn't want to get
involved. I also had to work tremendously hard at becoming
an actor, whereas O'Toole's aptitude was far more apparent.
It was second nature to him. No, no, my flirtations in the
early days were restricted to trying it on jokingly with old
Daphers. But I remember a brief conversation I had with
O'Toole shortly after we became mates about this very subject. I thought it was quite telling.

'How do you feel being surrounded by all these beautiful
women, Brian? Aren't you tempted?' he asked me.

'Yes, of course I am,' I said. 'I've spent the last two years
in the army surrounded by nothing but men! I'm a bit unsure
about it all, though. I'm not terribly experienced.'

This made him quite happy all of a sudden.

'I felt the same at RADA, love!' he said. It was almost as
if I'd somehow validated him feeling unsure of himself. 'Two

years at sea with the signals and then all of a sudden there were beautiful women everywhere. I didn't know what to do either.'

It was all very, very innocent; like having a conversation with a slightly jumpy teenager whose balls had only just dropped. O'Toole was more of a romantic than he was a womanizer. He'd have a woman on each arm at parties, of course, but as opposed to disappearing into a bedroom with them, he would just charm them all evening before heading off with his cronies to smash up a bar or something. He did visit a prostitute occasionally, though, which I suppose makes sense given the above.

For a man who drank, fought and swore his way through Soho, Hollywood and beyond – and over many, many decades – O'Toole could be shocked by the very strangest of things. One of the girls at the school walked back with him from a party one evening and, as they went through the local graveyard, she decided to stop and pinch some flowers for her room. I won't name her because she might feel embarrassed, but she later told me that O'Toole went off his box at what she'd done. Said he'd never been so shocked by anything in his entire life.

The best thing I saw O'Toole do at Bristol was the play *Look Back in Anger* by John Osborne. Never in my life have I witnessed acting quite like that. I'd seen the original production with Kenneth Haigh at the Royal Court Theatre but O'Toole really opened Jimmy Porter up. He played him with an element of humour – which made the character seem a lot more unpredictable – and that made Osborne's original 'angry young man' far, far more interesting and watchable. That's just my opinion, of course, but you have to remember that O'Toole was not like other actors. If Kenneth Haigh had tried to throw an element of humour into the mix, it almost certainly wouldn't have worked. His Jimmy Porter was basically John Osborne and the director Tony Richardson's creation, although it was a very fine performance. O'Toole, on the other hand, had the confidence and ability to mould the character and create his own interpretation, and that's a very brave thing to do with such a big, established character; especially when you're only in your mid-twenties. People expect to see an 'angry young man' and so if you are going to experiment with things you need to be certain it's going to work.

O'Toole took this to outrageous extremes during one matinee performance, when – upon seeing that I was in the front row – he called a halt to the show before jumping off the stage and having a chat with me. He actually sat down in the next seat!

'You enjoying it, love?' he asked, ever so nonchalantly. 'This next bit's good. Bit heavy going, don't you think? How're you keeping?'

But the moment he finished chatting to me, something equally bizarre happened: he actually stood up and jumped straight back onto the stage – and from a standing start! He was at least three feet away from the stage, which itself was about four feet from the bloody ground. I couldn't believe it! He was the most flexible and dexterous actor I've ever seen. Later on in the show, he threw off his shoes, climbed on top of the mantelpiece and stood there on the toes of one foot; all the time delivering line after line after line. And it worked!

According to Rudi Shelly, O'Toole was famous for his dexterity, and in addition to that could make all his different body parts move. He could roll his eyes in different directions at the same time and if you asked him very nicely, he'd move his biceps up and down his arms for you. He could be the perfect clown as well as the perfect actor. His personality was staggering.

His impressive plasticity of movement could be mirrored verbally, of course, in that he seemed to have voices within voices within voices, and it was while playing Hamlet that this all came together. He was at the height of his powers as Hamlet, and absolutely nothing went to waste. He bounced off the flaming walls! The best Hamlet I've ever seen, bar none. Olivier made him too straight and woolly for my liking, and O'Toole always agreed with me. Although O'Toole admired Olivier's contribution to the theatre, he had a very definite opinion of him as an actor, and he always expressed this using a cricket analogy.

'Larry plays with a straight bat, love. Sure and sound. Not great for me!'

I was at odds with O'Toole over this. Despite not being a fan of Olivier's Hamlet, in my eyes he was not only a great actor, but also a marvellous director. I couldn't stand the way O'Toole used to dismiss him. It made my blood boil! Anyway, we came to blows over this at a party one evening. I was using Olivier's film adaptation of *Richard III* to get my argument across; something O'Toole had dismissed out of hand.

This, I'm afraid, sent me into an almighty rage.

'Olivier has an eye for style,' I bellowed. 'And what is style, O'Toole? Casting off the superfluous! His film *Henry V* starts in Elizabethan theatre, moves to reality and then moves back to Elizabethan theatre. Pure bloody genius! Could you do that? You direct nothing, O'Toole. Olivier is the best Restoration actor this country has ever seen and has one of the finest imaginations known to man! You, on the other hand, are just a pissed-up buffoon from Hunslet.'

O'Toole howled like a banshee at this, then collapsed with laughter.

The only actor O'Toole ever really admired was Wilfred Lawson, a heavy-drinking character actor from Bradford who had appeared in literally hundreds of West End plays and the same amount of films and TV shows. He was a seriously intense man and could scare the living daylights out of you with just one look. He was the only one O'Toole ever really went to see.

While Olivier may have played with a straight bat, that was the one thing you could never accuse O'Toole of doing, particularly when it came to drinking. What a forty-two-carat bloody nightmare he was. Now, I'm not going to go on and on about O'Toole's drinking, because I don't want to help perpetuate the myth that he was just a bit of a hellraiser, but I will tell you a couple of stories for the simple reason they're quite entertaining, and demonstrate brilliantly the power he held over theatres, film directors and studios.

He was constantly being thrown into the cells by police, and quite rightly. It didn't matter what night of the week it was, the moment he left the theatre he and his cronies would be off terrorizing the people of Bristol. They destroyed restaurants, they destroyed bars, and because the Fulbright students were all terribly wealthy, they paid for all the damage with pocketfuls of cash. They'd just slap it down on a table – if they could find one that hadn't been smashed.

'How much do you want? A hundred pounds? OK, here you go.'

When this was going on, O'Toole would usually be on his knees vomiting somewhere. He was a consummate vomiter, O'Toole. I once saw him in the middle of Blackboy Hill, which is the road leading up to the university, waving his arms around trying to stop all the buses, while covered head to toe in vomit. He looked like a bloody tramp! This man, who was blessed by God with an amazing talent, was pissing it up against the wall, and that's what made me loathe Peter O'Toole. That's what made me hate his bloody guts sometimes.

Mr Moody pleaded with him to curb his behaviour, but O'Toole refused outright. After all, he was the star of the company; the actor everyone came to see. If he went, ticket sales would plummet, and the only person who knew that more than Moody was O'Toole. He had no respect for Moody whatsoever. No respect for authority.

Incidentally, the people O'Toole disapproved of most in life were stage directors, especially if they had no experience of acting.

'When they've trodden the boards for ten or fifteen years, then they can suggest something. Until then, they should go and play with the bloody lights or something. If you can't act on stage, you shouldn't be allowed to direct on stage. Clowns, love.'

These days, we have far more actor/directors – or directors who can act – but back then it wasn't the case.

Anyway, where was I? Ah yes.

Richard Harris, Oliver Reed and Richard Burton – all actors notorious for their exploits offstage – didn't compare to O'Toole, who was a real fighter. His cronies weren't there to keep him *out* of trouble – oh no! O'Toole had them to help him get *into* bloody trouble. I assume the definition of a hellraiser is somebody who quite literally 'raises hell'? Well, if that's the case then O'Toole is the only genuine article. Harris, Reed and Burton merely drank a lot, threw a few punches and got on everyone's nerves.

I once had reason to warn Oliver Reed about his behaviour for the sake of some fellow actors and actresses. We were making a film together called *Prisoners of Honour*, and he and I were playing generals alongside Peter Vaughan and my old mate Jeremy Kemp. I knew Jeremy from *Z Cars* and on the first day of filming he expressed concerns to me about working with Reed.

'He's a nutcase, Brian! And he's friends with the director. He'll be able to get away with anything. If I'm honest, I'm dreading this.'

Jeremy wasn't the only actor present experiencing Reed-dread, and so when Oliver arrived on set, I took him to one side.

'They're all scared of you, Oliver, do you know that? They're all scared that you're going to get pissed and spoil things for everyone. Do you actually enjoy having that effect on your fellow actors?'

He was sober at the time and seemed surprised and a little hurt by my outburst.

'If I smell alcohol on you, or if you start threatening people, I'll kick your teeth down your throat and get one of your cronies to pull them out of your arse. I swear to you, Oliver, you'll never act again.'

You see, without the drink, Oliver was just a sweet little Englishman. Charm personified, in fact. He was horrified by my threat and tried desperately to assure me that no drink would be consumed and that no harm would come to anybody.

'Every morning you report to me, Oliver, OK? And if you're pissed, I'll stop this film. I promise you I'll stop it being made, and it'll be your fault.'

Anyway, it did the trick. He behaved marvellously.

He was a terribly good actor, Oliver Reed, and basically a nice guy, but once he'd had a drink he turned into a bully. He might have made a few people laugh occasionally by getting his cock out and whatnot, but more often than not he scared people and made their lives a misery, and I'm afraid I won't put up with that.

Incidentally, back in the mid-1970s whilst making the film *Royal Flash*, Oliver Reed decided it would be a good idea to throw a punch at Henry Cooper. Henry told me all about this, years later.

'He was a strong boy, Oliver Reed,' said Henry, 'but he couldn't punch for toffee. Anyway, I thought I'd teach him a lesson and so I threw him a left hook. I pulled it, but he still dropped like a sack of shit. I knew he would . . .'

Good old 'Enry!

So the other three so-called hellraisers from the drama

world made a lot of threats. They'd throw stones and chuck spears at the castle, whereas O'Toole would pull down the drawbridge, charge in screaming and start swinging from the flaming chandeliers! He was the director's cut, love!

Before we leave Bristol for good, I must quickly tell you about the pantomime they had on at the Old Vic back in 1957; one of the most wonderful experiences of my entire life. The whole company was in it, of course, as well as four students from the theatre school. Luckily for me, one of the four parts they'd earmarked for us students was a Singing Robber, and because I had such a good tenor voice they offered it to me. I suppose that was my first professional role. I got ten quid a week!

O'Toole played Mrs Millie Baba, the pantomime dame, and I'll tell you what: he absolutely hated it. He had to wear a great big flowery dress, a huge red wig and lots and lots of lipstick and eyeliner.

I remember the first rehearsal. The other students and I literally ran all the way from our digs to the theatre. We were so excited! The first thing we did was a read-through, which is customary on these occasions. There we all sat in a big circle, students eyeing up the professionals and vice versa. *Hang on a second*, I thought. *Where the hell's O'Toole?* Just at that moment, the door opened and in he fell, three sheets to the wind, and carrying a cigarette holder the size of a snooker cue.

John Moody, who was directing the show, just looked at him as if to say 'you horrible arse!' We students were loving this, of course. Great entertainment!

Two minutes into the read-through, O'Toole was fast asleep on his chair, wearing the biggest grin you've ever seen in your entire life. Christ knows what he'd been up to. Those unfortunate enough to be sitting next to him had to shift their chairs in order to escape the stench. This meant that on one side of the room you had a group of slightly concerned actors, and on the other side was O'Toole, far from fresh and far from conscious.

'Shall we continue?' said John. 'I'll read Peter's lines.'

And so on we went.

Now, there was a live donkey in this particular panto- mime, but because it wasn't going to be present until the dress rehearsal, somebody had to shout 'Eee-orr!' every time it was mentioned in the script. I think it was one of the stu- dents who had to do this. Anyway, when the first cue arrived somebody duly shouted, 'Eee-orr!' and, as they did, O'Toole woke up with a jolt. He looked at me, crossed his eyes and said, '*This* is ART, love!'

And then he got up and walked out.

I think he turned up to about three rehearsals in all, the last of which he had to be dragged to. This was because he'd been late and somebody had told John Moody that he was at his prostitute's house. Finally reaching the end of his tether, John Moody jumped in a cab and went to fetch him. When he finally stumbled in, O'Toole was obviously still reprimanding Moody.

'I take a very dim view of being dragged out of bed for this shit!' he said.

But the lack of rehearsal time with our drunken dame made everybody slightly nervous about what was going to happen come the opening night. I suffered more than most with this as I was the one delivering his cue. 'Look, here comes Mrs Millie Baba' was the line. After that, O'Toole was supposed to enter the stage riding a bicycle, which his char- acter Mrs Baba sold ice creams from. It had 'Wall's of Jericho' on the front, which I thought was rather amusing.

At first, everything went according to plan. I delivered the line and then on came O'Toole. He even stopped exactly where he'd been told to. The thing was, he was travelling at about twenty miles per hour, which meant that, even though the bicycle came to a halt, he didn't. O'Toole went straight over the handlebars and landed right in the middle of the first row. How nobody was killed, I'll never know. When he eventually managed to untangle himself, he'd lost his wig and most of his dress, but instead of apologizing to the audience and seeing if anyone had been hurt, he started grabbing people's arses.

'Where's my wig, love? Where's my bloody wig? You're hiding it, aren't you? Come on, give it me back.'

Somebody eventually found the wig and when O'Toole got back on stage he turned to the audience and shouted, 'I represent Wall's of Jericho, love. There you go, there's your first laugh.'

Absolute silence from the audience.

All the way through the first half, he kept on feeding the donkey sugar lumps. His pockets were full of them and at every opportunity he'd throw a handful into its mouth. Now, sugar in large quantities will do two things to a donkey: it will make it 'Eee-orr' a lot more than usual and it will make it shit. And sure enough, about five minutes into the second half, the stage was full of shit and the air full of 'Eee-orr's. O'Toole came out and, pointing at the donkey, said, 'There is not only an artist, there is a critic!' What an absolute disaster . . .

Later on, when the two main robbers were telling some of their jokes – you know the kind of thing, 'What's a Grecian urn?' 'About thirty bob a week' – we suddenly began to hear roars of laughter coming from the Royal Box. It was O'Toole. There he was with his feet up – a bottle of beer in one hand and a fag in the other – and he was laughing like a drain and shouting at the actors.

'Marvellous, love! Thank God I'm not wearing any knickers, otherwise they'd be soaked!'

The final insult of the evening happened just before the end, when Mrs Baba was supposed to lead a big line of oilmen onto the stage. The story was that they'd found oil on

Ali Baba's land or something. Anyway, setting off from the back of the auditorium, they simply had to make their way to the front, hop up the steps and it would be a job well done. This route was not for O'Toole, though. That would be too boring. Basically, he led a kind of 'conga' through every single row in the stalls, whilst singing 'Payday in old Baghdad'!

So a lot of O'Toole's wildness was actually natural. There was a demon, of course, which appeared when he was drunk, but I think a lot of the unpredictability and disobedience was inherent. And he was always forgiven, somehow. It didn't matter what he did at Bristol, whether it was turning up to rehearsals drunk or forcing a donkey to shit everywhere and make a noise – it was always forgotten about. Yes, they were frightened of losing him, but I think what really stopped them from murdering the bastard was that he was absolutely magnificent. Twenty-five per cent of Peter O'Toole was indeed donkey shit, but the other seventy-five was just pure gold. A great, great actor was born.

I kept in touch with O'Toole after we left Bristol, and we continued our very unique relationship. We were polar opposites in so many ways, yet in the right conditions we would cling together like limpets. In the late sixties and early seventies, we even made a couple of films together. The first was *Country Dance*, which we filmed in Dún Laoghaire in Ireland in 1969. O'Toole and Susannah York were the stars and I played a character called 'Jock the Cock', would you believe? When I arrived on the set Peter grabbed me and gleefully told me that he had spent the night in police cells after a wild fight in a pub. To make matters worse he tried to wrestle me. You see, he wanted to find out if I could still beat him physically. Within seconds of him lunging at me I had him on his back on the floor, holding him down with a vice-like grip. Then

I realized the director, J. Lee Thompson, was watching and clearly thinking, 'Why the hell have I employed this guy Blessed? He's worse than O'Toole.'

Nevertheless, after this episode things quietened down and the film went smoothly. In fact, it was a delightful experience. Once again O'Toole gave an absolutely marvellous performance.

At this time I frequently went out with Peter to restaurants and nightclubs, where he'd take up the whole floor, madly gyrating like a dancing dervish before exploding into his 'Groanee' song.

'Oh death, darkness, nuclear war, radiation, killing whales, elephants, tigers, pygmy hippos, pollution, acid rain, starvation, cruelty and lasting torture and hell.'

At this point he'd collapse on the floor, lying senseless for a few seconds before bouncing up again.

'Ah well,' he'd shout with a great smile, 'might as well live. Sod it, let's celebrate with a happy dance.' And he'd call over to me, 'Love ingratitude, Brian Blessed. Love ingratitude.'

After ten weeks the film was complete and the final celebration party was held in a magnificent country house just outside of Dublin. Our host was a charming old lord, who was justly proud of his home, which was full of antiques. Cast and crew were dancing happily to the sound of the bagpipes and the drums when the great doors were flung open and there stood the terror of the universe − O'Toole! As Shakespeare so brilliantly put it, 'Cry havoc! And let slip the dogs of war!' The dogs in question were his wild minders, who were as drunk as he was.

To everyone's astonishment O'Toole grabbed one of the bagpipes and commenced playing them brilliantly. There was no end to his talents. After huge applause, he bowed and threw the pipes straight through a glass window. It was the signal for mayhem. Carpets, chairs, tables were flung all over the place. Tapestries were torn off the walls, and paintings too. J. Lee Thompson and the producer of the film, with the distraught owner of the house by their side, begged me to do something. I saw Peter Perkins, O'Toole's assistant, standing on the sidelines watching.

'Can't you do something?' I urged Perkins.

'It's more than my job's worth, Brian,' he replied.

As more furniture crashed to the floor, I stepped forward to confront Peter.

'STOP THIS, O'TOOLE!' I roared.

Peter turned and glared at me. He was virtually unrecognizable, his eyes wide and bloodshot.

'Listen to me, listen to me. Stop this now, do you hear me, Peter?' I begged.

He raised his leg to knee me, and froze like a statue on the spot.

'You try and knee me, Peter,' I continued, 'and I promise you that you won't be able to walk for months. You can kiss your acting career goodbye.'

'You are a miserable fucker, Blessed,' he rasped and walked out of the house.

I spent the early hours of the morning comforting the old lord and trying to comprehend how such a great actor and wonderful human being could turn into such a violent monster.

A few years later, in 1971, we were in Rome filming a musical called *The Man of La Mancha* (1972), which also starred Sophia Loren and the great Harry Andrews. O'Toole played Don Quixote and gave a brilliant performance. Mesmerizing. I played Pedro the villain. I was the only one of the cast who could sing! In fact, I had to sing Harry Andrews' song for him, 'Knight of the Woeful Countenance', because he couldn't bloody sing either.

Anyway, one lovely evening I was having a quiet dinner

at the Piccolo Mondo restaurant with the likes of Ian Richardson, Harry Andrews and the composer Larry Rosenthal
when our peace was shattered by the appearance of O'Toole
and three of his minders. Quite frankly Peter was pissed out
of his mind, breaking glasses, pouring wine over the table
and threatening everyone within sight.

'I'm leaving, Peter,' I said, standing up.

'You are bloody going nowhere!' O'Toole screamed at the
top of his voice, at the same time instructing his three tough
guys to bar my way. One of them was called Fausto, and had
once fought for the light-heavyweight boxing championship
in Italy.

There was a short stand-off while his three minders glared
at me.

'Peter,' I said quietly, 'I'll tell you what I'll do, I'll flatten
these silly buggers and then I'll kick your teeth down your
throat.'

After another pause, he waved his hand and his tor-
pedoes finally moved out of my way and I left.

Ian Richardson told me the next day that Peter treated
them like dirt for the remainder of the evening.

The next time I saw Peter for more than a few minutes
after *Man of La Mancha* was during the making of the BBC
series *I, Claudius* in the mid-seventies. He was married to the
beautiful Welsh actress Siân Phillips at the time, who played
my wife Livia, and we were about to start filming episode
four. This, for me, was my most important episode, as it's
when I discover that my daughter has been sleeping with all
the senators. I had to try and create an atmosphere of extreme
fear in the scene, as I lined the senators up to interrogate
them.

Now, Siân was always a very private person and rarely
talked about her home life, but that morning, before filming
began, she told me that she'd been up all night with Peter.

'I honestly thought he was going to die, Brian. His body

just broke down. It stopped working. The doctors had to balance his chemistry or something. It was quite awful.'

I actually looked this up later on that day and found out that the body's chemistry can actually be balanced, just like a car's mechanics. I found it all quite fascinating.

Anyway, according to poor Siân, Peter had been screaming with pain and she genuinely thought he was finished. He'd had a rough time, had Peter, what with operations for cancer and so on. I'd been told about those by some close friends of his; he'd had a shocking period.

'How is he now?' I asked.

'Well, he's weak, but at least he's alive. The doctors say that if he even has a drop of alcohol it might kill him.'

'Why not bring him in here?' I said. 'There's no point him being at home all day. Bring the daft bugger in here while we're filming and rehearsing. I'll keep him entertained.'

And I'm very pleased to say that's precisely what Siân did. The next day, a few seconds after she walked through the door, this little head appeared.

'Hello, Brian, you big rough bastard.'

'Get in here, you diseased shit! And don't go fucking up our rehearsals, otherwise I'll chin you! Actually, I might pour a gallon of whisky down your bloody throat!'

Immediately, he brightened up. 'Stop it, you big bastard! I'm not supposed to laugh.'

Over the next few days, I laid into Peter like you would not believe. Every time he nodded off, I was on him like a flash.

'What's the matter with you, you Irish fuckwit? The acting not good enough for you? You fall asleep again and I'll ram your shoes and socks so far up your arse you'll be able to tap-dance on your fucking teeth!'

'Sorry, love, sorry! Won't happen again. I'm here, love, I'm back in the room!'

Everyone else was so respectful and considerate, and

although it was all well-meant, that wasn't what he needed. O'Toole needed buckets of abuse. He needed to laugh! Occasionally, he'd try offering bits of advice here and there, which merely offered me yet another opportunity to pounce.

'Shut your bloody mouth, you ponce. Lawrence of Arabia? You look more like Catherine of Aragon. You know nothing about acting, O'Toole; in fact I have never seen a more untalented human being. You've got no face, you've got no voice and you have about as much presence as a vole's cock! Look at you there, all shrivelled up. You're fecked, mate!'

It did the trick. Put some much-needed colour in his cheeks! He'd have done exactly the same for me.

About three years after *I, Claudius*, while I was halfway through filming *The Little World of Don Camillo* for the BBC, in which I played the lead role of Peppone, I received a telephone call out of the blue.

'Hello, Brian? It's me, O'Toole.'

'What do you want, Peter?'

Despite our badinage on *I, Claudius*, I'm afraid I was in no mood for him at the time. I'd seen yet more examples of him pissing on his talent in the Sunday papers and it had left me vexed.

'I'm doing *Macbeth*. I want you to come over, Brian, I want you to come over. I'm shaking with excitement, love. I'm doing *Macbeth* and I want you to be Banquo.'

'Banquo's a boring part. Ask me to play Macduff, and then I'll come for you. Banquo, though? You Irish chancer!'

'No, no,' he said, 'I play Macbeth quite sickly – from fragility, remember – and I want Jeremy Kemp to play Macduff. He's slight and does sickly very well. I want Banquo to be a golden king! The power behind the entire show.'

'Honestly, Peter,' I said, 'I don't want to work with you. I don't want to work with someone who behaves like you behave. In fact, I'll tell you what, I'll come over to Hampstead now and I'll tell you exactly why I never want to work with a twat like you ever again.'

So I went over to Hampstead and was met by Peter at the door. 'Come in, old love, come in. It's so wonderful to see you, Brian.'

I had feared that seeing him in person might have softened my mood somewhat, but if anything it made me even angrier. In fact, I went absolutely ballistic. Off the Richter scale, love!

I got him in the front room of his house and I said, 'I have come here, Peter, because I am ashamed of you as an artist. Did you hear me? I am ashamed of you! Actors work all their lives, they work on their body, they work on their voice, they work on their studies and examine everything. They do all kinds of things to develop their voices and build confidence. They study and study and study to try and better themselves, and they haven't got a fraction of your talent. You have a God-given talent, a talent that has come from the edge of nowhere, yet all you do is piss on it. All the time you're either off your face, angry or violent. You bully people and you manipulate people. Then, suddenly, you're marvellous for a time, and then you're ugly once again. You shit on your fellow actors and you shit on your gifts.'

While I was saying all this I dragged him all over the room. I dragged him by his jacket and I dragged him by his shirt. I dragged him all over his house. I bounced him off the bloody walls!

'You're a shit, O'Toole. You're a good-for-nothing shit. That's what I've come to tell you!'

And all the time he was weeping. He was crying his eyes out.

'Brian, I love you, I love you. You're the only person who makes any sense. You're the only person who fazes me. Please play Banquo for me, please, Brian. Please play Banquo, please. I must walk on that stage with you by my side, Macbeth and Banquo together. I can't go on without you.'

Peter O'Toole was begging ME to appear in his production and promising me all kinds of everything. It made no mark on me, though. I continued to drag him round by his shirt before eventually throwing him over a sofa.

'So you now know why I won't work with you, Peter, because you have shat on your fucking talent.'

And, with that, I left him.

I felt no remorse about what had just happened. It was something I should have done over twenty years before. When I arrived home that evening, my wife Hildegard called me into the kitchen.

'I've had Peter on the phone crying. He said you came round and threw him all over the house. He said you beat him up! What on earth have you been doing, Brian? I'm worried. The man is distraught.'

Peter and I talked again later that evening and, finally, I agreed to play Banquo. He was going to go ahead with the production regardless, and although I was apoplectic with the gangly twat, I was also worried, tremendously worried; as was Hildegard. Peter could also be tremendously seductive, you see. All that Irish charm!

So eventually I said to him, 'Alright Peter, I will play Banquo for you. As you know, I am filming and I won't be able to make the rehearsals. In fact, I will only be free just three days before opening night. You produce your *Macbeth*, I will finish filming, and then we'll just fit my Banquo into all the choreography and direction on the stage.'

So I did: I came back after I finished *Don Camillo* and I went straight into rehearsals.

There Peter was to greet me outside Waterloo station with his three beautiful witches. Peter was kindness itself throughout this time. He was very loving. Whenever we met, he threw his arms around me and I thought, *Ah, marvellous Peter has returned. I wonder how long this'll last?*

But when I arrived at the Old Vic, it was like some kind of epic disaster had taken place. Peter came straight to see me in my dressing room.

'Come and watch it, Brian. We'll do a run-through with your understudy and then we'll start to fit you in.' Well, that seemed fair enough.

Then I discovered, just before the run-through, that he had sacked the wardrobe four times, he'd sacked several directors, he'd got rid of this, he'd got rid of that; he'd got rid of every bugger! Bob Crowley, the stage designer – gone. Jack Gold, the director – gone. There was no one there!

He'd brought in Bryan Forbes as director, who had never directed for the stage before, and Forbes had brought with him the set from *The Slipper and the Rose*, a live-action Cinderella movie he'd made several years before. He'd had it brought all the way from Pinewood Studios and had it put on the stage at the Old Vic. The Slipper and the sodding Rose? The set from a romantic musical for one of Shakespeare's greatest tragedies? It was ridiculous.

By the way, this *Slipper and the Rose* debacle all happened after they'd got rid of the inflatable scenery O'Toole had originally wanted to use. I kid you not, dear reader. He had ordered inflatable scenery!

And so I watched the run-through. It lasted four hours. Four bloody hours, when it should have lasted two.

I said, 'It's dreadful, Peter, and the set is ridiculous.'

I watched him trying to listen to me, but he didn't know where he was.

'Your eyes are twitching; you don't know where you are. Look at me. LOOK AT ME! You've got to get rid of this bloody set. Tell Bryan to get some lorries and take the whole lot away. Take it to a dump, take it to Pinewood, just get rid of it, Peter, it's wrong – IT IS WRONG!'

He still looked out of it, but I had to carry on.

'Now look,' I said, 'I saw in Bristol many years ago some students play *Macbeth* and all they had were some white curtains at the back of the stage and they all went to Marks & Spencer and bought white shirts and black trousers. That's all they had. There were no props and it was AMAZING! And this was all over in two hours.

'This is a thriller, Peter; it should be done in one hour fifty – two hours at the most. Yours is lasting four hours! You've got people coming onto the set and having to walk up hills just to get on. It's shit. People should be revealed, Peter. A light should come on and they should be revealed. They shouldn't have to walk up bloody hills. That's the great thing about *Macbeth*: it is a thriller, and it must be done quickly. Now get some white curtains.'

'I can't, I can't. This is what we want. This is right.'

'It's not bloody right. It's all bloody wrong, now get it off.'

'I can't, I can't, I can't, it's all been agreed.'

So the silly sod kept the set. *The Slipper and the Rose*! Jesus wept.

Well, come the first night I'd had about five hours' rehearsal and didn't even have a costume. I knew the lines, though. I thought, *It'll be fine*. And so off I went to see wardrobe about a costume.

'We've washed our hands with bloody costumes,' they said. 'Blame Peter O'Toole. There *are* no costumes – he's sacked the entire department!'

So I went into the wardrobe storeroom where they kept all the costumes and I picked out a bit of something from 1938 and then something else from 1955, and after a few minutes I'd made myself a costume. I thought, *OK, I've got some boots and a sword and I've got chainmail across my body, I'm good to go on*, and so that was me done.

For the first night, Peter had painted his dressing room

red. His room was bright flaming red. Once my eyes had recovered, I said to him, 'If I smell drink on you or see you've been taking drugs, I will reserve the right to walk out. I will neither tolerate nor work with somebody who is on drugs.'

Now, I don't think he was on drugs at the time, but he was certainly out of his mind with fear. Out of his mind!

And then, about a quarter of an hour before curtain up, I saw Bryan Forbes standing outside Peter's dressing room knocking back triple brandies.

'What the hell's wrong with you?' I said to him.

'Brian, I don't know what to do. You're going to have to talk to him; you're the only one he'll listen to. Peter's going to go on half-naked. He's going on half-naked, Brian! He's going to go on in red tights, parachute boots and nothing else. Please, I'm begging you, it's beyond the quarter. Please speak to him!'

'I'm not doing a thing. Not a damn thing!'

'Oh, please, Brian, you have to. It's going to be a disaster. People are here from all over the world. This could finish him!'

'For heavens' sake!' I roared. 'OK, OK. I'll speak to him.'

So I went away to the scarlet dressing room – and there's Peter naked to the waist, almost skeletal, and there's a great scar right across his stomach where they cut the cancer out. There had been rumours that he'd had cancer, but at this point nobody, other than close friends, really knew for sure.

'Pete,' I said, 'when you go on like that, the whole audience won't applaud you, they'll just say, "Ah, so he *did* have cancer! He *did* have an operation," and that's all they'll talk about when we walk on. Listen to me, Peter!'

Then I looked at him again – and saw that he'd painted fucking diamonds on his eyes.

'Right, Pete, you know bugger all about make-up. Charlie Parker always makes you up in your films, and even with all your genius and brilliance, *you know bugger all about make-up*. Remember Bristol! I'm going to wipe it all off – all this shit on your face – and I'm going to give you a foundation of number 9. Then I'm going to do something to bring your eyes out, OK, and I'm going to recommend you wear a beard, because you looked very good in *The Lion in Winter*.'

'I don't want a beard, I want my face to be as it is now!' he cried.

'Alright, but you'll look a twat. You'll be naked to the waist wearing parachute boots, and when I walk on alongside you, we'll look like Laurel and Hardy. Listen to me, Peter, we can save this production. Let me clean your face, let me clean it for you, because no other bugger's going to help you, Peter. No one else can help you now. You must let me clean your face and then you must let me put some simple make-up on you. I've got some chainmail here, and a garment to cover your body. It's deep red, so it will match your tights. Put that on. There we are: it looks splendid, doesn't it? Alright, and now I shall just put this chainmail over your shoulders. This will suggest "The Warrior" to the audience.'

'OK, Brian,' he heaved; he was already exhausted, emotionally and physically. Totally destroyed. 'OK, Brian. OK. Thank you. Thank you, Brian.'

When it came to curtain up, O'Toole had said to me previously, 'We'll be waiting for the line: "A drum, a drum, Macbeth doth come."' Peter had said, 'When we hear that line, you and I will walk onto that stage, and the West End will stand still. You and me, mate, together as Macbeth and Banquo.'

But when the moment came, we were still in his bloody dressing room. The line had been delivered two minutes ago!

'The line has been delivered, Pete! We were due on stage five minutes ago!'

And then he started: 'I can't go on, I can't go on, Brian. I can't do it, I can't go on.'

Well, I dragged him down the corridor. I dragged him

and dragged him and I threw him on that bloody stage, and when he arrived – silence.

The shock of how he looked, despite my best efforts, had obviously unnerved the audience, and things hadn't exactly been going well beforehand. It was THE BIGGEST DIS-ASTER. What really capped it all, though, was the bath. Yes, you read that correctly – the bath!

He'd had a bath put onstage and they'd paid somebody 3,000 quid to fill it with fake blood. And what happened after he killed Duncan? He got into the bath and then almost bloody drowned in the stuff. It covered his entire body! This really brought the house down. It brought the house down with laughter!

For you see, after he got out, there was blood all over the stage – so when people came running on during different scenes, they slipped on the blood and went arse over tit. The audience laughed and laughed and laughed.

The press murdered him, of course, and what's more, they enjoyed murdering him.

O'Toole's career had been a giant success. He had Oscar nominations coming out of every pore and Christ knows how many Golden Globes, yet they sought to destroy him. This was the man who at Stratford had taught Dame Peggy Ash-croft how to play comedy, when they did *The Taming of the Shrew* at Stratford-upon-Avon and the National Theatre. He taught Peggy Ashcroft how to do it! Astonishing perform-ances.

But the press now butchered O'Toole, even though they knew he was ill. They knew he was out of his mind, yet they all jumped on him. They all attempted to kill the man.

Anyway, a few weeks later, he decided he would ask them all back again for a second press night. I didn't know he'd done it until afterwards and it was a stupid thing to do, but, oh, they all came back. By God, they did.

'That's another four hours of our lives we've wasted,' they

said. 'Why did we bother to sit through this MacDEATH for a second time, starring this hopeless actor?'

Do you know, Peter made the headlines on the huge stockmarket boards in Times Square. He had the headlines! 'O'Toole in West End failure', 'MacDEATH a tragedy', 'MacDEATH a farce'.

Who's ever had that? Olivier, Gielgud . . . none of 'em! He was all over Times Square. The *Daily Telegraph* ran an entire page on it, as did the *Evening Standard*. It was WORLD NEWS. He brought them back and they butchered him again.

The day after they'd butchered him again, I came in to find it was a packed house. Of course it was: they'd all come to see him suffer. When I got to my dressing room, Peter was there waiting for me. He was on his knees and he had no voice. In fact, as far as I was concerned, he was dying. All the veins were sticking out of his head, and I was standing in front of him gently pushing them back into his skull. I was standing in front of Peter O'Toole and I was trying to push his veins back into his skull. I find this difficult to describe and painful to recall. It was as if his skull was open and his brain and his neocortex were hanging out of his head.

He then spoke, but he spoke as if he were about to die. There was almost nothing coming from his mouth.

'Brian, have you seen what they've written about me? I can't take it any more.'

He was sobbing his eyes out. He was on the brink of death that night. I said, 'Come here, Peter, come here,' and I picked him up, I put my arms around him and I kissed him on the lips, I kissed him on both eyes and I began stroking his head. 'It's OK, Peter, come on.' I then rocked him back and forth in my arms. I rocked him gently for half an hour and sang to him. I sang a gentle lullaby to him and I soothed him in my arms. 'Peter, I think you're dying. I am going to go down onto the stage and I am going to tell the audience to go home, and that you are not going to play this role again.'

'Oh, no, don't, you can't,' he pleaded.

As I walked down the corridor towards the stage, he followed me on all fours, like some demented ape, gripping me and saying, 'I have to go on, Brian, please let me go on, I have to go on. If I don't, I WILL die.'

He eventually went on, and the show lasted almost five hours. After Banquo died, I stayed on the stage. I just stood there at the side, ready to collect him. He had no voice, nothing. There was no life in him. But he went on to complete that run. The mark of a man, it is always said, is that he completes the job, and he completed the job. He finished it. Never in my life have I witnessed such courage. I couldn't have done it!

Years later, I was playing Captain Hook in pantomime and, about halfway through the first half, I spotted O'Toole in the audience. *You old bugger*, I thought. Anyway, I mouthed to him to come back afterwards and he did. Hildegard was destroyed with emotion as she watched him hug me and hold me: 'My friend, my friend, my only dear friend.' The room was full of nothing but love and admiration: the result of a forty-year friendship that had both fired and flattened us both. He had his son Lorcan with him, who was obviously the apple of his eye, and for the first time since I'd known him he actually seemed happy. He was still smoking like a bloody chimney, of course, and I dare say he enjoyed the odd glass of wine occasionally, but the madness had gone. Happy was the man.

The last time I saw him?

Well, in about 2009, I was walking down Wardour Street in Soho after doing a voice-over when I suddenly realized I was being sworn at.

'Blessed, you big rough bastard! Over here!'

I looked up and there, standing right in the middle of the

road, was O'Toole, arms in the air, looking as though he'd been dragged through a hedge backwards.

'Look at you, you big lovely fucker,' he shouted. 'Come here, come and give me a hug.'

'Where on earth are you going to, O'Toole?' I asked.

'I'm off to the Groucho Club, love, off to pick up some award or something. Come here, you big marvellous bugger. Look at me, I'm fucked, and look at fucking you, you look wonderful. You bastard, I'm going to knock you out!'

He threw a gentle punch and then I grabbed him, lifted him into the air, slowly lowered him onto the pavement and I pinned him.

'You big rough bugger. Watcha go and do that for?'

The taxi drivers and tourists passing by didn't know what to think.

'Submit?'

'Of course I fucking submit. I can't move!'

With that, I picked him up, dusted him off, gave him a big hug and a huge kiss – and then away he went to the Groucho Club. Before he turned the corner onto Old Compton Street, he looked back and gestured as if to say, 'I'll call you.'

He never did, nor I him – and that's the last time we ever saw each other.

It had been just like the old days: profane, confrontational and fun. I miss him dreadfully. With his death a great light has gone out on this planet. We shall never see his like again.

3

GET IT DOWN IN THE BOOK, LAD

Before I tell you about my first brush with fame and fortune, and how I nearly lost my birthday tackle to a crowd of ravening fans, there are the wilderness years to cover – when it looked as if I had become the pariah of the acting world. Things could have turned out very differently indeed. It all started quite promisingly, though, at Nottingham Rep.

Now, there will undoubtedly be some among you who are not familiar with what a 'Rep' is, so very quickly: 'Rep' is short for repertory company, and is where I and countless other actors and actresses learned our craft. All the towns and cities used to have them. Drama school was where we were given the tools, if you like, but it was at Rep where we learned how to use them. Let's call it 'work experience for dedicated artists'!

But the crux behind the importance of Rep – certainly to an actor straight out of drama school, like yours truly – was the sheer volume and variety of output: a different play a week, a fortnight or a month depending on which company you belonged to. So, from the moment you arrived at the theatre until the moment you left, you never stopped learning. And it wasn't all Shakespeare, by the way. Good God, no! We did all kinds of bloody everything, from *Present Laughter*, *The Cherry Orchard* and *Coriolanus* to *An Inspector Calls*, *Mother Courage* and *Death of a Salesman*. So you can imagine the work involved; learning lines and rehearsing, and so on. Tremendous fun, though, and of course you learned an awful lot, very, very quickly. Anyway, so that's Rep. Everybody on the same page now?

I'd gone straight from Bristol to Nottingham Rep, but despite being fairly well-off creatively there, I'm afraid that from a fiscal point of view things were never quite as prosperous. Or, to use a technical term, I was always bloody skint! You see, out of my four pounds, nineteen shillings and sixpence a week, two pounds ten shillings went straight to my digs (which was run by a hunchback and his mother), so I only had two pounds to live on, or thereabouts. That wasn't enough to feed a gnat on a gnat's back, let alone a sixteen-stone Yorkshireman with the appetite of a brontosaurus, and so I'm ashamed to say that the penury that then blighted my life often drove me to become somewhat larcenous on occasion. I took food from the stores at the theatre as well as the odd pair of trousers from the wardrobe department. It was either that or I starve to death whilst walking around Nottingham with my bits hanging out! I simply had to do it to get by.

I was there for fourteen months in all. Almost starved! Then, just as I was plotting my next raid on the underwear drawer in wardrobe, I got a chance to join Birmingham Rep, which at the time was probably the most respected repertory theatre company in the UK. Still is today, in fact. One of the few left.

I'd been spotted playing Matt of the Mint in *The Beggar's Opera* (which is a very showy part) by Sir Barry Jackson, who was the founder and head of Birmingham Rep. Sir Barry had been incredibly impressed by my performance and after seeing me again in *The Rape of the Belt*, in which I played Zeus, he invited me over to Birmingham to have a chat.

Now, the alumni at Birmingham were second to none. Sir Laurence Olivier, Sir Ralph Richardson, Dame Edith Evans and Dame Peggy Ashcroft all made their professional debuts there. I went on to goose them all, of course. Four of the most respected arses in show business. Impressive stuff!

At the time, Albert Finney had been one of their leading actors, as had the great Paul Scofield, but as they were both about to move on, the theatre company was preparing to re-cast for the forthcoming season. What names, though! Together with the Bristol Old Vic, Birmingham really was the crème de la crème. Peter O'Toole and Eric Porter dominated Bristol, and Finney and Scofield Birmingham. These were the two companies that every actor in the country wanted to work for.

So off I went to Birmingham, where I was immediately introduced to Sir Barry's assistant, Nancy Berman, and to his new director, the famous character actor Bernard Hepton. Hepton was a wonderful actor (he's still alive but now retired, I think) and later appeared as, amongst others, the Komman-dant in *Colditz* and one of the leads in *Smiley's People*. I always thought that his becoming director at Birmingham Rep was a great loss to the acting world. That said, he was good at it and I was lucky to work with him.

Strangely enough, I never auditioned for Birmingham, which was definitely not the norm, and when I first met Ber-nard and Nancy alone at a casting meeting, I got the feeling they'd had their noses put out a little, almost as if I'd been forced on them.

'Barry is enamoured of you, Brian,' said Bernard. 'And on this occasion we have had to trust his judgement. We're about to cast our first production and have seen five actors includ-ing yourself. All have credentials as good as yours.'

'I completely understand, Bernard,' I said. 'Whatever Sir Barry thinks of me, the role must go to the actor you think most appropriate.'

'Yes, but who *is* that actor, Brian?' countered Bernard, softening a bit. 'We've been impressed by all five of you and are having difficulty making our decision. Is there anything you'd like to say that might influence us? We've asked the other actors the same question.'

This is my chance, I thought. I stood up and said with great passion, 'Yes, there is! For months now I've been living on brown bread and bloody soup, and I'm fed up with it. I've had to borrow clothes from the wardrobe department so that my underwear isn't on show every time I go for a newspaper and I'm living with a hunchback and his mother. I even had to thumb a lift to get here. I'm telling you: I need this role!'

Bernard almost fell off his chair. 'You've got the job, Brian. That's the most original and honest·answer we've ever had, so the job's yours. We can't leave an actor on queer street!'

Apparently, the other four had come out with the usual 'Well, I'm very good at Restoration comedy' or 'I'm very good at Chekhov', etc., but I was bloody well starving! I needed some meat and vegetables in my diet. That's a very important ingredient in professional life though, I think. You have to *need* it, as well as want it.

Anyway, I got £15 a week, almost four times what I was earning at Nottingham. A bloody fortune! The production in question, by the way, was *Henry IV – Part 1*, in which I played Sir Walter Blunt, and it premiered in Birmingham on 16 February 1960.

After a few months of being there, Sir Barry and Bernard began casting me in leading roles; usually as characters much older than myself – sometimes twenty or thirty years older.

I remember my first lead at Birmingham as if it were yesterday. It was in a play called *The Bastard Country* that had been written by Anthony Coburn, who went on to write the first ever episodes of *Doctor Who*. It was Anthony's first effort as a playwright and he described it as 'a human story in which all things common to men are included – tragedy, pathos, humour and, above all else, love'. Hmmmm.

Although it didn't go on to break any box-office records, *The Bastard Country* presented me with the perfect opportunity to try my luck as a leading man – and, all things considered, it went well. The show got decent notices, as did I. I was cock-a-hoop with happiness! The only other actor I can think of who appeared in *The Bastard Country* and became famous was a man called Arthur Pentelow, who went on to play Mr Wilks in *Emmerdale Farm*. It was a powerful company and full of tremendous actors.

The lead in *The Bastard Country* was supposed to be at least sixty-five years of age, and I was only twenty-three. Stranger still, everyone else appearing in the play was at least ten years older than I was. It was a rum state of affairs. Completely arse-about-face, really. This became a bit of a running theme at Birmingham, and as time went on I carried on being cast in, shall we say, slightly more senior roles. This came to a head one day when Sir Barry, obviously deciding that I was born to play pensioners, decided that my next role should be King Lear.

'What? But I'm too young to play Lear, Sir Barry,' I pleaded. 'And by about fifty bloody years! I'm all for playing older parts, but Lear, at twenty-three?'

Sir Barry reluctantly accepted my decision and so it was forgotten about. It would have been a disaster! I think Sir Barry had been influenced by the fact that I had the ability to explode on stage with seismic effect. The Birmingham critic J. C. Trewin said of me at the time: 'This is a living volcano we have here at Birmingham Rep, something quite different to what we're used to.'

Now, as a seed for what comes later in this chapter, I must expand on something about my character that I mentioned earlier: the fact that, ever since I was a child, there have been times when I cannot stand to be with other human beings. It doesn't matter who they are – friends, family, school pupils or teachers – for as long as the compulsion is with me, I simply cannot be in the same room as other people. It is something that, to be honest, I don't quite understand. It is neither depression nor anxiety; in fact it does not upset me in any way whatsoever. But its hold on me is strong, and it has, at times, got me into all kinds of trouble. As a child I used to take myself off on a walk for a few hours . . . which was precisely what I did while at Birmingham Rep when I was supposed to be attending a full day's rehearsal. I went for a walk to Cannock Wood, to be exact, leaving the entire cast and crew high and dry.

Of course, I was hauled up in front of the management, and rightly so. Nancy Berman went absolutely ballistic!

'I've never known behaviour like this, Brian. Explain yourself. Is it stage fright?'

'No. I've never had that. I just couldn't face acting or actors, Nancy. I couldn't be bothered really. I needed to be alone!'

That was quite an ill-judged reply, if memory serves. I was simply being honest, though. At that point, my yearning was to be on my own, preferably out in the open air. After about the third time of this happening, I received what could have been my final warning.

'Brian, you are destroying what we believe to be an extremely promising career,' said Nancy Berman. She was so attractive when she was angry. She had a strange haunting face with an intense beauty of its own. 'This is the third time this has happened. You don't drink and you don't smoke. You say you're not depressed or anxious about anything. What's wrong with you?'

'I just feel terribly detached, and for as long as the feeling is upon me, I have no desire whatsoever to act. Don't worry, though, I'll turn up for the performance.'

After that, something obviously clicked and I was a good boy for a few years. Well, about two, to be exact. It all started again while I was in Z Cars, and Christ did I get into trouble then. I'll come to that in a bit.

Anyway, back to Brum.

The security I felt being at Birmingham was immensely powerful, and after a while I felt that I needed to break it. We were all terribly well looked after there, and I was in danger of feeling too safe. Where was the danger? The risk? In the end, I thought, *Bugger it, if I don't do it now, I never bloody will*, and so I left Birmingham Rep and decided to move down to London, rent myself a room, get myself an agent, and seek my fortune. Television was becoming ever more popular at the time and the West End was thriving. Surely this was the perfect time? Even if I was a human volcano that went walkabout occasionally.

My first two ambitions were realized almost immediately. I found a nice room in Golders Green and was then taken on by the Mary Harris agency, one of the best in the business. *A good start*, I thought.

Oh, the innocence of youth.

Yes, I got the auditions. My time at Birmingham saw to that. But could I get a part? Could I buggery!

At the time I had two partners in crime, John Thaw and Keith Barron. I'd first met Keith as a teenager while attending drama courses in Yorkshire, and had got to know John simply by attending the same auditions. Between the three of us we went for every single part available. None of us ever seemed to get a bloody look-in though. There was a set routine. In the morning we'd all go off to our respective auditions and meetings, sometimes for the same parts, and then all meet for tea at the Interval Club in Soho. There we'd sit – three Northerners with no parts. Not even small ones.

Although our reactions varied by degree, each had his own style when it came to expressing the injustice of it all. I would become indignant. Wild with rage!

'What do they mean by giving the part to so-and-so? He's as camp as bloody Christmas, and at least a foot shorter than they were asking for. It's a disgrace. We should have shoved that script up that director's arse there and then!'

While poor old John Thaw would just sit there, shaking his head and looking dour.

'I'll never work again, Brian. Nobody wants me!'

He did OK in the end, of course.

Keith Barron, on the other hand, who has the most marvellous sense of humour, would just explode.

'Who did that director think he was? What a complete wazzock! There's more talent in my beard than there is in his entire bloody cast. He wouldn't know a good actor if God Himself had recommended him.'

'Alright, Keith, calm down. Have another cup of tea, love. It'll all work out in the end.'

'Well. The stuck-up tosspot! He doesn't know his arse from his bloody elbow.'

It was terribly frustrating, though. We'd all come from playing leads in Rep – me at Birmingham, Keith at Sheffield and John at Liverpool – and now we couldn't even get a walk-on role in a bloody advert. We'd thought the West End was going to bow down in front of us and offer us instant stardom!

We all soldiered on, of course, and as time went on both Keith and John found parts, which just left me. But before I could become even more indignant, I got a call one morning from my agent.

'Orson Welles is holding open auditions for a new film he's making called *Chimes of Midnight*. They're taking place at Wyndham's Theatre. Would you like to go along?'

I didn't need asking twice.

'The great Orson Welles? Yes, I'm in, love, I'm in. I'll be there.'

I flatter myself, but we're actually quite similar, Orson Welles and I; certainly with regards to physique. Just picture him now in your head, a huge bear of a man with a beard. And now picture me. Do you see? We could have been twins.

So off I went to Wyndham's Theatre at the speed of light.

When I got there though – Jesus Christ! There must have been enough actors and actresses to stretch from here to Mars – thousands of them, and all begging for work. I'll tell you what, it's no fun being an out-of-work actor. I thought, *I can't be arsed with all this. I'll be waiting here for a week!*

Also, if I did wait in line, the chances were that, should I get seen, it wouldn't be until right at the end of the day, when everyone involved would be tired and irritable, including Welles. No: *Balls to that*, I thought. *I've got to see him now!* Luckily, I knew the manager at Wyndham's quite well and so went to the box office to have a word.

'Look, do us a favour, me old son, and get me to the front of this queue, would you? I won't stand a fucking chance otherwise.'

'Follow me,' he said – and within about two minutes I was standing on the side of the stage, waiting to go on.

'Oh shit,' I said. 'I haven't thought about what I'll read! What am I going to read?'

'Well, you've got about three minutes to think of something,' said the manager. 'You're on next but one.'

We all had millions of audition pieces prepared, but it had to be the right one. *Bugger it*, I thought. *Perhaps I should have waited my turn and thought about it. Bollocks!*

There was no point – or time – to worry about it. Suddenly I felt a tap on my shoulder.

'You're next, off you go.'

So out I strode onto the stage. It was all quite dark and I remember looking out to see who was watching. At first glance I couldn't see a thing, and then, as my eyes acclimatized, I saw, about ten rows back, a heavy-set bearded man wearing a white three-piece suit. He seemed to be about the size of a rhino. Absolutely enormous, he was, and smoking a cigar that looked more like a log.

'What's your name, young man?'

'Blessed, Mr Welles. My name is Brian Blessed.'

'Blessed, eh? Same spelling as "blessed", I take it?'

'That's right, Mr Welles, yes.'

'Fascinating. Well, I think that's rather splendid. What have you got for me, Mr Blessed?'

'Well, I'm going to do Aaron's speech from *Titus Andronicus*. Act two, scene one. "Now climbeth Tamora Olympus' top".'

He immediately jumped up with a roar.

'May I say, that's a very good choice, young man? I've been sick to death of listening to Hamlet, Romeo and Richard II. This will make a refreshing change. OK, as soon as you're ready.'

> Now climbeth Tamora Olympus' top,
> Safe out of fortune's shot; and sits aloft,
> Secure of thunder's crack or lightning flash;
> Advanced above pale envy's threatening reach.
> As when the golden sun salutes the morn,
> And, having gilt the ocean with his beams,
> Gallops the zodiac in his glistering coach,
> And overlooks the highest-peering hills;
> So Tamora . . .

'Excellent, Mr Blessed. You're quite a heavyweight, aren't you? Now look, I'm casting the role of Hotspur. You show me how heavy and powerful you can be. Can you be sharp, Mr Blessed? Can you be sharp? Hotspur is sharp.'

'I know the character well, Mr Welles,' I said. 'I played him several times at drama school. Which speech would you like? "My liege, I did deny no prisoners"?'

'Yes, that would be splendid.' I could see he was impressed.

'And how do you see him, Mr Welles? How do *you* see Hotspur?'

What happened next I shall remember for the rest of my

days. After pausing for just a moment, the great man rose slowly to his feet.

'I see him as—' He paused again, before looking towards the stage. 'HOT,' he growled, his face turning crimson.

'HOT,' he said again, but now much louder.

'HOT!'

Jesus Christ, I thought. *The man's going to explode!*

And then the grand finale.

'HOT-SPUUUUUUUUUUUUUUUUUUUUR!' he screamed.

And they called *me* the human volcano? I was a mere hillock compared to this man. I'll tell you, Mount Vesuvius had nothing on Orson Welles. Nothing! What an eruption!

But he wasn't finished. Simmering back to a growl, he continued.

'Hotspur should be mad, Mr Blessed – aflame with rage! And, as I said before, he should be sharp – very sharp. This is a man who has had to give up his prisoners to, as you English would say, a poof. A man smothered in perfumes – and this infuriates him! That is how I see Hotspur.'

What had originally meant to be an audition had in fact turned into a masterclass. Well, I wasn't going to let this slip through my fingers. *Right, you bugger*, I thought. *Just you watch this. If you want mad, I'll give you mad*. And I launched into my speech.

BOOOOM!

> My liege, I did deny no prisoners.
> But I remember, when the fight was done,
> When I was dry with rage and extreme toil . . .

About three minutes later there I stood, centre stage at Wyndham's, totally and utterly exhausted and drenched with sweat. I had given it everything.

'My word, Mr Blessed, you are indeed Hotspur. That was magnificent. Come back in an hour and we'll have some tea together in my dressing room.'

So about an hour later, there I am having tea with Orson bloody Welles, post masterclass! Sitting with us were two friends of his from the Abbey Theatre, Dublin – Micheál Mac Liammóir and Hilton Edwards.

'OK, Brian,' he began. 'You don't mind me calling you Brian, do you?'

'Not at all, Mr Welles.'

'Thank you, Brian. Look, I'd like you to play Hotspur in *Chimes of Midnight*. What do you say?'

'I say yes, Mr Welles. I say yes!'

Just then, the great Russian-born Hollywood actor and Welles's long-time collaborator Akim Tamiroff walked in.

'Hello guys. Do you mind if I join you?' he said, in a thick Russian accent.

'No, come in, Akim, come in. Brian, this is Akim. Akim, Brian. Brian's going to be playing Hotspur in *Chimes*.'

'Congratulations, young man,' he said warmly.

'Akim's going to be sitting in on rehearsals this afternoon,' said Mr Welles.

'Oh, that's nice,' I said.

THAT'S NICE?! Oh Jesus. Compose yourself, Blessed, I thought, *compose your bloody self!*

And compose myself I did, thank the Lord. So, as opposed to me making a complete tit of myself and being told I was no longer required, I managed to engage these two cinematic giants in a discussion concerning – amongst other things – a shared fascination of Captain Ahab, *The Third Man*, *Citizen Kane* and *The Trial*. What a day! It was like going for a job on Mount Olympus and being interviewed by Zeus himself.

Unfortunately, as is so often the way with these things, the call confirming my engagement never materialized. I waited and waited . . . but nothing. I even turned down one or two jobs in anticipation of it going ahead, but I'm afraid Mr Welles remained silent. Eventually, I could wait no more, and so returned as best I could to normality: auditions,

Interval Club, shouting session – auditions, Interval Club, shouting session – auditions, Interval Club, shouting session, *ad infinitum*. I managed to scrape by with the occasional odd voice-over, but it was no way for a future great to live!

Life carried on that way for another year or so, after which time I wasn't the only one becoming exasperated. My agents in particular were now at the end of their tether. Fortunately, though, as opposed to simply dumping me, they decided to tout me to all and sundry.

'Right, Brian,' said John Ingram, the chap who looked after me at the agency. 'We're going to invest a bit of money in you. It's about time you started making a name for yourself. Somebody with your pedigree should be working flat out so we're going to take you out to meet as many of the big boys as possible. We're arranging meetings at Pinewood, Shepperton and at Elstree. You're going to see the lot. Every director, actor and producer we can get in front of. First meeting's tomorrow with John Mills up at Pinewood.'

'OK!' I enthused. 'Thank you, John, that sounds fabulous!'

Except it wasn't fabulous. In fact, I hated every minute of it. I felt like some kind of exhibit; something people pick up and fondle at a ruddy antiques market. Don't get me wrong, I knew exactly why the agency was doing it, and I appreciated their efforts. It just didn't sit with me as a person. I may indeed be the size of a small bull, but I don't expect to be treated like one; being paraded in front of potential 'buyers' like that. All day long I was taken from bigwig to bigwig.

'Johnny, this is Brian Blessed, our new star, fresh from Birmingham Rep.'

'Pleased to meet you, young man.'

Then, once they'd looked you up and down, you were shunted off to the next one.

'Dickie, old thing! I'd like you to meet Brian Blessed, our new star from blah blah blah . . .'

It was a damned awful experience.

Anyway, perhaps sensing my extreme dissatisfaction with the proceedings, not one of the bigwigs got back to them. Not a single enquiry. We were back to square one.

'We can't flog you for love nor money, Brian,' grumbled John Ingram.

Then he had a lightbulb moment – of sorts.

'How about changing your name?' he suggested. 'Blessed's an odd name. It doesn't seem to stick. I'll tell you what, how about Benedict? Brian Benedict.'

My response was a very firm – 'NO!'

'OK, no name change then.'

Well, in the words of the great Greek philosopher Heraclitus, 'the only thing that is constant is change'; *sooner or later*, I thought, *my luck will have to*. And so it did.

Two days later, I received yet another call from John Ingram, this time bearing potentially better news.

'Brian, there's a chap at Television Centre who wants to see you called David Rose. He's casting some semi-documentary police thing called *Z Cars*. That's all I know I'm afraid. Anyway, you're in to see him tomorrow at 11 a.m., OK? Good luck.'

I could tell by the tone of his voice that he didn't think I stood a cat in hell's chance. And to tell you the truth, neither did I. But along I went to Television Centre as requested. That in itself was a revelation. What a building that is! I have to say that on seeing it I absolutely fell in love with the place. It's an astounding piece of architecture, really: brave, diverse, but in its own way very beautiful and soulful.

So off I went to the fourth floor, where I duly met this David Rose chap – a great tall gangly fellow, fortyish, and very friendly, who appeared ultra-sensitive and nervous.

Now, for those of you who have never actually seen *Z Cars*, which is basically all those under the age of about eighty, I'd better bring you quickly up to speed. Created by Troy Kennedy Martin and John McGrath, *Z Cars* portrayed the imaginary Victor Division of the Seaforth and Newtown constabulary on Merseyside. The main cast consisted of four police constables (two in each car), a sergeant and an inspector and staff at HQ, and each show would disclose what had happened to them on their various patrols, etc. It was like an early version of *The Bill*, I suppose, except a hell of a lot better. Sorry *Bill*!

The theme music, which is worth a quick mention, was arranged by Fritz Spiegl and is, as I'm sure many of you know, played before every Everton home match, as it is before every Tranmere Rovers and every Watford match. So there you are, *Z Cars* in a nutshell. You'll learn the rest as I go.

After David Rose told me what they had planned with *Z Cars*, I began telling him who I was and what I'd been up to, which wasn't very much. Suddenly, he sat up.

'Sorry for interrupting, Brian, but there's a very good part here in episode five; in an episode called "The Whalers". The character's a Norwegian whaler, would you mind reading it?'

I didn't need to be asked twice.

'Of course, I'd be delighted,' I said. And so I began reading. After a few lines, David stopped me.

'That's great, Brian. I think we can offer you that role.'

Bloody hell, I thought – *television. The promised land. At last, I've got a job!*

I shook David warmly by the hand and was just walking out of the room when he stopped me.

'Hang on a minute, Brian, hang on. I've got an idea. Have you got ten minutes?'

I thought, *I've got ten bloody days, love*, but didn't let on.

'Yes, of course, Mr Rose. Fire away.'

'OK. Of the four main constable roles in *Z Cars*, we've got one called "Fancy" Smith. To a certain extent you've upset the apple cart, really, because we'd all but decided on whom to cast—'

I didn't let him go any further, just in case he went back the other way and talked himself out of it.

'Pass me a script and I'll read him,' I interrupted. 'What kind of a man is he?'

'Well,' said David, passing over a script. 'He's described as being tall and thin with pointed shoes. An Italian type and a bit of a teddy boy.'

'Well, that's not really me,' I said, slightly deflated. 'If anything, I'm described as a rugby type.'

'Never mind all that,' he said, 'just read the part.'

So I read it for him, after which he just sat there looking rather confused. 'Read it again, would you?' he asked.

So I read the part again, only for him to look even more confused.

'I'm going to fetch a couple of my colleagues. I'd like them to hear you read. Is that OK?'

'Of course, the more the merrier,' I replied.

And so, after a few minutes, David walked back into the room, closely followed by Robert Barr, the executive producer of Z Cars, and Troy Kennedy Martin, one of the main writers. I read the part again, after which David said, 'What's coming over to me is that you fancy yourself as a tough guy, despite what you're reading, which is quite contrary to what we've been playing with so far. You come over big-headed and sure of yourself physically, as opposed to aesthetically, and I think this is much more interesting.'

Fortunately for me, Robert and Troy seemed to be in agreement with David.

'Would you mind leaving the room for a few minutes, Brian? I think the three of us need to have a chat.'

So I left the room as he asked, but within about thirty seconds was called back in again.

'We'd like to offer you "Fancy" Smith, Brian. You're going to be one of the boys, one of the regulars.'

'Thank you!' I said, shaking all of them by the hand, and trying desperately to hide my enormous relief.

I couldn't believe it. I'd gone from being a complete no-hoper – the Jonah of the Mary Harris agency – to a regular in what was about to become the biggest programme on British television. Pick the bloody bones out of that! My salary was £34 a week, the equivalent of about £750 these days. *Not bad*, I thought. It was enough to keep me in Sugar Puffs for a bit.

After receiving the scripts, I then learned who my co-stars would be. With me in Z-Victor 1 would be the Scottish actor Joseph Brady, playing PC Jock Weir. We shared the same birthday, Joseph and I, and he was a lovely man. Over in Z-Victor 2 you had Jeremy Kemp, who played PC Bob Steele, and Jimmy Ellis, who played PC Bert Lynch, and then back at the station were Stratford Johns, who played Chief Inspector Barlow – our boss, basically – and Frank Windsor, who played Sergeant John Watt. All five of these actors were a few years older than me, and all five had done television before, so I'm not ashamed to say that I was more than a little daunted about working with them.

There were also six or seven semi-regular parts too, of course – what were then called subsidiary roles. You had Sergeant Twentyman, who was played by Leonard Williams, who had a long reddish face and was already one of the best-known actors on television. He'd done a tremendous amount of work, even in 1962, and was also a big star on radio at the time, appearing in, amongst other things, quite a few episodes of *The Clitheroe Kid*. And there was PC Sweet, who was played by Terence Edmond. When it came to acting talent, we were certainly very wealthy as a show – but when it came to writers? Oh my God, we were billionaires, love. You see, this was a very big show for the BBC – the UK's first-ever hard-hitting police drama – and so it had to be good. We had

Allan Prior, Bill Barron, Alan Plater, Adele Rose and John Hopkins, to name but a few.

The only police drama produced prior to *Z Cars* had been *Dixon of Dock Green*, and as popular as that show was, it could never in a million years be described as either 'hard-hitting' or realistic. It was about as hard-hitting as a sodding feather duster! So while Jack Warner as Dixon was teaching us all to be nice to old people and suchlike, Joseph Brady and I would be kicking the crap out of an armed robber or some other toerag. This was real life.

Role secured, it was on to the first read-through! This was to take place in St Helen's Church in Ladbroke Grove. Now bearing in mind I was yet to meet any of the cast members, directors or writers, it's safe to say that I was a bag of nerves. And, as it later turned out, I had very good reason to be. First of all, I was only just on time, so as I entered the room just a minute or so before 12 p.m., thirty people stopped what they were doing and stared straight at me. It seemed like an age before David Rose broke the silence.

'Brian, come in, come in. This is Brian Blessed, everyone. He's playing "Fancy" Smith, our tough guy in Z-Victor 1.'

To say the response was muted would have been a ginormous bloody understatement. I thought, *I hope they warm up a bit!*

Down the centre of the room was a huge table with chairs around it, and there were scripts everywhere of course. Gradually, as I was introduced to Jimmy and to Joseph and Frank, I started to relax a bit. *They seem like a nice bunch*, I thought, *it's going to be OK*. Just then, David Rose spoiled it all by explaining how the show would be filmed and broadcast.

'Basically, we'll pre-record the location shots during the week up in Lancashire, which will be about ten minutes' worth of scenes, and the rest will broadcast live from Television Centre.'

Forty minutes live! FORTY MINUTES! Bloody hellfire. What a rude awakening that was.

Just to compound my fear, I then decided to ask what is commonly known as 'a stupid bloody question'.

'Excuse me,' I said. I think I even put my bloody hand up. 'Excuse me, but should I bring my make-up with me when we're shooting on location?'

Fortunately – although there were around thirty people who were desperate to – nobody laughed out loud. I must have been the greenest thing they'd ever come across!

'It's OK, Brian,' said David. 'The BBC looks after that sort of thing. It means you can concentrate on the script.' David would eventually prove to be a terrifically kind director/ producer.

How was I supposed to know? I'd come straight from Rep and had always done my own make-up. I had no idea there were departments full of people to do it for you in TV.

Anyway, a few days after the read-through (which did in fact go very well), I was duly called up to Liverpool, where I was introduced to the director, Shaun Sutton. Now, not putting too fine a point on it, Shaun Sutton was one of the most important figures in the history of British television, and I'll tell you what, I miss him terribly. As a director he worked on all kinds of ground-breaking stuff, such as *Z Cars*, of course, as well as *The Last Man Out* and *The Troubleshooters*. But it was as Head of Serials at the BBC that he really made his name, commissioning such legendary series as *I, Claudius*, *The Forsyte Saga*, *Play for Today* and *Pennies From Heaven*. The man was a genial genius. He had a noble heart and was a beautiful human being.

So that's Shaun, our director.

Eventually, it was time for me to deliver my first lines. My first ever lines on television! I kept saying to myself over and over again, *Don't bugger it up, Brian. For God's sake, don't screw it up*. Shaun could obviously see I was nervous and so took me to one side.

'Are you OK, Brian?' he asked.

'I've never done television before. I don't know what to do.'

'It's quite simple, dear boy,' he said. 'When I shout, "Action!" you pause for a moment and then say your lines. When you've finished, you pause again and I'll say, "Cut." After that, hold your position and the cameraman will love you. Mark my words, dear boy, you'll be a great success.'

We filmed the scene and I did exactly as he said.

'Delightful!' said Shaun. 'You see, that's all there is to it, Brian.'

From then on, Shaun Sutton became my TV father, if you like, and I became a BBC boy. I was begat by the BBC, in that I used to listen to it all as a child, and now here I was actually working for them as an actor. It felt good.

After we finished the outdoor shots, we then had to film the driving scenes. Now, the other three actors playing constables had all learned to drive several years previously, which meant that when it came to filming these scenes, they looked like – and indeed did – know exactly what they were doing. Jeremy Kemp had a wonderful sports car if memory serves. A real whiz-kid, he was.

Brian Blessed, on the other hand, didn't know a handbrake from a flaming windscreen wiper, nor an emergency stop from a three-point bloody turn. All Greek to me, love. I was OK when it came to steering, of course. I mean that's easy, isn't it, turning a wheel every so often. But it was the pedals and the bloody gears that I just couldn't get my head around. Didn't have a bloody clue! In the end, they got a chap called Stan Hollingsworth to act as my kind of 'pedal-and-gears car dwarf'. So I used to sit there, steering away and saying my lines and suchlike, while poor old Stan would work the pedals and the gears. It sounds bloody ridiculous, but I promise you it worked.

Well, it worked to a point. You see, I used to have a habit of getting excited occasionally, especially if it was a good storyline. And in such a situation, as opposed to keeping my feet as far away from the pedals (and Stan) as possible, I'd start working the bloody things with my feet and, subsequently, trampling Stan half to bloody death. He'd have my feet in his face and up his arse. I once kicked him very hard in the bollocks.

Then there was Joseph's wind problem. He could have – and probably did at some time in his life – fart for Great Britain and all her colonies; so, not only did poor Stan have to suffer my feet in his bollocks, but he also got a mouthful of Joe's farts occasionally. In the end, the BBC took pity on Stan and demanded I take driving lessons.

'He'll take us to bloody court if we don't do something. You almost brought his sex life to an end last week and he's at his wits' end. They're still quite numb, apparently.'

'Fair enough,' I said. 'At least you're paying for the lessons. That'll do for me.'

So off I went for lessons with, as luck would have it, Lancashire Police Force. Now, there were two absolute legends in the force up there at the time, one of whom I partly based my character of Fancy Smith on. He was called William Palfrey, and was the Chief Constable of Lancashire Police Force. He was a terrifying man, six foot six with a big gruff voice, and he had an army of about 17,000 policemen and women – which, at the time, was the biggest force outside of London. What's more, he had the respect, so I was told, of every single one of them. He was a remarkable man. His assistant was a man called Pendergrass, and he was even more bloody terrifying. But they were also the advisors on *Z Cars*, which is why it was always so true to life.

Now, at the time of me starting my lessons with the Lancashire Constabulary, a man from Blackpool had just shot a policeman dead. Today, of course, it occurs far more regularly, but back in the 1960s it was almost unheard of. A policeman shot dead on duty? The headlines were full of it. I remember Palfrey going on television not long after it happened to be interviewed. It was the *Ten O'Clock News*.

'How do you feel?' asked the presenter.

'How do I feel?' growled the dangerous Chief Constable Palfrey. And then he leaned forward just inches from the interviewer's face. 'How do I feel? One of my policemen is dead!'

His face contorted into a mixture of Frankenstein's monster and the Kraken. Watching it, I thought, *I wouldn't be that gunman for love nor money*.

A few days later, they arrested the man who did it, and the next time I saw Chief Constable Palfrey I asked him how they'd managed to catch him so quickly.

'I went to the underworld, lad,' he replied.

'Really?' I said, not knowing whether to believe him or not.

'I did. I went to the underworld and I said, "If you don't cough up that man to me within two days, I'll close you. I'll close your nightclubs and I'll close your pubs. I'll close every single business and racket you lot run and I'll finish every single one of you. Cough him up or you're finished."'

'And they coughed him up, just like that?'

'Of course they did. I was serious, lad. They knew I meant every bloody word.'

I smiled later on and thought, *And this man's helping to teach me how to drive?*

He also had a nickname, did Chief Constable Palfrey. He was known, rather affectionately, as '51 Bodies'. I remember the reply he gave me when I plucked up the courage to ask him how he'd come about it.

'I've discovered fifty-one bodies in my time, Brian. I've discovered fifty-one bodies and do you know what? My men and I have captured all but three that killed them. All but three, lad.'

I was impressed and, it has to be said, slightly terrified.

'I once collared a man who I believed was responsible for a recent murder,' he went on. 'I knew he'd done it, so I got a team of men and we scoured every inch of land surrounding the body. Seven acres, lad; seven bloody acres. When we came up with nowt, I told them to burn the grass until there's nothing but topsoil. "We'll find the knife, lads," I said. "We'll find it." And we did. We got him, lad.'

Flaming hell, I thought. *What's he going to be like if I take a wrong turn or something?*

When it came to my actual test, I had Pendergrass sitting in the passenger seat, growling like a bloody bear, and Palfrey in the back. This was a Police Advanced Driving Test, by the way, not the usual civilian one. Didn't I mention that? Yes, indeed: there were skids, handbrake turns and all kinds of bloody stuff, which is why I had our two advisors testing me. They were already involved with the show so it seemed to make sense.

The test lasted about an hour, and from the moment I first checked my mirror, all I got was a barrage of abuse.

'No, lad, no, lad! Yer doin' it all wrong!'

'Sorry, Mr Pendergrass, I'm trying my best.'

'Left here, Blessed. I said left, you daft sod!'

'Sorry, I lost it for a minute there.'

'OK now, let's try a handbrake turn. No no no, I said a handbrake turn, not an emergency stop!'

'Sorry!'

'You're a dickhead, Blessed.'

'I am, Mr Pendergrass, yes.'

'Why didn't you signal at that last junction?'

'Well, you didn't give me time, Chief Constable.'

'You've always got bloody time, lad!'

'Yes, Mr Palfrey.'

Finally, after what had seemed like an age, Mr Pendergrass barked the final order.

'Right, pull in, lad, pull in. Thank God that's over with. Right, Mr Blessed, did you have any idea what you were doing that last hour or so?'

'Yes, of course.'

'Well, that's good, because no bugger else did. Get out, lad, you've passed.'

With that, we all got out of the car and they clapped me on the back. What an experience!

Incidentally, shortly before I started taking lessons, somebody at the BBC leaked to the press that I couldn't drive. This became a big embarrassment to the BBC; after all, we were all supposed to be ace drivers. Kings of the bloody road! Anyway, as soon as I passed they got me on some entertainment show and had me doing all kinds of skids and things. Now I really was tough guy Fancy Smith – king of the road!

Anyway, that's enough about bloody cars and bodies. Back to the show. The morning after the first episode went out, we all got the train back to Liverpool to begin shooting more location scenes. At that point, it hadn't really dawned on us what had taken place the night before. We simply got the train as usual and began chatting about this, that and the other – all perfectly normal. It was only when we pulled in at Liverpool Lime Street that we realized that all was not as it should be. The press were there in tonnage, as were the police, and it was pandemonium! But the police weren't there simply to protect us from the throng. Oh no, they were there to protest – to us!

Apparently, some members of the police force considered the show *too* real, and were demanding that it be removed from the schedules immediately! They were insisting on this right there on the platform, by the way. It was chaos. They'd been used to *Dixon of Dock Green* you see, which had always portrayed life and the police through a soft lens. *Z Cars*, on the other hand, showed it warts and all. If memory serves, what had really wound the police up was a scene in which Jeremy Kemp (from Z-Victor 2) threw something at his wife which had resulted in her getting a black eye. A policeman had inflicted an injury on his wife! It was provocative alright. An incendiary scene if ever there was one, and on the first bloody episode! I remember the headline in the press was '*Z Cars* Storm!' And I'll tell you what, it was everywhere. The *Daily Herald*: '*Z Cars* Storm'. The *Mirror*: '*Z Cars* Storm'. The *Express*: '*Z Cars* Storm'. Even the broadsheets carried the story! Later on, when things had calmed down a little, I asked David Rose if the show would be pulled.

'Pull the show with this kind of publicity? No chance!'

The BBC refused to bow to the pressure, fortunately, and the police seemed to be split down the middle. Not all of them wanted the show pulled, but the ones who did were vociferous in their protestations and, in a way, I can understand why. You see, prior to *Z Cars* there was always an air of mystery surrounding the police; an aura of untouchable anonymity. So, in a way, it must have felt like having your veil removed.

In the end, to try and quell the unrest, Palfrey and Pendergrass went on television to express their admiration for the show, as well as their appreciation of its realism, both personally and professionally. The police who claimed to hate the show seemed to be concentrating solely on the negative events, which in actual fact were heavily outnumbered by far more positive goings-on; such is real life! Bad things happen, but then so do good things!

One additional factor which I firmly believe added to both the positive and the negative feedback we received was the fact that the show was broadcast live, or most of it. That undoubtedly enhanced the realism of the show further still, in that you were actually watching something that was happening there and then. This obviously made some people watching the show quite nervous, and understandably so. And for us actors and actresses, the sense of excitement and danger we felt performing live was sometimes almost overwhelming. It's far more akin to performing live theatre – especially repertory theatre – except that as opposed to performing different plays in front of an audience of hundreds, you're performing one in front of millions; in our case often over 20 million! When that red light went on, you were live! There was no hiding place; no prompt; no 'Oh, I'm so sorry. This is a very difficult play, though. Bear with me and I'll be right with you.' Could you imagine doing that on live television? Looking into the camera and asking for a few minutes' grace while you pull your arse into gear? Bollocks to that!

Some of the regulars got used to it after a while – dicing with disaster week after week after week – but not Stratford Johns. He used to vomit for about an hour before every single show. Throw his guts up! That's live TV for you, though. Such adrenalin! Joe Brady and I used to try and block it out by over-joking. We'd become stand-up comedians for a while, and it used to work. It was similar to being on Everest. We used to joke about the perils of being there; of what could happen to us. It was our way of coping.

But it was a nightmare for the guests. You see, we had hundreds of guests on *Z Cars* over the years and very few of them had any experience of working in live television. Everyone wanted to be in it – the show was the biggest thing on TV at the time – but once they were stood in front of that bloody camera they were terrified.

Anyway, seven or eight weeks after being on air, the police who'd originally taken umbrage with us gradually began to come round a little, and from then on we were considered their champions. We were adored by the police, and by the press. There were stories almost every day of the week in the papers, and all positive; articles about storylines and about the cast. As I've already said, we had well over 20 million people tuning in every week. Twenty-odd million people! That was over half the adult population of Britain! About 250 full Wembley Stadiums, every week.

Now, this may sound rather fanciful to some, but back in 1962 and 1963 we were as big as the Beatles. That's honestly no exaggeration. You ask anyone who was around at the time: *Z Cars* was ab-so-lutely-flipping-enormous, and we regular actors, to all intents and purposes, were the show. We couldn't go anywhere! Pop down the road for a pint? Impossible. Go for a walk in Richmond Park? You wouldn't last five minutes, love.

At the end of every day, I used to do what I'd called 'The Woolly Run'. By now, I'd bought a delightful little cottage in Richmond, and when I arrived home at around 5 p.m., I'd put on some kind of disguise and run like the wind down to Woolworth's. Then I'd grab some groceries, pay for them, and run back again. It didn't always work. If there was a queue at the tills, I was for it: when people start to recognize you, they just grab you.

'Oh my God, it's Fancy Smith.'

There was no attempt at conversation. In fact, the majority didn't even ask for an autograph. They would simply grab you as hard as they could and stare at you. I think they were in shock more than anything. Remember: there was only BBC1 and ITV then.

I remember once being asked to open a bookshop in Derby. We used to get asked to do hundreds of personal appearances back then and although I wasn't terribly keen on them, the money was bloody good. And a man's got to live! Anyway, I was free that day and so got in my car first thing and drove up there.

At the time, Sean Connery was appearing in the second

James Bond film, *From Russia with Love*. The film had just opened and it was the biggest thing the cinema had seen for eons. Broke all kinds of box-office records! When I eventually arrived in the centre of Derby, there were people everywhere – thousands upon thousands of them. I thought, *They must be here to see the film*. There'd been queues around the cinema in Leicester Square. There was no way I could drive through them. *Bugger it*, I thought, *I'd better walk*, and so I parked up and carried on towards the bookshop on foot. As I didn't have a map with me, I decided to stop somebody in the street and ask for directions.

'Excuse me,' I said. 'Could you tell me the way to—'

'IT'S HIM!' the woman screamed. 'IT'S HIM, HE'S HERE, HE'S HERE!'

Apparently, I was only a stone's throw away from the bookshop – and the crowds were all there to see me. So it wasn't Sean Connery and it wasn't *From Russia with Love* that had caused absolute pandemonium: it was Brian Blessed, Fancy Smith off *Z Cars*! I was there for eleven hours signing autographs. Eleven bloody hours! I had a police guard and everything.

So anyway, all this fame meant I actually became a bit of a prisoner. Now don't get me wrong, I love it when people stop me in the street for a chat these days.

'Gordon's alive, Brian!' they shout, referencing my famous line in *Flash Gordon*.

'Yes, of course he is, love. God bless you, love, God bless you!'

I have 'em in fits of laughter, and they me. You see, it's good for the soul! But the kind of fame which I enjoy today is very different to the one that was thrust upon me in *Z Cars*. I'll give you an example . . .

About a year into the show, I was asked to take part in a big charity football match at Hillsborough in Sheffield. I did a lot of these kinds of things at the time, and would always

My mother, Hilda,
aged twenty-one.

Aged one and in the Probert
Avenue communal pram, by Seven
Fields, Bolton-on-Dearne.

Goldthorpe as I remember it growing up, with the
Picture House on the left and the Empire behind it. As a child
I'd walk around and around them, trying to see inside.

Mum and Dad outside our new council house
in Bolton-on-Dearne, 1948.

Me, aged eleven, with my
four-year-old brother, Alan.

Twelve-year-old Alan
with our mother.

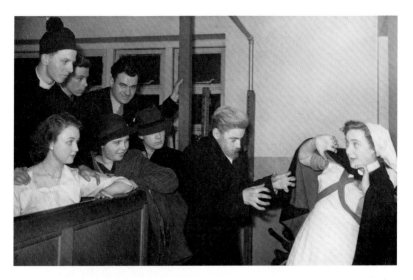

The Bolton-on-Dearne Youth Centre production
of *The Second Visit*. I'm the one in the beard looking
suitably nasty. Mr Fred Lawson, the youth leader,
has his hand on the post.

Cutting a cake after winning 'best actor of the season'
for my role as Branwell Brontë.

Aged eighteen and fresh from playing Heathcliff. My eyes were firmly set on the Bristol Old Vic Theatre School as soon as I'd finished my national service.

Playing Lopakhin with Elizabeth Spriggs in *The Cherry Orchard* at Birmingham Rep. Birmingham liked to cast me in, shall we say, slightly more senior roles.

With the Demon Actor O'Toole in *Country Dance* in 1969 – enormous fun to film once we'd sorted a few things out.

O'Toole as Macbeth. The press butchered him
and never in my life have I witnessed such courage
as O'Toole showed in finishing the run.

The first ever photograph of *Z Cars*. Joe Brady (as Jock Weir) and myself (as Fancy Smith) outside the Mersey tunnel.

On the set of *Z Cars* with (*l–r*): Terence Edmond (PC Sweet), Diane Aubrey (Sally Clarkson), Leonard Williams (Sgt Twentyman), James Ellis (PC Lynch), Jeremy Kemp (PC Steele), Dudley Foster (DI Dunn), myself, and, seated, Stratford Johns (DCI Barlow) and Joe Brady (Jock Weir).

I was overwhelmed to meet Jack Dempsey, the Manassa Mauler, on a promotional trip to New York. From left to right: Joe Brady, Jack Dempsey and myself at Dempsey's restaurant.

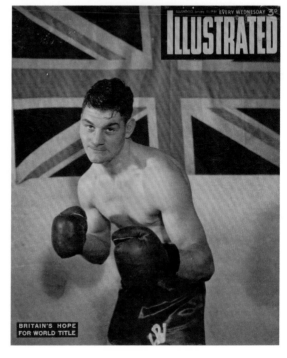

Bruce Woodcock on the front of the January 1946 edition of *Illustrated*. He was a childhood hero.

The first confrontation between Katharine Hepburn (Hecuba) and myself (Talthybius) on *The Trojan Women*.

A beautiful shot of Katharine Hepburn as she waited to be called on set.

Myself with Geneviève Bujold, who played Cassandra.

turn up and score eight or nine goals. This was always fixed, of course, and nearly all the goals were offside. You see I was Fancy Smith – cock of the bloody North! And so I always played centre forward and I always scored a hatful of goals. The crowds loved it! Anyway, there were about 30,000 people there that day. The police were there, of course, and as well as myself there were a host of celebrities and professional footballers. It was a great occasion!

Now, usually these games were very closely supervised by the police. They had to be. But for some unknown reason they decided that, at the end of this particular game, they'd simply allow the fans to run onto the pitch and seek out one or two autographs. What a disaster that was! How I came away with skin on my body I shall never, ever know. It was a miracle!

At the final whistle, these fans rushed onto the pitch as expected, but as opposed to spreading themselves evenly among the players and forming nice orderly queues, they came straight towards me – and, believe me, they wanted blood, or at least some kind of souvenir or memento. Suddenly they piled onto me and I went straight down like a sack of potatoes. Bang! Then they began grabbing for my shirt – which was torn off within a couple of seconds – and then it was my shorts, followed by my socks. After about a minute flat, I was lying on the pitch stark bollock naked with what felt like twenty elephants landing on me, and I was in danger of being torn to bloody shreds. How I've still got a penis, I will never know. That poor old thing was yanked more times than I've had hot dinners. Yes, I said yanked! It must have thought that all its Christmases had come at once. Eventually, the police realized what was happening and managed to make a channel to where I was. But I'll tell you this: if they hadn't done it when they did, I'd have been in serious trouble. As it was, I was in an absolutely shocking state. I was covered in blood, had hardly any hair left and only half a penis.

So that is what it was like working on *Z Cars*. Absolutely mental! Needless to say, I never did another charity football match again. I was scarred for life.

Incidentally, it was at about this time that I received a very welcome yet at the same time frustrating telephone call. I was at home with my feet up when the telephone rang.

'Is that Brian Blessed?' asked the caller.

'Yes. Yes, it is. Who is this?'

'This is Orson Welles. I hope you remember me, Brian.'

What a shock!

'Yes, of course I do, Mr Welles.'

'Look, Brian,' he said. 'First, I want to apologize. Getting *Chimes at Midnight* off the ground has taken me far longer than I first anticipated. But listen, Brian, let me cut to the chase. Are you still interested in playing Hotspur for me?'

I was interested, alright, but in the end I had to refuse. A lot of effort had gone into finding me a regular role; not just by me, but by my agent. I couldn't give all that up just for a couple of weeks on a film, even if it was for Orson Welles.

Such is life!

Of course, the overriding thing about *Z Cars* was that it made an awful lot of people very, very happy. First there were the people who watched the programme, week in and week out. It was *their* show, really. Then there were the newspapers. Everyone in the country wanted to know about the show and the only way to find out – apart from watching – was to read the papers.

From a personal point of view, it was wonderful, despite being almost torn limb from limb! For a start I got to work with all these marvellous people, not to mention the experience of working on live television, and on such a ground-breaking show! It set me up for life. But there were also my parents' and my brother Alan's reactions to the show.

It made them so very, very proud. They couldn't believe how famous I was. What tickled them all most, I think, was seeing me on the cover of the *Radio Times*. We were on the front of the *Radio Times* every other week, or that's how it seemed. Anyway, they loved all that. Yes, a huge amount of good came out of that show.

I feel I must talk a little bit more about my character in *Z Cars*, Fancy Smith. You see, the production team of *Z Cars* were actually very intrigued by Fancy Smith; this character I had based partly on the power of Chief Constable Palfrey. He was different to the other PCs. He was young, and although he often came across as being a bully or a tough guy, he was in fact a gentle soul and used to beat up bullies and the like and protect children. Many of the social issues which had to be handled by the writers were conveyed in episodes featuring Fancy Smith. My partner, Jock Weir, was like a restraining influence on Fancy, so there was also a very interesting dynamic between the two cops. And it was the same in Z-Victor 2. Jeremy Kemp's character, PC Bob Steele, was very much like Jock Weir, a strong silent type, whereas Jimmy Ellis's character, PC Bert Lynch, was cheeky and bold; a bit more of a loose cannon. There was also this great rivalry between the two cars (although it was a healthy rivalry): which car could apprehend the most robbers and suchlike. And there were catchphrases, of course. Every great show produces at least one memorable catchphrase, and with *Z Cars* it came from Sergeant Twentyman. He was always based on the front desk back at the station and whenever a crime was reported he would always say to PC Sweet, 'Get it down in the book, lad, get it down in the book!'

And so that became *Z Cars'* first catchphrase. All over the country, people would wait for an opportunity to use it. It became second nature to them, and to us!

Stratford Johns, I think, was probably the most impressive character in *Z Cars*. He was the father figure, if you like, whereas me and the other three lads were the 'glamour'! But it was Frank Windsor, the constables' boss, who had to work the hardest. He was in every other scene, poor old Frank, and always seemed to have the most to do. He was the engine of the series. A terrific actor with a classical background.

One thing I forgot to tell you about my partner Joe Brady is that he was very short, about five foot two I think, and so the BBC decided to have a special pair of shoes made for him with soles about five inches bloody deep. They were quite soft, too, like a huge black training shoe. Anyway, during the show one week we had to chase after a burglar through a great pile of mud. I forget exactly what the scene was about, but the whole studio was covered in mud. This was live, remember. So off we ran after this felon and, about five metres in, Joe got stuck and lost his shoes. He had to carry on without them! Anyway, come the next scene, he was inches bloody shorter than he was before. He was on his tiptoes, bless him, with the rest of us controlling our laughter.

Another thing I remember in *Z Cars* is that my character was always arguing with Inspector Barlow. Fancy Smith didn't take too kindly to authority, you see, and Barlow was a real disciplinarian. The writers I think warmed to our conflicting attitudes and so as time went on the rows became more and more frequent. 'How dare you speak to me like that, Smith?' Barlow would snap at me. 'Just you watch your lip, lad.'

During one such scene, disaster almost happened. Barlow and I were at each other's throats as usual, when all of a sudden I felt something heavy resting on the back of my head. *Jesus Christ*, I thought, *it's the flaming scenery!* And sure enough it was. Some of the weights had come loose from the back of one of the walls and it had all fallen forward. At that very moment in time, I was the only thing stopping it from crashing onto Stratford Johns. I thought, *What the hell am I going to do?*

Meanwhile the director was sending increasingly frantic messages to the staff from the director's gallery above. 'Why isn't Brian moving around like he should be?' I heard him whisper. 'Get him to move, somebody!' Eventually, the director realized what was happening and the workforce rushed in to adjust the scenery with more weights.

Disaster narrowly averted, thank heavens.

Anyway, let's go through a couple of guests, shall we? One I remember was a chap called Toke Townley, who later went on to play Sam Pearson, Annie Sugden's father in *Emmerdale Farm*. He too had been at Birmingham Rep (although long before me) but, like so many of the occasional callers on *Z Cars*, he had no experience of live television. I remember this scene as if it were yesterday. I had to interrogate old Toke. I had to break him down until he confessed to a crime. It was supposed to last about ten minutes, this scene, almost a quarter of the episode, so it was a big one. Huge, in fact. We'd rehearsed it for hours.

At the start of proceedings, I had to say something like, 'Nar then, lad, I want a word with you,' and be as menacing as I could. 'Where were you last night between the hours of 8 p.m. and midnight?'

'I'm guilty,' came his reply.

Bloody Nora! I thought. *He's gone straight to the end of the bloody scene!* Poor old Toke. It was the only line he could remember.

'Oh, guilty are you?' I laughed, desperately trying to think of a way out. 'Guilty, you say. Well, we'll see who's guilty. You just wait there, my lad.'

And with that I quickly went off-camera to one of the assistant directors, a man called Tim Vignals.

'Cue the next scene!' I said. 'He's dried. Cue the next bloody scene!' Then I turned back on camera. 'Right then, you'd better come with me!'

And with that I grabbed him by the scruff of the neck and

dragged him out. The news went out about ten minutes early that night. This happened quite regularly, I'm afraid, and it was always because of scenes that I was in.

Of course, in the studio we never had working cars, only shells. For front-on driving scenes, we'd have a camera on the bonnet and a backdrop at the reverse of the car, which would show some film of a country lane or wherever it was we were supposed to be driving, to give the viewer the impression that we were actually out and about. Quite a crude technique by today's standards, I grant you, but back then it was all we had. To make it look more authentic, the carpenters would stand either side of the car and rock it occasionally. And there were no windscreens, of course. This used to fox me every time, I'm afraid, and whenever I was being filmed standing just outside the car and had to fetch something from inside, I'd simply stick my hand through the front where the glass was supposed to be. A couple of days later, there'd be a barrage of letters asking why our police cars didn't have any windscreens, to which the BBC would reply that the viewers must have been imagining it. No repeats, you see, and a long way off videos and DVDs, thank God!

Sometimes the scripted dialogue would finish before the red light went off, which meant that the cameras would still be rolling. If this happened, you had no choice but to ad-lib for a few seconds. In mine and Joe's case, we'd sing a song or talk about what had happened at Everton the previous week. We became quite good at it after a while.

One day, we had an old man in the car with us and were supposed to be driving through Seaforth. Once again, the dialogue finished a few seconds early, but instead of waiting for the red light to go off, the old man started to get out of the car. We were supposed to be travelling at about fifty miles per hour! Anyhow, because the red light was still on, I had to act quickly.

'Don't get out of the car,' I whispered, with 20 million viewers looking at my face. Another illusion shattered! I'm afraid it didn't register, though, and in a blind panic he started to get out. The thing was, I was supposed to be driving the car at the time and the old man was sitting alongside me, so when he started to get out I had to take one of my hands off the wheel so that I could reach across and restrain him. That then got me into all kinds of trouble with the police, as it was forbidden for them to drive one-handed. Worse was still to come, though. For you see, once I'd got the old boy back in his seat, he simply sat back up and did it again, except this time I missed him and he got out of the car at 50 miles per hour!

'Good night, officer,' he said sweetly.

I'll give you good bloody night, I thought. What a pillock! Fortunately, this happened only a second or so before the red light went off, but some people must have seen it. They probably thought they were hallucinating.

Looking back, you could have driven an articulated lorry through some of the holes in *Z Cars*, but that was live television for you, and in its infancy. It was never going to be perfect. I'll tell you what, though; it couldn't be done much better today. I am quite convinced that some of the episodes of *Z Cars* are among the best TV ever!

The Queen used to visit the studios all the time, and was a huge fan of the show. She was also, it was rumoured, an even bigger fan of Fancy Smith. We all read it in one of the Sunday papers. 'PC Fancy Smith has kept Queen Elizabeth very happy during her pregnancy.' This must have been when she was having Prince Edward. So glad I could be of service, Ma'am!

About a week later, Prime Minister Harold Macmillan came for a look around. That raised slightly less excitement; in fact, he was about as animated as a curling stone, though seemed to move slightly slower.

Anyway, it wasn't just royalty and sluggish prime ministers who wanted a piece of *Z Cars*. The crème de la crème of the British acting fraternity also wanted a look-in. Just have a look at this list. Over the years we had in the cast Joss Ackland, Leonard Rossiter, Malcolm McDowell, Brian Cox, Esmond Knight, Robert Powell, Diana Dors, Alison Steadman, Brenda Fricker, Martin Shaw, Judi Dench, Arthur Lowe, Kathleen Byron, Frank Finlay, John Hurt, Warren Mitchell, Patricia Routledge, Nicol Williamson, James Bolam, Eileen Atkins, David Warner, Ian McShane, John Laurie, Bob Peck – and masses more. Not bad, eh? You'd be hard-pushed to find a guest list like that anywhere else.

Then, in October 1964, I was approached by my mate, the great Shaun Sutton. In fact, he apprehended me in a corridor at Broadcasting House.

'Brian, we're doing an episode in about five weeks' time. It's virtually a two-hander and you're involved. We have Barlow and Watt at the beginning, then after that Fancy Smith goes off to help a woman who has locked herself in her house. She's late middle-aged and is about to go through a horrifying nervous breakdown. She changes personality literally dozens of times and because Jock is ill, Barlow sends you round to investigate.'

'And you're sending Fancy Smith to go and talk her round?' I asked dubiously.

'That's all part of the plot, Brian,' said Shaun. 'It's where Fancy Smith grows up. It's been written by John Hopkins and is based on a true story.'

I have to say, I'd already become incredibly intrigued by this time. Shaun carried on with the plot.

'As I said, Jock's off sick and so Smith goes in on his own; the *least* likely person to handle a situation like this. That's what makes it really interesting. Normally, you'd need Sigmund Freud or Marjorie Proops, but this time it's Fancy

Smith, the tough police constable. So you have this entire episode with the woman as she's changing personality.'

'A great part for the woman,' I said. 'Who's playing her?'

'We've offered it to Wendy Hiller,' said Shaun.

'What, as in two-Oscars Wendy Hiller?'

'Yes, of course. She loved the script and sees it as a real challenge.'

Now, once again, for all you lovely kiddiewinkies out there, Wendy Hiller — or Dame Wendy Hiller as she later became — was a giant of the cinema. She'd won her first Oscar playing Eliza Doolittle in the 1938 adaptation of *Pygmalion* opposite Leslie Howard, and her second playing Pat Cooper in *Separate Tables* opposite David Niven. This woman really was acting royalty, just as Dame Maggie Smith and Dame Judi Dench are today. I was beside myself with excitement.

'There's just one thing,' said Shaun. 'She insists on being called Miss Hiller. You don't mind, do you?'

'No, of course,' I replied obediently.

Now, at the time in *Z Cars*, one or two new characters had been introduced, including a character called Sergeant Blackitt, who was played by Robert Keegan. He was replacing the wonderful Leonard Williams (Sergeant Twentyman), who had recently died.

After the other actors learned about Wendy Hiller appearing in the show, and more importantly that only I would be playing alongside her, I'm sorry to say that a certain amount of jealousy began to spread through the camp. Bob Keegan seemed to have the biggest issue, and before filming began he decided to approach me.

'I thought you were supposed to be the tough guy, Brian. Not just as Fancy Smith, but in real life. I was told by the others that nothing fazed you, yet I hear the moment Wendy Hiller asked you to call her Miss, you fell to your knees and agreed. That's not strong, Brian. That's just sucking up to the establishment.'

'Bugger off, Bob,' I said. 'That's the most ridiculous thing I've ever heard in my life.'

I was shocked more than angry. That was the first time I'd ever had a set-to with a cast member on *Z Cars*, and over something so absurd.

Anyway, Wendy Hiller, or Miss Hiller, duly turned up a few days later and we began rehearsing; and, my word, what an amazing actress she was! She was staggering in that role, staggering. I remember receiving some really good write-ups after that, but hers were from a different bloody planet. What a tour de force. 'Historic performances' said the critics.

After about a week of rehearsal (we had two weeks in all), it became impossible for me to carry on calling her Miss Hiller. Our relationship had developed and because many of the scenes were so heavy and intense, it just didn't feel right. Eventually, I made my appeal.

'Miss Hiller, would you mind if, while we rehearse, I could call you Wendy please? I have to say I'm finding it a bit difficult using Miss Hiller. It's like a barrier for me.'

'Of course you can, Brian,' she said. 'You can call me anything you like, my dear. You can even call me—'

I'm going to leave that until the end of the story.

At the end of the second week's rehearsal, we had a full run-through in one of the main rehearsal rooms, and every member of the *Z Cars* team turned up to watch. Everybody wanted to see it. They were intrigued. So there they all were, the *Z Cars* boys and girls, and all the heads of BBC Television; people like Norman Rutherford, Huw Weldon, Elwyn Jones and the Director-General. It was a big, big occasion!

The run-through went marvellously, thank God, and afterwards everybody congratulated us. 'That was wonderful, Miss Hiller! Thank you for gracing our little show with your presence.' I managed to just about hold my own with her, and did OK in the end. It really was a masterclass from her though. Taught me a huge amount! Anyway, while all the arse-kissing was going on, Bob Keegan came up to me.

'She was bloody marvellous, Brian. Marvellous!'

'Really, Bob?' I said. 'Well, since you've told me, why don't you go over and tell her? Go over and say, "Wendy, I thought you were bloody marvellous."'

'I will,' he replied. 'Just you watch this.'

So off he trotted over to Wendy, took her by the hand and said, 'I thought you were bloody marvellous, Wendy.'

But the moment he said the word 'Wendy', she pulled her hand away from him and shouted, 'MY NAME IS MRS GOW!'

That was her married name, of course. She was married to Ronald Gow, the writer.

Bob walked back over to me, obviously feeling two inches tall. He was very badly shaken. I smiled gently.

'Do you know what I call her, Bob? I call her Ducky.'

And, with that, I walked off.

What a wonderful woman, though. We became good friends after that and I sometimes attended film premieres with her. We had a great relationship, and I'll tell you what, she was wonderful to go to awards ceremonies with. I remember one in particular. It might have been the BAFTAs; it was definitely one of the biggies. Anyway, so we're sitting there in our finery, Wendy in a beautiful chiffon gown and me in my dinner jacket, and suddenly they're ready to announce the Best Actress award.

'And the award for Best Actress goes to . . .'

I can't say the actress's name, so for argument's sake, let's call her Milly Jones.

'The award for Best Actress goes to . . . Milly Jones!'

And as everybody started applauding, Wendy stood up and shouted, 'Oh no! She must have got it for staying power!' Silenced the whole room. I just sat there with a napkin over my head!

So anyway, we're just about at the end of this chapter. I had a huge amount of fun on *Z Cars*. We all did. But as the saying goes, all good things must come to an end. Not my favourite saying of all time, but it fits here.

Anyway, Jeremy Kemp was the first to leave the show. All of us apart from him had signed a two-year deal, whereas he'd just signed the one. He was adamant that he wanted to go after that, and sure enough he bloody did. He went on to great things, of course: *The Blue Max*, *A Bridge Too Far* and *Operation Crossbow*. It was a great loss to the show, Jeremy leaving, and I've always had a lot of time for him. Marvellous actor!

Jeremy's replacement on *Z Cars* was a chap called Colin Welland. He looked a bit like me did Colin, apart from the fact he had buck teeth, and he too played quite a roughish, tough-guy character. Anyway, because of the similarity it wasn't too long before people started getting us muddled up.

'I saw you last night. It broke my heart when your dog died. What a wonderful actor you are.'

'It's very kind of you, my dear, but that was the other one.'

'What other one?'

'PC Graham – Colin Welland. The chap in Z-Victor 2. I'm in Z-Victor 1.'

'Z-Victor what?'

'Oh forget it.'

I remember Colin one day approaching me with a couple of scripts he'd written for *Z Cars*. I had no idea he was a budding writer as well as an actor, so agreed to take them home with me and have a look at them. I'll tell you what, I was absolutely flabbergasted. It was some of the best stuff I'd ever read for television; as good as any of the scripts Allan Prior and John McGrath had written, and their stuff was absolute dynamite. He was obviously a talented man, our Colin. So anyway, I told him to take them to David Rose, which he duly did, but they were turned down flat. I couldn't believe it! He was very upset, was Colin, but to his credit he didn't let it get to him. In fact, he ended up winning a bloody Oscar for writing *Chariots of Fire*. How about that?

I remember watching the BAFTA Awards that year and I couldn't wait for them to get to Best Screenplay. Now, whenever people are up for awards, especially on television, they always have to get ready to put a face on, don't they? Not Wendy Hiller, of course, but most people. Then, when they don't win, they can smile and start clapping and mouthing all kinds of disingenuous platitudes. 'Oh, he deserves it far more than I. Wonderful, darling, wonderful!' It's a farce! Anyway, eventually it was time for Colin.

'We now present the award for Best Original Screenplay.'

Cut to shots of all the different nominees at their tables, trying to look calm and serene.

'And the winner is . . . Bill Forsyth for *Gregory's Girl*.'

The camera then went straight onto Colin Welland's face and, in close-up, he roared, 'Oh fuck off!'

I died with laughter. I'd never admired a writer so much in all my life. Quite right, Colin – what guts!

Now, I really will finish off this chapter in a moment, but before I do, I have to marry up what I said about going AWOL all the time. Do you remember that I said it didn't happen again until I was in *Z Cars*? Well, I'll just tell you about that and then we'll all move on.

About eighteen months after *Z Cars* started they brought in a new director, an Austrian-born gentleman named Herbert Wise. He was a brilliant director, Herbert – had a touch of genius about him. He was a medium-sized man with dark hair and deep penetrating eyes, and he was a great disciplinarian. My God, you did not mess with him. Not with Herbert.

Now Stratford Johns, who as I said had become quite a superstar as Inspector Barlow, and rightly so, was a couple of minutes late for rehearsal one afternoon; he'd been doing some promotion for the show, an interview with a local paper, I think. Anyway, nobody usually gave a damn really, but then this was Herbert's rehearsal. When Stratford entered the room, Herbie stood up and made a funny noise with his nose. He always did that when he was pissed off, a kind of violent sniff.

'What time do you call this? You're two minutes late.'

'I'm so sorry, I was doing an interview and I'm afraid it ran over slightly.'

'You've already cost us all two minutes. Now I have to talk to you about it, and that's another two minutes. Who do you think you are, Stratford? Don't you ever, ever be late for me again, OK?'

Poor old Stratford was completely taken aback – paralysed with a mixture of fear and incredulity. He was the heart of *Z Cars*. He was Inspector Barlow! It didn't escalate into anything, and we all just got on with it, but Herbert had laid down a marker. He was a force to be reckoned with.

Anyway, after we'd done about three episodes with Herbie Wise, I'm afraid that my 'wandering affliction' began to raise its strange head once again. Now, I wasn't really Herbie's cup of tea to start with – he thought I played Fancy Smith far too aggressively and didn't like me as an actor generally – so when it first happened, you can imagine what occurred. We were due in for an all-day rehearsal and I'm afraid that I simply didn't turn up. I didn't want to act and had an overwhelming compulsion to be as far away from people as possible – so, instead of travelling up from Richmond to the rehearsal, I hired a rowing boat and rowed up and down the Thames all day.

I heard later from Joe Brady that Herbie Wise went off his bloody box. There was Frank Windsor, Stratford Johns, Jimmy Ellis and Joe Brady, but no Brian Blessed; and I wasn't a minute late, I was hours late. In fact, I didn't turn up till

about five-a-bloody-clock! According to Joe, Herbie's dia-
tribe was of gargantuan proportions.

'I will sack him I will sack him I will sack him I will sack
him! I want him out out out out out!'

The man was sweating blood, apparently!

'Nobody has treated me like this. That big-headed egotistical bastard! I will cut his bloody bollocks off when I see
him. I will rip his fucking throat out. He is the worst kind of
actor and the worst kind of fucking person. It's all about
vanity, vanity, vanity, vanity. I WILL KILL HIM! Nobody
does this to me. His ego is uncontrollable! I will phone Elwyn
Jones and have him sacked on the spot.'

'I promise you, when Brian arrives you won't be able to
say a word,' Frank told him.

After about an hour, Joe and Frank managed to calm him
down a bit, but he was still capable of – at the very least –
castration.

At about 5 p.m., when there were only thirty minutes
left, I arrived at the rehearsal room. I thought, *If you're going
to tell a lie, tell a whopper, Brian*, and so I stormed through
the door, sank to my knees and screamed, 'MY MOTHER'S
DEAD! MY MOTHER'S HAD A HEART ATTACK AND
SHE'S DEAD! I'VE BEEN UP AND DOWN THE MOTORWAY
TO DONCASTER INFIRMARY. SHE'S GONE, THOUGH,
MOTHER'S GONE!'

Herbie stood there open-mouthed.

'MY POOR OLD DAD'S THERE,' I continued, 'AND
WHEN HE SAW HER LYING THERE HE HAD A HEART
ATTACK TOO! WHAT AM I GOING TO DO, HERBIE? WHAT
AM I GOING TO DO? MY MUM'S DEAD AND MY DAD'S
LYING THERE DYING!'

'D'you see?' Frank said. 'You can't say anything!'

Herbie just looked at me. He obviously didn't know
what to believe. 'I'm sorry, Brian,' he said. 'Let's continue
rehearsals.'

I was always killing my mother when I felt I needed a cop-out. Dad would usually have had a heart attack or broken a leg or something, but I'm afraid that Mother would always end up on the slab. In fact, in the late 1970s I remember receiving a telephone call from her asking me to stop.

'You've got to stop telling people I'm dead, Brian, you've got to stop. I've had people ringing me up again, asking if I'm OK. Now you either stop this altogether, or you find somebody else to kill, is that clear?'

'Yes, Mum, sorry.'

Anyway, after my performance in the rehearsal room that day, I quite naturally assumed that my professional relationship with Herbie would cease to be. He'd have to tolerate me until his run on *Z Cars* had finished, of course, but after that? I thought he wouldn't piss on me if I was on bloody fire. In fact, he'd probably walk over and pour some more petrol on me!

Well, it just goes to show how wrong you can be. You see, in late 1975, I received a telephone call from my agent.

'Would you be interested in playing Caesar Augustus in a new adaptation of *I, Claudius*?'

The question threw me a little.

'I'm not really Augustus Caesar material,' I said. 'Caesar was a middle-aged king. Wouldn't somebody like Alec Guinness or Paul Scofield be better suited for that role? I'd be better playing Tiberius.'

'No, the BBC bigwigs are adamant. Apparently the director has *insisted* that you play Augustus. He won't direct the show otherwise.'

'Who *is* this director?'

'Herbert Wise.'

As the words came through the receiver, I could feel every single muscle in my face collapse.

'Pull the other one,' I said. 'Herbie Wise hates me. I buggered him up on *Z Cars*. He can't stand me.'

'No. He's asked specifically for you, Brian. Apparently he won't take no for an answer.'

'Well, then tell him I'll do it, love. Tell him I'll do it!'

To say I was surprised would be underplaying the situation more than somewhat, not only because I thought Herbie wanted my head on a bloody stick, but because I just didn't feel I was right for the role.

Anyway, it all went ahead as planned and a few weeks later I was asked to attend a press launch for *I, Claudius*, along with Herbie, Derek Jacobi, Siân Phillips, George Baker, John Hurt and one or two of the other leading actors and actresses. It wasn't really my cup of tea to be honest but, determined as I was to get off on the right foot with Herbie, I decided to go along and smile for the cameras. When it came to us all taking questions from the press, it seemed that they too had been a little perplexed by Herbie's choice.

'Why did you choose Brian Blessed for Augustus?' they asked.

Herbie smiled suddenly, as if he'd been reminded of something from the past.

'Because nobody can shoot crap like Brian Blessed,' he said.

Touché, Herbie.

4

THE WITCH HAZEL QUEEN

'Always try and say "yes" to life. And don't
obey all the rules. If you obey all the rules, you
miss all the fun.'

Katharine Hepburn

Working with Katharine Hepburn would be at the vanguard
of anyone's career, but actually becoming her friend is a
different thing altogether. You see, in addition to making
an almost immeasurable contribution to the film industry,
Katharine Hepburn was one of the most intelligent and
fiercely independent women Hollywood — if not the world
— has ever seen. She was Boudicca in slacks, you might say.
She found the concept of celebrity both tiresome and super-
ficial and lived by her belief that we should be kind to each
other and help other people whenever we can. Simple but
salient words.

She was opinionated and outspoken, yet could back up
every single word that came out of her mouth. We discussed
literally hundreds of subjects during our time together, and
even though I was fairly well versed in many of them, I was
still the pupil to her teacher. She taught me so much *about* so
much, and lived her life with passion and conviction.

Actually, perhaps I should just get on with it? OK, then.

In the spring of 1971, I was experiencing a real sense of

frustration. I wasn't unhappy, you understand — life was being marvellous to me. I was having a wonderful time playing TV and stage leads here, there and everywhere, and I had my lovely little cottage in Richmond; but there was still something amiss for me professionally. You see, at that time I'd been all set to make a film about the life and career of Bruce Woodcock, the former British and European heavyweight boxing champion whom I'd first met when I was just seven years of age — but things were not going well. I shall tell you all about that in the next chapter.

To rid myself of some of the frustration I was feeling, I started frequenting a brand new gymnasium that had opened on Hill Street in Mayfair, which was just a stone's throw from my agents' offices on Berkeley Square. They had all kinds of heavy bags and things at this gym and so I spent hours there, attacking and hitting everything in sight. It was enormous fun, and to a certain extent it made me feel better, at least about the film going tits up. I felt like I was just waiting for something big to come along, and in the meantime I channelled all my energies into pounding the living daylights out of canvas bags the size of small humans.

Now, just a few doors away from this gym were the offices of an executive producer named Josef Shaftel. Shaftel was quite big in Hollywood at the time and was about to make a new film with the director Michael Cacoyannis, who had made, amongst other things, *Zorba the Greek*. Cacoyannis was one of the most celebrated directors in the world and had been auditioning this film, *The Trojan Women*, for quite some time. Based on a play by the Greek tragedian Euripides, *The Trojan Women* follows the fates of the women of Troy after their city has been ransacked and their men killed. It's a cheery little piece, then, and even though it was considered to be a great play, it wasn't exactly what you'd call box-office material. In order to counteract the fact that nobody was likely to come and see the film, Cacoyannis and Shaftel had drafted in four big stars to play the female leads: Katharine Hepburn would be playing Hecuba, Vanessa Redgrave Andromache, Greek actress and singer Irene Papas played Helen of Troy and Geneviève Bujold, an Oscar-winning Canadian actress, played Cassandra. The boys had done well. Four absolutely world-class actresses!

Cacoyannis and Shaftel were chuffed to bits with their four leading ladies and I remember there was great excitement surrounding the film. Newspapers reported on it the world over and the filming dates had been set in stone. The only problem was Talthybius, the only male lead in the film – or, rather, the lack of Talthybius. They couldn't find an actor to play him for love nor money! Apparently Cacoyannis had been auditioning this role for months; and not just in England, but all over Europe. He'd tried every actor in Christendom, or so they said.

Talthybius was King Agamemnon's officer-at-arms, and when the Trojan War had ended, it had been his job to look after the women. All he really did was put them onto ships and sell them into slavery, but he was still one of the good guys and had the ears of all the kings. Even Odysseus used to kiss his arse. What a guy! In the play he wants to get rid of the women as soon as possible so he can stop being a bloody minder and get on with being a warrior again, but he's still good to them. He was a tough man but had great sensitivity.

Now, luckily for me, the casting director on *The Trojan Women* was a woman named Maude Spector, and she was an absolute legend within the industry. She'd cast hundreds of films and television plays over the years – and, crucially, was also a big admirer of mine. In fact, she'd offered me all kinds of wonderful stuff, most of which I'd taken.

She'd been called into Shaftel's office for an emergency meeting with Cacoyannis one morning, as apparently he'd all but given up trying to cast Talthybius in England and was worried they'd have to cancel the film. He could be a bit of a headache, Cacoyannis; he had a huge temper and, according to Maude, he had decided to vent his considerable frustrations on everyone in sight.

Poor old Maude couldn't do a thing about it, and so just had to sit it out.

'You've seen just about everybody, Michael,' pleaded poor Maude. 'I can't help it if none of them are right.'

And indeed he *had* seen everybody. He'd seen Charlton flaming Heston and he'd seen Laurence Olivier and Robert Shaw. He'd seen James Mason, Richard Harris and Nigel Davenport. He'd seen all the big stars in all the big films. Every bugger! Even the Austrian actor Maximilian Schell. He didn't want them though.

Suddenly, the marvellous Ms Spector had a thought.

'I'll tell you what, Michael, there's an actor I've just seen round the corner who might be worth five minutes of your time. He's called Brian Blessed. You won't know him as he hasn't done many films but I've cast him in quite a few things over the years. He's very big on TV.'

'Mmmm, I don't know, I don't watch British television. I want a big name. We need a big name! Mind you, Blessed? What an interesting name. Yes, actually, yes! What a beautiful name. I don't care if he's famous or not, so long as he's right.'

'Well, he's a very good actor. I think he's in the gym next door at the moment. You could see him now if you like.'

'Oh, I don't know. I've already arranged my taxi. It will be here soon.'

'Oh come on, Michael, he's only round the corner. I'll fetch him.'

Thank goodness Maude was so persistent. Five minutes later, there I was, standing in front of Michael Cacoyannis, the world-famous Oscar-winning film director. I was wearing a blue tracksuit and because Maude had caught me mid-workout I was sweating like a deviant in a fucking bush.

I have to say Michael was a strange-looking man. He was quite short, had a very high forehead and the most piercing eyes I'd ever seen.

'Sit down,' he hissed. 'OK, Maude says you're good so I'm going to give you a chance. One chance! And if you bugger it up, I suggest you leave this room very quickly.'

I have to say I didn't like his tone but I respected him as a director and so decided to go along with it for a bit. I'd hit the bastard later if I had to.

'By the way, I like your name. Is that your real name or a stage name?'

'No, it's not a stage name, it's my real name,' I replied.

Suddenly, he stood up.

'OK. I'm going to give you one line to say, and I'll tell you this, if you say it like Nigel Davenport, James Mason or Lawrence Olivier, I'll throw a bloody chair at you. They're all so tediously English!'

He then proceeded to go through the list of every single actor he'd seen, and I swear there must have been at least thirty, and all of them big film stars.

'But I too am English,' I said.

At which he exploded. 'Well, you better start thinking about how *not* to say the fucking line then!'

Excitable buggers, these Greeks, I thought. And then, after telling me a little bit about the character, Cacoyannis gave me the line.

'OK, Brian, are you listening? OK, this is your line, and you are delivering it to Hecuba, the Queen of Troy. "You go with Odysseus. His wife's a good wise woman, so they say."

'Remember what I told you, Brian. The last actor I saw was Nigel Davenport and he delivered the line like he was in the Foreign Office. I don't want any of this idiotic English subtlety! If you deliver it like him, I promise, I'll throw the bloody chair at you. Now, begin.'

Oh bloody hell! I thought. But while Cacoyannis had been talking, I had indeed been thinking. I'd remembered that the great poet Pindar had always said that the Ancient Greeks were bald in their expression, almost monotone. They neither embellished nor embroidered the spoken or the written word. If they were describing a mountain, it would either be a big mountain or a small mountain, and so on. And so, with Pindar's words in mind, I delivered the line as an Ancient Greek would have – as Talthybius would have – stentorian but without expression. Total simplicity.

It's hard to express on paper exactly how I delivered the line, so you'll just have to try and imagine it. Strength with honesty.

'You go with Odysseus. His wife's a good wise woman, so they say.'

I stood there like a statue, the last words suspended in the air. It was all over and done with in about three seconds.

Cacoyannis grunted. 'OK, do it again.'

'You go with Odysseus. His wife's a good wise woman, so they say.'

'OK, thank you, Brian,' said Cacoyannis. 'OK, sit down. Would you like a coffee? Come on, have a coffee, have a coffee before I go.'

His demeanour had now changed somewhat. His ex-asperated and dictatorial manner had disappeared. At that moment, the executive producer, Josef Shaftel, walked in. 'OK Michael, are you ready? Your taxi is here.' He saw me sitting there in my sweaty blue tracksuit. 'Oh, I'm so sorry, who's this?'

'This is Brian Blessed, Josef,' said Cacoyannis. 'HE IS GOING TO BE PLAYING TALTHYBIUS!'

'Oh my God – at last!' shouted Shaftel.

'OK Brian,' said Cacoyannis. 'I am going to send you to

Covent Garden to see Nicholas Georgiadis. He makes the costumes for all of my films and he is a genius. The costume he will make for you will fit your body as if you've worn it for a million years. We also have for this part a white and blue horse. In Spain they have horses like this. Horses like you have never seen before. Can you ride, Brian?'

'Yes, I can ride, Mr Cacoyannis. I was in *The Three Musketeers* a few years ago and I can ride very well.'

'Can you ride bareback?'

'Yes, of course.'

'Gooooooood,' he growled. 'Now, you go to Georgiadis in Covent Garden. Maude will give you the address.'

Maude Spector looked like somebody who'd been given the all-clear at the clap clinic.

'Thank you!' she mouthed.

I just smiled at her. I couldn't believe it! With that, we all shook hands and I was ushered out of the door, but before I left Mr Cacoyannis had one final piece of advice for me.

'Brian, my boy. You play Talthybius like that and I will love you forever. Promise: no subtle English acting!'

So there you are, you see. Something big *did* come along!

When the door closed behind me I started to grin, and then, as the realization of what had just occurred took hold, I began to laugh, but not your run-of-the-mill laugh. Oh no, this was a 'I've just been offered a leading role in a film with an Oscar-winning director and four of the world's most fabulous actresses' laugh. And then, floating down the stairs like a fairy, I proceeded to dance in the direction of Covent Garden. Honestly, I did. I was so happy that I danced through Mayfair like a little girl on her way to the zoo! I had never in my life felt such joy. When I told my agent, John Miller, he actually screamed!

I was going to have a minimum of thirteen scenes with Katharine Hepburn and goodness knows how many with Vanessa Redgrave and the rest of them.

A week or so later, after the contracts had been signed, I was summoned to go to Madrid for solo rehearsals with Cacoyannis. We all had solo rehearsals to begin with, me and my four leading ladies; and for the first week or so we were deliberately kept apart from each other. I had a full beard by now and was looking very Greek.

The producer on *The Trojan Women* was a now-deceased man named Anis Nohra, or Bloody Nora, a legend in the east! He was Lebanese, I think, and probably the most extravagant character I have ever met. He used to speak in a kind of eccentric whine, like a Lebanese Peter Lorre. People think I'm eccentric but I'm telling you now, Anis Nohra was me times fucking ten! He actually reminds me a bit of Dino De Laurentiis, my producer on *Flash Gordon*. You'll read all about Dino later, but I had a very similar relationship with him as I did with Anis.

I remember Anis greeting me when I first arrived at the hotel.

'Aaaah, he is here! The Barnsley bastard is here! Ooooh, he is expensive. He is costing me a lot of money. Hello you Barnsley bastard!'

I'd never met the gentleman before in my life, remember. But as he's saying all this, he's jumping around the foyer like a madman.

'They tell me you're fantastic, Brian, you big Barnsley bastard. Michael loves you! He says you are even more Greek than Anthony Quinn.'

See what I mean? Off his box.

In actual fact, I was being paid just less than a thousand pounds for *The Trojan Women* as it had an absolutely minuscule budget. Even Katharine Hepburn was only being paid a thousand.

'You will receive gold of a different kind,' Cacoyannis had assured me.

When he'd finished jumping, Anis sat me down, grabbed me by the lapels and began telling me about my horse.

'You think you can ride, Mr Barnsley bastard? You think you can ride? My expert will show you how to ride. Where I come from, we ride bareback at forty miles an hour and we can pick up pennies from the ground without slowing down. That's fucking riding, Brian, you big Barnsley bastard. You think you can do that, eh?'

'Yes, of course I can,' I lied. 'Easy!' I was a little bit less confident then than I was, in time, on *Flash Gordon*. Had it been Dino, I'd have told him to shove his horse up his arse. Fortunately, Cacoyannis walked through the doors at that moment and came to my rescue.

'Brian! Oh Jesus Christ, I see you have met Anis. Put him down, Anis, put him down!'

I hadn't seen Michael since the audition five weeks ago and somehow he seemed a little put out.

'You do realize that I very nearly recast you, Brian?'

'No, Michael, I had no idea,' I replied.

'Yes, I did. You were supposed to go straight round to see Georgiadis, but you didn't. Why did you not go and see Georgiadis?'

'Well, I was going to, Michael, but I was so happy I just couldn't be bothered to go and see Georgiadis.'

And that's what had happened. I'd set off to Covent Garden, but had ended up going back to Richmond instead. Anis Nohra went off his bloody head on hearing this and began roaring with laughter. And rolling all over the floor.

'YAAAAAAH HEE HA HEE HA HEE HA! I LOVE HIM, MICHAEL! NOBODY WOULD GIVE YOU A REPLY LIKE THAT! WHAT A MAAARVELLOUS EXCUSE! I LOVE THIS BIG BASTARD, I LOVE HIM!'

Fortunately for me, Michael seemed amused by my explanation.

'OK Brian,' he said. 'That makes sense. I was right to continue.'

The following morning, I had my first solo rehearsal with Cacoyannis, and what an eye-opener that was.

'Now, before we begin, I want to talk to you, Brian,' he began. 'I think you know by now that I am a man of great honesty. You know actors are so diplomatic, and they lie. They lie in silence. So throughout this production, Brian, I don't care who you are acting with, Hepburn or Redgrave – whoever – I want you to be perfectly honest. If the scene doesn't go well, you must speak up. I don't want you to give a fuck about anything other than being honest, OK? And now I will teach you how to become Talthybius.'

I remember that lesson as if it were yesterday. Halfway through delivering my first speech, he stopped me.

'No, no, no, Brian. You're going to be terrible. I had Katharine Hepburn in here half an hour ago and she's going to act you off the screen. When I ask her to deliver a speech, she just does it, there and then. She starts immediately, whereas you prepare. You straighten your body, clear your throat, check yourself over and then you begin. That is not organic, Brian. That is contrived. It is unnatural. Just do it!'

And so I did. I started again the moment he finished speaking.

'Yes, Brian!' he said. 'That's better. Just one thing, though, you sometimes lick your lips before you speak. Irene Papas does the same. I have worked with her many times and she still does it. Geneviève Bujold also clears her throat. You see this is all unnatural, Brian, it is preparation. Watch Spencer Tracy. He is the most natural of them all. Get this right and you will match Hepburn, OK? Finally, Brian, never ever close your mouth on screen. If you deliver a line and then close your mouth, you kill the scene dead. Then, when you deliver your next line, it looks like you were waiting for it to happen, like a fucking robot, Brian. Always leave it slightly open, OK? It looks far more natural.'

That was a big lesson; something I'd never been taught at drama school. I tell you I learned so much from Cacoyannis. I don't think I was a bad actor before I appeared in *The Trojan Women*, in fact I could hold my own with the best of them. But after spending just a few days with him I became a more rounded performer and, as he'd requested, I attained an ability to deliver my lines far more naturally.

But the lesson hadn't finished. In fact, he'd only just started!

'Now, I need you to trust me completely, Brian. I know it's not easy to trust another human being but I need you to try, Brian, OK? I have talked about honesty and now I will talk about trust. You see, I am the reincarnation of Euripides. I am Euripides, and because I am Euripides, I understand Euripides and know exactly what I'm talking about, OK? That is why you can trust me, Brian. It is my play; probably the greatest play ever written and the one of which I am most proud. But it is also an important play, Brian, as it proves the strength of mankind is its women.'

You may recognize that particular line from when I began talking about my mother at the very beginning of this book. That's where it came from. How true, though?

It was an extraordinary thing for Cacoyannis to say, of course, that he thought he was the reincarnation of Euripides, but he was being deadly serious. Whether this was just a habit of his and he became the reincarnation of every playwright whose work he adapted I've honestly no idea, but I went away from that lesson knowing exactly what he wanted, and set about trying to get it right.

Over the following days 'Euripides Cacoyannis' and I went through every line and every movement of every scene; but without me ever meeting any of the other leading players. Only Redgrave hadn't arrived yet as I believe she was finishing off another film, but Katharine Hepburn, Geneviève Bujold and Irene Papas were all seeing Michael at different times. This segregation was a deliberate plan and extended far beyond these initial rehearsals; Cacoyannis told me that even the 2,000 extras playing the women of Troy weren't allowed to see me until I rode towards them during the first shot.

'I want them to be afraid of you, Brian,' he told me. 'I want to see the fear and curiosity on their faces as you ride towards them on Morales.'

There were two people with Cacoyannis during rehearsals. Stavros Konstandarakos, who was his first assistant director on the film, and Takis Emmanuel, who was a friend of Michael's. Takis I found bloody tiresome at times and I came perilously close to thumping the bugger on more than one occasion. He was a bit of a legend in Greece, apparently, and was subsequently a bit of a bighead; and I can't abide bigheads, I'm afraid.

Anyway, a few days later, Michael called me over to his offices at the film studios.

'We want to run some tests on your face and with your costume, Brian, but before that I want you to meet some people, OK?'

And so off I went to the studios. On arriving outside Cacoyannis's office, it suddenly dawned on me who 'some people' might be, and as I knocked and entered there was, indeed, the legend Katharine Hepburn sitting in an enormous black leather chair. She turned and smiled, fixing me with an intense gaze. 'Hello, hello, hello, who is this, Michael?' she said.

'This is Brian Blessed, Katharine. He's our Talthybius.'

'Oh, hello, hello, hello, Brian, I'm Katharine. Very pleased to meet you.

'Have you had your test yet, Brian?' she continued. 'Michael says he doesn't want anybody in the film wearing make-up, but you see I have trouble with my skin, Brian. I have millions of freckles, and so I have to apply a little bit of witch hazel every now and then. Witch hazel gets rid of them for a while.'

She wasn't lying. Some of these freckles were about two inches in diameter. Her neck was covered in them. The other three actresses were furious. They thought it was unfair that Hepburn be allowed to wear make-up and later complained bitterly to Michael. It was the only bit of friction on the film, I think. Poor Katharine, though. Foundation was hardly make-up and she was twice their age!

'And my eyes, Brian,' she continued again. 'Ever since they had to pull me out of the canal in Venice when I was making *Summertime* with Rossano Brazzi, I've always had problems with my eyes. They water a lot these days.'

That's *why her eyes water*, I thought.

The last time I'd been at all star-struck was when I met Paul Robeson, the actor famous for his celebrated portrayal of Othello at Stratford-upon-Avon. I'm not really that kind of person, especially when it comes to actors; but with Hepburn I think I was, slightly. She represented the golden age of Hollywood and had worked with the very biggest names: Jimmy Stewart, Spencer Tracy, John Wayne and Humphrey Bogart, to name but a few. But she herself simply oozed quality. There was something terribly masterful about her, not unlike Cacoyannis in a way. She was an icon, of course, yet completely unpretentious.

When the tests came out, I went to another room to wait and there was Geneviève Bujold. She was effervescent, naughty and very, very beautiful. I'd seen her recently playing Anne Boleyn in *Anne of the Thousand Days*.

'Hello, Brian,' she purred. And, believe me, she did purr. What a woman! 'I saw you as St Peter in *Son of Man* with Colin Blakely. I'm a big fan of yours.'

'That's very kind of you, Miss Bujold,' I replied as I kissed her hand.

Sitting next to Geneviève was Irene Papas, who was shyer and more reserved than Geneviève but still very, very beautiful. She had deep, dark eyes and was to play Helen of Troy. In fact, it's doubtful whether Helen herself could have matched Irene's beauty.

Redgrave had already been in to shoot her tests and had had to leave Spain again, but I remember seeing her shots. My word, there she was: tall, thin and with long blonde hair; perfect for the role of Andromache.

Now, I have to admit that at the time I was never terribly comfortable around women. Not socially, at least. I was very much a man's man. I liked boxing and judo and fencing and suchlike and so, apart from my relationships, I rarely came into contact with women outside of what I was doing either on the stage or on TV. Michael, I think, could sense this apprehension, and so one evening tried to do something about it.

'Brian, have you played many love scenes in the past?' he asked.

'No, hardly any, Michael,' I replied.

'And do you ever mix with women? Socially, I mean?'

'To be honest, no, I don't.'

'Well, I'll tell you what, here's some money.' And with that he handed me this huge envelope full of cash. 'Tonight you're going to be mixing with three women socially. You're taking Katharine, Irene and Geneviève out to dinner, OK?'

Well, no, it wasn't OK!

'No, Michael,' I protested. 'Don't do this to me!'

'You are all booked in at a fabulous restaurant in Madrid,' he went on, blithely ignoring my panic, 'and Katharine and the girls know all about it. They're looking forward to it, Brian. You'll have a good time! Now off you go.'

I remember I was stiff-necked and aching with tension.

Like a bear with rigor mortis! The restaurant was beautiful, though, and served all kinds of wonderful seafood. Being a hearty eater, that helped to take my mind off things a bit, and so I tried my best to relax. Every now and then, Katharine would look over and nod to me, as if to say, 'Are you OK, Brian?'

Cacoyannis had obviously told them that I was not too comfortable around women, and each had a different way of reacting to this. Katharine was occasionally attentive and a bit concerned, Geneviève was inquisitive, constantly asking me what kind of women I liked and whether I was a randy bugger, and Irene was just rather dismissive of me. Now, I don't mean that disparagingly, because Irene and I eventually got along marvellously, but at first I think she just saw me as some rather stereotypical Englishman. You know, the type who wears a bowler hat and swings an umbrella. Because of this misapprehension, Irene thought it would be fun to start talking about sex, thinking of course that this would shock me.

'I am told an English girlfriend visited you here in Madrid the other day, Brian. She has blonde hair – a true English rose. I am offended. You import your sex and overlook the Greeks. When it comes to love-making I am a sexual, mystical sorceress. You would never be able to resist my siren call.' As Katherine and Geneviève sat like statues, totally expressionless, Irene leaned a little closer. 'So Brian, how do *you* fuck?'

I pondered a while, before replying, 'Well, these days, love, I prefer to have a good shit!'

Hepburn nearly fell off her chair, Geneviève got up and ran around the restaurant, and Papas almost exploded with laughter!

'That serves you right, Irene,' said Katharine. 'You weren't expecting that, were you?'

Irene was terribly apologetic. 'Oh I'm so sorry, Brian,' she said. 'I just couldn't resist it!' And then kissed me sweetly on the temple in forgiveness.

'What the hell do you think Englishmen are, Irene?' I said. 'We're Romans, we're Anglo-Saxons and we're Danes! We're a mixture of everything.'

So all in all, and against the odds, my night out with the girls was a roaring bloody success. I'll tell you what, though: handling all those amazing women was really something. I was relieved to have survived unscathed. Anyway, a few days later Vanessa arrived at the hotel, after which we all left Madrid for Atienza, where we would shoot the majority of the film.

Now, we were all in awe of Hepburn. She was very graceful and quiet but also very kind and considerate. By this time, she was beginning to talk a lot about Spencer Tracy; generally praising him and talking about how wonderful he was. *Fair enough*, I thought. After all, they had been together a long time before he'd died a few years earlier, and he was indeed a great actor. One of the best. But I'm afraid she did go on about him like a broken record; as and when anyone so much as mentioned another actor, Katharine would automatically compare them, unfavourably of course, to good old Spencer.

The first time I remember it grating on everybody was at dinner one evening. All the main cast and crew were present and I was on a table with Katharine, Michael, Irene and Vanessa.

'Do you know,' said Michael, about halfway through the evening. 'I've always been a great admirer of Fredric March. He has to be one of Hollywood's most versatile actors.'

Already I could see Katharine's hackles were up.

'Really?' barked Katharine. 'Fredric March? You honestly think so? He didn't have the subtlety of Spencer, or the talent, or the refinement. And I can tell you this: when he talks to you, he scratches his bollocks. So don't you try and tell me he's a better actor than Spencer.'

Talk about getting shot down in flames! She slaughtered him.

'Oh no,' said Michael hastily. 'I didn't say I thought he was better than Spencer. I just said I thought he was a good actor, that's all.'

So that was it, you see. To get in hot water with Katharine Hepburn you didn't even have to *suggest* that somebody was better than Spencer Tracy; you just had to say they were good. And then – BAM! 'Not as good as Spencer!'

Anyway, the filming schedules were tight, to say the least, which meant we began filming almost as soon as we arrived in Atienza. My first assignment was to be introduced to and hopefully befriend my trusty steed, Morales. Everything our lunatic producer had said was correct; Morales *was* a kind of blue colour. She was an astonishing-looking creature! I rode her bareback right from the beginning, gripping her mane and the inside of her mouth as we rode. This may sound slightly barbaric to some of you, but Morales was used to being ridden like this; and it was authentic to the Ancient Greeks, of course.

Morales and I took to each other like you wouldn't believe. Within a day I could also ride her at forty miles an hour, jump with her at any angle and stop her on a button – and make her rear up marvellously too.

Two days later, filming began, and one of the first scenes to be shot was my introduction. This was the scene I was telling you about earlier, the one with the 2,000 actresses and extras who hadn't been allowed to see me; and if you watch the film back, it really works. Exactly how much of that was down to us all being kept apart I've no idea, but I think it certainly helped create an atmosphere of fear and trepidation. Either that or it was just the sight of me on a horse.

Incidentally, I was also told by Michael Cacoyannis that

he recommended that under no circumstances did I sleep with any of these women . . .

'Quite, Michael,' I responded. 'If I slept with one, I'd be insulting the rest. Anyway, I'm here to work, not to have sex. All you Greeks talk about is sex!'

Anyway, in this opening scene, when the women of Troy see me riding towards them they realize they're about to learn their fate, and so as I get nearer they become more and more agitated and fearful, and eventually begin to scatter. All their men and boys are dead, of course; except for Astyanax, the three-year-old son of Andromache.

Talthybius wasn't a baddie, remember, and although he has orders to sell the women into slavery, he is sensitive to their plight and possesses a certain amount of sympathy for them. So I had to deliver my lines thus: with authority, sensitivity and empathy.

As I dismounted from Morales I was approached by Hecuba, or Miss Hepburn.

'You know me, Hecuba,' I began. 'I've often come to Troy with messages from the Greek camp. I am Talthybius.'

Then I commenced to give her the appalling news: that one of her daughters has been taken by Agamemnon as a concubine and another has been sacrificed. The rest of the Trojan women will be put on ships and sold into slavery.

Eventually, we reached the end of the scene.

'Cut!' shouted Michael. 'How do you think that went, Brian?'

'Well, I think that I was pretty lousy,' I said honestly.

Katharine seemed astonished by what I'd said – and then took a defensive stance.

'You don't think I was pretty lousy too?' she said.

'Yes, Katharine, as a matter of fact, I do.'

Her hackles were now positively rigid!

'And WHY do you think I was lousy?' she asked.

'Well, I don't need to tell you anything, because you're

not the Queen of Troy any more! Unless you irritate me and really upset me, how can I tell you that your daughter's been sacrificed? I give the information reluctantly. You need to extort this information from me. You need to pressurize me!'

Katharine looked at me, then at Cacoyannis, and then at me again. 'Well, well, well, Mr Blessed. You said a lot of things there, didn't you?'

There then followed a pause which felt like it lasted a year, but was probably closer to thirty seconds.

'OK,' said Katharine. 'Michael, we go again?'

So I took Morales down to the start, rode in at great speed – Trojan women scattering everywhere – and as I did so, Hepburn went off her rocker. She irritated the horse, she irritated me; she grabbed my legs and she grabbed the horse's mane; and all the time she was shouting, 'Where's my daughter?'

'Your daughter's dead, your daughter's dead!' I finally yelled. And it was out of genuine anger and frustration that I gave her the line; I didn't have to act.

'Cut!'

'How was *that*, Mr Blessed?' enquired an evidently fortified Miss Hepburn.

'Bloody marvellous,' I replied.

I made a point of not going too far with my praise. After all, I was simply being honest.

'Michael, what did you think?' she asked.

'Good. Definitely a better take,' he said.

From that day on, whenever I had a scene with Katharine and something went awry, either she or I would accuse the other of being lousy and it would be put right immediately. Not 'drab' or 'rubbish', but 'lousy'. So right from the beginning we had this wonderfully honest relationship.

I remember Katharine used to be very fond of Vanessa. She was fascinated by her hair and used to wash it and style it for her while on set. But as well as liking and admiring

Vanessa, I believe Katharine also felt quite maternal towards her; almost responsible for her welfare, somehow. She thought little of Vanessa's father, for instance, the great Sir Michael Redgrave, and would openly criticize his parenting skills.

'Her father never looked after her. He never looked after any of his children. He was too busy misbehaving. Awful man! How can you have a child like Vanessa and all but ignore her? She's an angel!'

But it wasn't just Michael Redgrave who had incurred Katharine's wrath. In fact, save for the great Spencer, of course, I got the distinct feeling that the whole of mankind had pissed her off.

Geneviève Bujold became like a sister to me on the set and would hold my hand and ask me all kinds of questions about the Bristol Old Vic and suchlike. She was a real theatre buff, not to mention a terrific actress, so we always had plenty to talk about. She too had benefited enormously from her solo sessions with Michael and, like me, was excited about working with all these wonderful people. That is, however, until it came to filming her final scene.

The role of Cassandra is the smallest of the four leading female roles and she leaves the film quite early on. Quite frankly, she's an absolute pain in the arse, prophesying doom for the Greeks and things, and so Talthybius puts her on a ship as soon as possible and sends her on her merry way. She actually goes insane in the end.

Anyway, this final scene of hers took place in a cave and, as it was her last, we all turned up to watch. She had a very long speech, which was delivered to the Trojan women. Basically, she tells them that their husbands died happy because they were married to them and had children; the Greeks were miserable because they were far from home and had ten years of misery and pestilence; and so not to worry, everything would be tickety-boo. It was actually a very demanding speech and it took all of Geneviève's marvellous acting ability to succeed in it. Delivering it was a terrible ordeal for her.

So, Geneviève tried this speech a couple of times – and it went really well. In fact, Hepburn and I both thought she was superb!

'How was that, Michael?' she enquired of our director. I think she already had one foot on the plane home.

'Mmmm, not quite right. We go again.'

And so they did go again, and again, and again – and again! Fourteen takes later, Geneviève was almost at breaking point.

'Michael, I *can't* do it again!'

'Look, I've printed three takes, OK?' said Michael. 'Just one more darling, please!'

When she began the final take of her final speech, she was almost breaking down, and that was *exactly* what Cacoyannis wanted. Euripides is very demanding. You can't just walk on set and do it. After the final take, Geneviève collapsed in tears and we all gave her a hug.

Anyway, back to me and Hepburn. During the filming of *The Trojan Women*, I was living in a town called Sigüenza, which is about thirty miles away from Atienza and quite a hike on a day-to-day basis. Katharine wasn't at all happy about this and so had me moved to a little apartment next door to the house they'd rented for her, which was close to where we were filming. She was quite blatant about it, really.

'I want Brian closer to me, Michael,' she'd said. 'Could you find him something as close to my house as possible please?'

I have to say that I did feel quite isolated out in Sigüenza and so went along with her request quite happily. And so began a relationship which I freely admit engulfed me for a time.

When neither of us was filming, she and I would walk all

over the wilds of Atienza looking for fossils. We'd spend six hours, sometimes, covering miles and miles and miles, just searching for these remnants of early life. Then, when either of us found one, we'd sit down and discuss what we thought they might have been when they were alive. They were geological field trips, I suppose, the kind my behemoth of a teacher Mrs Brown used to take us Woodentops on.

Ours was now slightly more than just a friendship. In fact, I'd go as far as to say that it was probably akin to an old-fashioned courtship. She was in her early sixties at the time, and I in my mid-thirties. We always held hands while we walked and talked together and when I saw her to her door at seven o'clock each evening, I would embrace her, tell her what a wonderful time I'd had and then I'd kiss her lightly on the cheek. She would reciprocate with some words about the day before kissing me either on the forehead or on the cheeks. So, yes, it was a courtship. We never, ever talked about sex or anything like that, but I always left her feeling buoyed and, if I'm honest, ever so slightly in love. I did find her very attractive and I enjoyed kissing her. It remained quite innocent, but nevertheless delightful.

On the days when I was called on set and Katharine wasn't, she would come up from her house and enquire when I was going to be free.

'Do you still need him, Michael? What time can he go?'

As soon as Michael gave me leave, she would take me by the hand like a twelve-year-old, lead me back to her house, sit me in a chair and make me bacon and eggs, shouting, 'Go on, live dangerously!'

When our roles were reversed and only she was needed on set, I would come and collect *her*, before cooking her either sausages or a steak on the extremely primitive cooking apparatus in her apartment. She was a real homebird, though, and liked nothing more than chatting over the issues of the day whilst making the evening meal.

'Spencer and I never went out to restaurants, you know, Brian,' she said. 'We always used to eat at home and just chat. Don't you prefer that, Brian? Don't you just love it?'

'Of course. I've never really enjoyed eating out.'

By the way, at this particular time a sixty-year-old lady called Phyllis was Katharine's constant companion. She was a charming, quiet and graceful figure in the background.

Off camera, Katharine always wore Spencer Tracy's clothes; his trousers and his shirts. She had about four pairs of trousers and at least six or seven shirts with her, and used to throw them on the moment she was out of costume. Some people may find this quite strange, but I have to say I never did. She was still terribly devoted to Spencer and had no intention of allowing time to heal her loss. She wanted to protect and perpetuate his memory; both to herself and to those around her. Wearing his clobber obviously went at least some way to fulfilling that desire, so why not?

'Spencer had a great capacity for a human relationship,' she once shouted to me as I had a bath!

So much of what she said about Spencer was quite stimulating. I remember her telling me how she handled the issue of his height, something about which he could apparently be very sensitive, and that led on to a very interesting confession.

'I think my first words to him, Brian, were, "Oh my, you're a lot shorter than I imagined," and he said, "Aww, don't worry, I'll soon cut you down to size." Then he gave me the evil eye. Have you ever been given the evil eye by an alcoholic, Brian? It's quite seductive. He then said, "Katharine, have you ever heard of Pandora's box?" and I told him that of course I had. He said, "I believe that everyone has a Pandora's box, and if you open that box and you take out the wrong thing, you're finished. You won't be able to resist it." And I said there was no denying that.

'I understood exactly what he was talking about, Brian

– and do you know why? Because when I smell whisky, I go absolutely out of my mind. Whisky is beauuuuuutiful. I smell whisky in a glass and I want it. I want it all and I want more. So you see, Brian, I understood every word of what Spencer said, because if I ever opened my Pandora's box and took out whisky, I'd be finished. I'd give up acting, I'd give up the studios and I'd give up everything. I'd drink whisky morning, noon and night until it killed me. So when I found out Spencer was an alcoholic, and when I fell in love with Spencer, I adored the smell of whisky even more. And why do you think that is? Because I had more to lose.'

That made the whole thing even more fascinating. The relationship between Katharine Hepburn and Spencer Tracy is the stuff of legend and is one of Hollywood's great love affairs. They were both outrageously strong characters and had an attraction to each other that was stronger than gravity.

No man had ever got to Hepburn before. She destroyed men – made mincemeat of them, both physically and mentally – but in Spencer Tracy she found her match and, in her, so had he. They stimulated each other *totally*. You could tell that just by watching them on screen. That wasn't acting. It was a consummation!

To demonstrate this, I shall tell you about a George Cukor film I saw back in the mid-1950s called *Pat and Mike*, in which Hepburn plays Pat Pemberton, a promising tennis and golf player. Despite her bright future, Pemberton's fiancé wants her to pack it all in so she can marry him and concentrate on being a good wife, which is of course the opposite of what she wants. Sticking to her guns, she enlists the help of a promoter called Mike Conovan (played by Tracy) and together they set about getting her to the top – before gradually falling in love, of course. It's an enjoyable enough film but the thing that always fascinated me most about *Pat and Mike* was one particular scene about halfway through, in which Tracy pays Hepburn a compliment about how she looks and moves. Now, I was always adamant that Tracy came off-script during that scene. One minute he's telling her how graceful she looks on the tennis court and the next he's almost sexing her up, telling her that watching her is like watching poetry in motion and so on. You can see him change in a split second and her response is absolutely astonishing. Suddenly, she doesn't know what to do and is completely unsettled. I'll tell you, it's an electric scene. I remember watching Tracy work her and I thought at the time, *This isn't in the script. There's no way this is in the script*. Naturally, I couldn't wait to ask her about this.

'Do you remember making *Pat and Mike*?' I said to her one day.

'Why yes, of course, Brian. Not my favourite film, but it was OK. Why do you ask?'

'Well, there's a scene about halfway through in which Spencer starts complimenting you on the way you move. Tell me, does he go off-script at all?'

As I was asking the question, I could see her start to fidget a bit, and by the time I'd finished she was almost flushed.

'Yes, I know the scene you're talking about, Brian, and yes that was *not* in the script. Spencer used to do that rather a lot. Fancy you noticing.'

Honestly, she couldn't change the subject quick enough! You see, he knew how to get to her and was the only man who ever could.

One evening I was sitting quietly with Katharine in her sitting room. That day we had watched Michael Cacoyannis lose his temper on the set, something he did quite frequently, what with being a perfectionist.

'He should be careful,' Katharine said to me. 'He's putting his whole heart and body under extreme stress. I told him to calm down or he'll not live much longer. You know, Brian,

Spencer died just like that. He was sitting up in bed, and I was sitting on the edge of the bed describing to him for the umpteenth time how I wanted to mount a production of *Coco Chanel*. He tolerated this moment with a gentle smile. I remember the lamplight shone on his darling, lovely features. Slowly his expression changed, his eyes grew dim and he died. He died of thrombosis. Just like that. It could happen to you, it could happen to me.' She was silent for a moment. 'I felt for his pulse and felt his heart. He was gone. I didn't need a doctor to tell me that. I sat looking at him for half an hour and then I phoned his wife.'

One of the more interesting yet difficult conversations I had with Katharine was about her decision never to have children. This, I believe, revealed the mark of Katharine Hepburn. She spoke with honesty, candour, empathy and consideration; four words that I believe sum her up perfectly. They were her bywords.

I remember what she said and will attempt to convey this to you now. I think you'll find it illuminating.

'I could not bear the thought of being a mother, Brian. I've been attacked for this over the years, attacked and pilloried by all kinds of people: journalists, politicians, fellow actors; even fans. And, do you know, I'm sick of it. I've had it up to here. Being a mother is the most important job in the world and it is probably the hardest job in the world, and I'm afraid that I just wasn't up to it. But at least I was honest enough to admit that. Do you know how many people have children because they believe they should, or because other people tell them they should? Millions. But the consequence of bringing a child into the world under those kinds of circumstances and in that kind of environment wasn't lost on me, Brian. It made me think and it made me act.

'A child needs to be loved unconditionally, but especially by its mother. When I was of child-bearing age, I was obsessed with my career. Nothing else mattered to me and I did a lot of things to further my career that I'm not proud of. Things I should never have done. Can you imagine what kind of life a child of mine would have had? Because, believe me, I could have given birth to a thousand children and not one of them would have dampened my ambition. There would have been precious little love for a child of mine, I'm ashamed to say; and no attention or affection. Just a room full of au pairs and a lifetime of resentment. Hollywood has been having these kinds of babies for years, Brian. It's abuse. It's child abuse. So that's why I decided never to have children and I stand by my decision. It doesn't matter to me any more because I'm over sixty now, but it still does to some.'

At the time, I didn't really know what to say, and so after she stopped talking we simply sat in silence for a while. For five or ten minutes, perhaps. What she said affected me deeply, though, and made me think very differently about parenthood. I suppose it gave my thoughts and opinions a responsible edge. There wasn't a hint of melancholy in what she said. There were no regrets. She'd done all her mothering as a child in Connecticut, looking after all those younger brothers and sisters of hers. No, all that remained was the resentment that after all these years she was still occasionally denounced for being responsible.

Anyway, on to something a little lighter! Remember earlier I told you about how Katharine was always going on and on about how wonderful Spencer was? Well, this all came to a head one day during a break in filming. In fact, it did more than come to a head: it went BOOM! Or, rather, I did. Poor Geneviève was the catalyst, God bless her. She planted the device, so to speak.

Michael had told everyone to take a break while the crew prepared for the next scene and so the three of us – Geneviève, Katharine and I – had decided to go off on a little walk together. I'd been riding Morales earlier on that day and had been rehearsing all kinds of jumps with him. Geneviève, who

I think had an interest in horses, had been impressed by what she'd seen – but made the fatal error of imparting her opinions to Katharine.

'Brian rides a horse marvellously, Katharine, don't you think?'

'Spencer rode a horse just as well. In fact, he was a natural with horses.'

Here we go, I thought. *Spencer's on!*

Geneviève should have stopped there, but she went on. And on!

'But you've got such big arms, Brian. Is that from riding horses or do you lift weights?'

'Spencer had big arms. And they were naturally big. He didn't have to lift weights.'

Five, four, three, two, one . . .

'THAT'S IT!' I yelled, throwing my hands in the air and pretending to be annoyed. 'THAT'S IT! I AM BORED TO DEATH OF HEARING ABOUT SPENCER BLOODY TRACY. IT DOESN'T MATTER WHETHER I'M RIDING A HORSE OR RUNNING A BATH, SPENCER COULD ALWAYS HAVE DONE IT BETTER. IT'S ALL SPENCER, SPENCER, SPEN-CER, SPENCER, SPENCER! IF HE'S IN HEAVEN, I DON'T KNOW HOW THE ANGELS WILL MATCH HIM.'

Katharine had obviously never heard anyone say any-thing rude about Spencer before, and so the look on her face was quite a picture. Total shock! She was completely and utterly mystified. Her reaction delighted me!

'IF SPENCER WAS HERE NOW I'D BREAK HIS NECK AND THEN I'D BREAK HIS FINGERS. I'D BREAK THEM ONE AFTER THE OTHER! I'M SICK OF HEARING HOW MARVELLOUS HE WAS. HE COULD NOT RIDE A HORSE AS WELL AS ME AND HIS ARMS WERE NOT AS BIG AS MINE! HE WOULDN'T LAST TWO BLOODY MINUTES WITH ME. END OF CONVERSATION!'

By this time, Katharine had her head in her hands and was weeping with laughter.

'Oh Lord, I get it. Am I really that bad?' she asked. And then we both exploded into laughter.

'You've always been so quiet, Brian. I wasn't expecting that. I promise, though, I'll try and give Spencer a rest.'

'Aaaaah,' I said, 'an hour's relief from Spencer!'

I was on a roll now, though, and so instead of just changing the subject, I decided to carry on confessing.

'I'll tell you something else, Katharine,' I said. 'For me you are still one of the sexiest and most desirable women on God's earth. I'll tell you what; I think I'll buy you! You're still for sale, aren't you?'

'And how much do you think I'm worth?' she enquired.

'Well,' I said, 'I will go to the deepest part of the Pacific ocean, the Mariana Trench, and I will dive to the bottom and bring back the rarest, most beautiful black pearl ever seen. Then I will sell the pearl and buy you with the proceeds. Ever since seeing *The Philadelphia Story*, I have found you strangely, weirdly and astonishingly sexually attractive.'

She looked at me long and hard, then whispered, with a smile, 'You're good. Oh yes, you're very good!'

We'd arrived back at the set by now and so this was in front of everybody. Cacoyannis heard it, Vanessa, Irene and Geneviève heard it; everyone did. I could see her blushing like mad and so just walked away.

Such was my devotion to her that on one of our walks one day she ran out of witch hazel – something that threw her into an enormous panic – and I ran five miles in forty-degree heat to get her some. Honestly, I was like Forrest Gump. Totally focused! I managed to find two bottles at a pharmacist and, when I eventually got them back to her, she wept with relief. It was the closest she ever got to vanity.

Katharine seemed to have an ongoing war with men. So much so that people often accused her of being a lesbian.

'I have high standards, Brian,' she explained, 'and some men don't take too kindly to being rejected. I have said no to thousands of men – thousands of very important men – and because I said no to them, and because I wear trousers as opposed to dresses and I don't attend galas and such things, I have always been branded a lesbian. That says more about all those important men than it does about me, don't you think, Brian?'

Absolutely.

Now, there are some very, very dramatic scenes in *The Trojan Women*. As I said at the start of the chapter, it was written by Euripides, and Euripides is the doyen of trage-dians. But by far the most heart-rending scene in the film and probably *the* most dramatic is when the Greek kings decide that Astyanax, the three-year-old son of Andromache, should be killed. He is the only male Trojan left and so the kings, in fear of him growing up to be like his father, decree that he must die. It is the job of Talthybius not only to tell Androm-ache, but also – worse still – to take the child from her. This order from the kings sends Talthybius into an almighty rage. He argues and argues that Astyanax should live, but the kings refuse to accept his plea. In history, it is recorded as The Rage of Talthybius.

So I had this entire scene with Vanessa, a scene which in my opinion is the hardest there is for a woman to act. It wasn't exactly a walk in the park for me, of course, but for her as Andromache, a woman who learns that her child has to be taken from her and executed? Well, to play that takes some skill, let me tell you.

I ride up at great speed on Morales and as I dismount all the women of Troy part like the Red Sea (again!), leaving only Hecuba and Andromache. Hecuba, who is of course the leader of the women and the person with whom I usually converse, walks towards me, but as she does so I step past her and walk towards Andromache, who is standing with Astyanax.

'Wife of the noblest man who was in Troy,' I begin. 'Wife of Hector. Do not hate me. Against my will, I have come to tell you that the people and the kings have all resolved.' And I try and fail to explain the terrible truth until my character is maddened. I just cannot find the words. 'I feel you are kind, Talthybius,' she says, 'but you have not good news.' Finally, I can bear it no more. It's like a disease eating away at me. I cannot say the words, I can only release them like a poison. 'Your child must die!' I scream. 'YOUR – CHILD – MUST – DIE!'

There is then a pause for a few seconds – the camera now on Vanessa – and as she looks at me with increasing horror and disbelief, she begins, very, very slowly, to let out the longest and loudest howl I have ever heard in my entire life.

'Ahh, ahh, ahh, aahhh, aaaahhhhhh, AAHHHH AAHHHH AAAAAHHHHHHH AAAAAAHHHHHHHH AAAHHHH-HHHHHHHHHHHHHHHHHHHHHHHHHHHHHH!'

It almost made my ears bleed! Then, as I try and snatch the boy from her, she picks him up and runs with him, but my soldiers stop her and form a large circle around her. Vanessa runs again at the soldiers, desperately trying to find a way through, but it's no use of course. I plead with her to give up her son or they will all be killed. Finally, she falls in the dust, still clinging to her son, and as she falls the women of Troy begin to charge at me. I hold them back with a shout, then after a moment, I walk over to where Vanessa and her child are lying, breathless and overcome.

'If you say words that make the army angry,' I tell her, 'the child will have no burial and will be killed without pity. So bear your fate as best you can.'

Finally, she stands.

'My bed, my bridal, all for misery,' she screams towards

the heavens. 'When long ago I came to bear my son, not for Greeks to slay.'

Now, if *The Trojan Women* had been written as a modern television drama they'd have had Talthybius or one of his soldiers snatch the child away at this juncture. But because it is Euripides, the Master, he makes the mother give up the child – and what mother can give up a child? This is Greek drama at its very best.

Talthybius allows Andromache two minutes to say good-bye to her son and, as everybody turns their backs to give them privacy, she rejects her little boy. He holds on to her like you wouldn't believe, but she will not embrace him. The boy then begins to cry and as he does so, she laughs at him, before pushing him towards the soldiers. So the only way she can give him up is to reject him.

My final words to her as I lead the boy away are, 'You must forgive us. We Greeks do things that are not Greek.' A wonderful line to end the scene.

Well! Dramatic beyond belief. Vanessa Redgrave was towering in that scene. Towering! See if you can get hold of the film and, if you can, you just marvel at her performance. Totally sensational and, most importantly, totally believable!

All the way through filming this scene, Katharine Hepburn stood watching from a hillside. Competitive? You bet your bloody life.

Because of the heat during filming, Katharine ended up buying umbrellas for everybody; in fact, she spent her entire fee on umbrellas! There were hundreds of them, for the entire cast and crew.

'I've decided to buy chocolates and umbrellas for everybody, Brian,' she said one day.

'Why on earth are you going to buy chocolates?' I asked. 'They'll melt within about five minutes.'

'My God, you're right. Umbrellas it is!'

A couple of days after filming Vanessa's big scene, I was

sharing a large umbrella with Katharine when Cacoyannis suddenly came up between us.

'You know, Katharine and Brian, that big scene yesterday? Vanessa was superb, but she could have done the last speech so much better if she had listened to me more. She doesn't trust me. She doesn't trust me! This is how she should have done the speech.'

And before Hepburn or I could say anything, Cacoyannis went through the entire scene right there under our umbrella. Every word! He did the howl, everything. He even tried to impersonate the soldiers forming a ring around Andromache, and when it came to the part where Vanessa laughs as she's rejecting Astyanax, he started cackling like a rabid hyena. It was horrendously bizarre! Like a demented Widow Twankey! The moment he finished, he just walked away with this satisfied look on his face.

Hepburn leant her head on my shoulder and, after a long pause, said, 'What a Goddamn pity he can't act.'

The next day, we filmed the scene in which I have the boy killed and then take his body to the Trojan women for burial; and that's something that was very important to the Greeks, as if you didn't receive the right burial, you wouldn't be welcomed by the gods. This scene also included a long speech that I had to deliver; a speech in which Cacoyannis had taken great interest.

After Astyanax has been killed, I appear slowly from behind a sand dune, carrying the boy's body on his father's shield. It's all extremely dramatic and I emerge in front of this enormous grey sky to all kinds of drums and things. Weeping Vanessa has been taken off to slavery by now and, as I carry the boy over the dune, standing there in front of me are all the women of Troy, all wailing like banshees.

Now, as you'd imagine I'm not somebody who normally feels the cold much. I've been up Everest three times! And I've trekked to the North Magnetic Pole. But all of a sudden, as I was walking over this dune, about to deliver my speech, the warm weather unexpectedly ceased, and in its place came a draught which could only be described as bitter. It was such a contrast to what we'd been used to that it made all the hairs on my arms and my legs stand on end. Had I been wearing normal clothes, I wouldn't have minded, but all I had on were a pair of sandals and my costume, which consisted of a skirt-type thing that the Greeks used to wear and a rather flimsy shirt. I was perishing! And I had this long speech to deliver, where Talthybius tries to explain the actions of his people. It's an amazing speech of apology, really; of mankind apologizing to woman. I knew the lines backwards, but about halfway through I just couldn't continue. My teeth wouldn't stop chattering. Michael was watching me very intently at this point and I thought, *Here we bloody go, he's going to explode*. Michael could be volcanic at times, but fortunately on this occasion he was very gentle and understanding.

'I just can't get the words out, Michael,' I said.

'OK, Brian, no problem. Let's take five, shall we, and you go and get warm.'

Katharine, who was opposite me in the scene, came to my rescue.

'Give me a minute with him, Michael, will you? Brian, you come with me.'

And, with that, she led me over to a little car they'd hired, in which her driver used to ferry her about. She opened the door, sat me in the front passenger seat and then got in the other side. Then, after rummaging under her seat for a while, she suddenly produced this huge bottle of whisky.

'Whisky?' I said. 'But I thought you said . . .'

'No, it's not mine, Brian. It belongs to my driver. Sometimes he lets me have a smell of it!'

After finding a cup in the glove compartment, she then poured me an enormous shot of the stuff.

'Here, drink this.'

'But I don't drink, Katharine.'

'I know you don't drink. Now drink it. All of it. Do as I say!'

So I drank this bloody treble whisky.

'Now come here, darling,' she said, and with that she put her arms around me and rubbed me for a quarter of an hour. She rubbed me and rubbed me and rubbed me. She rubbed my head, my stomach, my arse and my legs. She rubbed me until I was raging warm. Then she opened her door, came round to my side and helped me out, straight into a huddle. She completely enveloped me in her costume, which was all robes. Then she walked me back up the hill, still in a huddle, until we were on the set again.

'Are you OK now, Brian?' she asked.

'Yes, I'm wonderful, Katharine. Thank you.'

'OK, Michael, are you ready to go again now?'

'Yes, all ready.'

And with that she turned opposite me and started crying. She gave me tears and I did the speech.

After a slight pause, Michael said to me, 'When you do things like this, Brian, I love you very, very much.'

That was it: only one take!

The care and the kindness Katharine showed me was just staggering. She solved it. I owed it all to her. And, straight after dealing with me, she had to deliver a huge speech of her own, once again with tears. Unbelievable!

Half an hour later, as I was changing into my normal clothes, Anis Nohra poked his head round my door. He had a huge but mischievous smile on his face.

'Michael tells me the Barnsley bastard has just given one of the best performances he has ever seen. I'm glad we paid so much for you.'

'I'm glad to be of service to you, you randy man of the east,' I growled, beaming back at him. At one point in the filming, Cacoyannis stopped talking to Katharine, who was bemused by this and hurt.

'Why do you not talk to her between the scenes?' I asked Michael, hoping to smooth things over.

'She called me a son of a bitch!' he said.

'She calls everyone a son of a bitch. It's a term of endearment. She meant no offence. You are wise, Michael,' I said persuasively. 'You say you are Euripides. How can you not understand?'

He nodded, smiled and patted me on the head.

'Of course I understand, Brian. It's just that my mother is *not* a bitch!'

It was patched up, of course, life went on and normal filming was resumed. But, dear reader, beware what you say to Greeks.

A few days later I remember having a wonderfully positive conversation with Katharine one morning, about two days after she had rubbed me up. She was describing how happy she was, despite now being alone, and became extraordinarily animated as she tried to explain just how much life itself meant to her. She actually used to practise the philosopher Albert Schweitzer's theory of 'Reverence for Life', which was an ethical philosophy. Schweitzer said, 'Ethics is nothing other than Reverence for Life. Reverence for Life affords me my fundamental principle of morality; namely, that good consists in maintaining, assisting and enhancing life, and to destroy, to harm or to hinder life is evil.'

'I love life,' Katharine said to me. 'And I am lucky enough to enjoy a life that is full of privilege. I swim, I garden, I play tennis, I read, I paint, I talk and I laugh. I am privileged to be alive, Brian.'

She always veered towards the affirmative in life.

'Always try and say "yes" to life, Brian. And don't obey all the rules. If you obey all the rules, you miss all the fun.'

These are words I have lived by for the past forty-five years.

Katharine was a good painter, I remember, and would produce a canvas at every opportunity. But whenever she'd finished something, she would immediately give it away to a friend or somebody. People who worked with her used to clamour for one of these, as they knew that one day it would be worth a lot of money.

'Let me paint you something, Brian,' she said that morning. 'I'd love to. Please let me.'

'I'd really rather you didn't, Katharine. Please don't think me rude, but I don't want anything material from you. You have offered me friendship. I want nothing more.'

I genuinely did mean what I said. I didn't want anything from her – for the simple reason that she'd already given me so much. Her generosity knew no bounds and her friendship had been unconditional. I needed nothing more.

One of the funniest yet most telling things Katharine Hepburn ever said to me was, 'I have no problem with death, Brian. In fact, I'm quite looking forward to it. No more interviews!'

Which leads me on perfectly to my final story about the redoubtable Ms Hepburn.

Throughout her adult life, Katharine always claimed to be an atheist, and I heard her speak on the subject more than once; the last time being during an interview she gave towards the end of filming. It probably won't surprise you to learn that Katharine absolutely hated journalists, and only towards the end of her life did she start treating them like human beings. This attitude was hardly surprising, given what they'd written about her over the years, what with her affair with Spencer and the rumours of lesbianism and so on, but I did try and impress to her on more than one occasion that all of them were not in fact devils.

'They're simply doing their job, Katharine,' I used to say.

'What's more, it's a very important job. They help to promote us and they help to promote our work.'

'Rubbish, Brian! If that was all they did, then I'd have no problem, but at the end of the day all they want is sensationalist gossip. They're vermin, Brian!'

It wasn't like her to generalize but I understood why she did. As I said, she had suffered greatly at the hands of the gossip columnists and was at a point in her career when she no longer needed the press.

So when this poor wretch of a journalist flew in from Madrid, he never stood a cat in hell's chance. For a start, he looked like he'd been dragged through a hedge backwards; and Katharine despised untidiness. She wouldn't tolerate it with her friends – and so a journalist being scruffy? Well, it was the worst possible start. To be fair to him, he had travelled all the way from America to interview her and had been on about three planes, two buses and an open-topped jeep, so his appearance was understandably a tad tawdry. This made no difference, though, to Katharine Hepburn.

'Just before we start, I want to say that I'd like to choke you here and now,' she began, glaring right at him. 'Look at you. You're a modern man, yet you look like a tramp. You see those women over there?' She pointed to a nearby river, where some women were washing their clothes. 'You will not find a man, woman or child in this town who is not absolutely spotless.'

'Be nice, Katharine,' I whispered. I was sitting in on the interview, her constant companion as I was so often on that shoot. 'He's only young and he's come thousands of miles. Give him a chance.'

This seemed to placate her a tiny bit.

'OK, sit down,' she barked. 'What do you want to ask me?'

The poor lad was shaking like a leaf by this point, but he stood his ground. He had guts!

'Well, first of all, Miss Hepburn, I'd like to ask you about the film, of course.'

After no more than about ten minutes on *The Trojan Women*, our anxious young hack reverted to the list of questions he'd obviously been given by his editor. This was a bad move, as he should have stayed on the film for at least an hour.

'Thank you, Miss Hepburn, that's enough on the film. OK, I'd like to move on to the subject of God.'

Hackles were now rigid – obviously! I looked at him pityingly. Katharine sat bolt upright.

'Let me get this straight, young man,' she began. 'You have travelled thousands of miles to ask me about something in which I do not believe? Don't you think that's ridiculous? I think that's ridiculous. You asked me three questions about *The Trojan Women* – which, let's face it, is the only reason I agreed to see you – and now you want to know about God? If you want to hear about the God your editor is referring to, I suggest you go see a priest, because in my opinion God is just a tool; a tool which was invented by mankind – in his own pathetic image, of course – in order to wield power over the weak. Man is just a machine, young man; a vain, avaricious, self-interested machine, and God is his weapon of choice.'

She went on for about fifteen minutes, quoting all kinds of philosophers and scientists, and my word did she know her stuff. Like all really credible non-believers, she knew the Bible, the Torah and the Qur'an inside out and so could engage with virtually any argument thrown at her. She cut through this boy like a laser. It was a bombardment of irreligious brilliance!

'And now,' she said, once she'd finished with him, 'I think you should leave. Brian, would you please take me home?'

I'd never witnessed anything like it in my life. It was by

far the most convincing argument for atheism I'd ever heard.
When we got into the car, I just looked at her.

'Are you OK?' I asked.

'Me?' she beamed. 'Oh, I'm just perfect, Brian!'

Now, I couldn't quite put my finger on it at the time, but
the way she was acting, it was almost as if she'd broken the
bubble of the universe.

'Are you absolutely sure you're OK?'

'Never better!' she said, slapping my leg. 'Now, come on,
take me home, I'm hungry.'

Three days later, it was at last time for me to go home,
but what a wonderful time I'd had. Michael, Vanessa, Irene,
Geneviève and the entire cast had all been marvellous to me
and it was going to be such a pleasure having them all on my
CV. Even Anis had been a joy to work with, if a little eccentric perhaps. I think he was going to miss his Big Barnsley
Bastard! No, it had been a tremendous experience and, as I
said earlier, I arrived back in England a much better actor.

But it was, of course, Katharine who dominated my
thoughts at this time. She was the person I was really going
to miss. Thanks to her, the last three months of my life had
been some of the most fascinating and fulfilling I'd ever had,
or was ever likely to have. Believe me; she's up there with the
Dalai Lama.

Anyway, I was due to fly out from a small area close to
Sigüenza. On the morning of my departure, I heard a knock
at my door. It was Katharine.

'I'm driving you to the airport, Brian, and I won't take no
for an answer.'

And so, when the time came for me to leave, I packed my
bags into her little car and off we went. She cried as she drove
and so, to comfort her, I rested my hand on her shoulder.

'You'd better keep in touch, Brian,' she said threateningly.

'So had you!' I parried.

We remained silent for the rest of the journey. When we

arrived at the airport, there was my little plane, waiting to take me to Madrid.

'This is it then,' I said. 'Thank you for being such wonderful company.'

'It's been such a pleasure getting to know you, Brian. I'll never forget our time together.'

When we'd said our goodbyes, I turned to board the plane but, as I did, she stopped me and took me by the shoulders. She then stared deep into my eyes, her cheeks now streaming with tears.

'God be with you, Brian,' she said. 'God be with you, God love you and God take good care of you. Always keep God in your heart, Brian. Always keep God in your heart. I promise I'll pray for you.'

With that, she then planted little kisses all over my face. Just tiny little kisses, on my cheeks, my forehead and my lips.

'My God,' I said. 'You damn well covered that one up! What about Schopenhauer and all that "God is a weapon and man is a machine" stuff? I believed you!'

'Ha!' she said, grinning triumphantly. 'They'll always get Fanny Adams out of me.'

5

LIFE ITSELF IS A FIGHT

This particular chapter indulges my life-long passion for all things boxing. 'Oh no! Not more fisticuffs,' I hear you cry. 'We thought Brian was a lover, not a fighter?' Well I suppose I'm a bit of both really, but with the emphasis falling more on the lover part. Like it or not, though, boxing has played a very big part in my life and was to be the subject of one of the biggest films I *never* quite made.

I mentioned in the last chapter that I'd wanted to make a film about Bruce Woodcock, which fell through in the spring of 1971. Bruce had been a childhood hero of mine, and boxing a passion that was handed down to me through the generations. My father absolutely adored boxing. It was probably the most popular sport in Goldthorpe back in the 1940s, more popular even than football, and there were some huge teams back then. You had Bolton Wanderers and Wolverhampton Wanderers; and you had Arsenal, Manchester United and Blackpool. But boxing was what fascinated us Blessed men most.

We used to listen to a lot of boxing matches on the radio when I was a child. We'd sit there, my father and I, open-mouthed, riveted by the mesmeric commentaries delivered by Raymond Glendenning and W. Barrington Dalby. These days, you have awful laser beams and fireworks before a boxing match, which I think detracts from the actual bout. Too much razzmatazz! In my day, when the star attraction made his way to the ring, he did so to a Henry Bliss fanfare, but because we had no television then and could only listen via the radio, it was Glendenning and Barrington Dalby's job to bring it all to life.

'We're here at the Harringay Arena for the match between Freddie Mills and Gus Lesnevich. The actor Stewart Granger and his wife Jean Simmons are here, as is James Mason. Cary Grant is also here, I see. There really are film stars galore here tonight. And here's Winston Churchill. We're in for a marvellous evening's entertainment, don't you think, Barrington?'

'Absolutely, Raymond. I've just seen the world light heavyweight champion Gus Lesnevich make his way to the ring. My word, he's looking very dangerous indeed. He's the favourite tonight, not surprisingly, with Mills the challenger. Hold on, Raymond, the fanfare's started, I can hear it. I think I can see Mills? Is that him coming through the crowds? YES IT IS, IT'S MILLS! The crowd are on their feet and they're cheering him into the ring.'

Wonderful stuff!

The majority of you delightful readers probably remember the great Harry Carpenter, more than Glendenning and Barrington Dalby. He was their contemporary, of course, and a damn fine commentator.

Anyway, my passion for boxing wasn't limited to listening to it on the wireless. I was a live-action kind of boy – I'm a live-action kind of man, for that matter – and I soon found myself following in the footsteps of my fighting heroes. I always had hobnail boots when I was a child, and these came in very useful if I ever got into a tussle; which I almost always did. Then, when I arrived home, my mother would cover all my cuts and bruises with yellow iodine, which used to sting to high heaven. I can feel it now! My word, it was painful.

I remember a neighbour of ours complaining to my mother about my fighting one day. I'd been involved in a scrap with her two sons and had given them both a right pasting! I had a reputation to keep. I was junior school champion!

'All children fight, Hilda,' she said, 'but your Brian just goes out looking for trouble.'

She was right, I'm afraid, and although I was no bully – I used to beat those bullies up by the dozen – I did get into fights wherever humanly possible. It was a huge adrenalin rush.

Young Tommy Burns, who was the leader of a rival gang close to Probert Avenue, once set his entire mob on me on the way home from the junior school one day. There were about eight of them, but with the help of a rudimentary but nevertheless burgeoning knowledge of the noble art of boxing, a few pints of adrenalin and my hobnail boots, I never let them get anywhere near me. I was like a whirling dervish!

'Come on, you bastards!' I shouted. 'I'll chin the lot of you!'

Well, I chinned and kicked at least five of them before they realized that I was liable to end up maiming them all.

The next day at school, an argument broke out between me and Tommy Burns and so I ended up taking on his gang again! This time, though, I got into trouble; in fact I got caned in front of the entire school. That didn't bother me, though. I just went home, got myself covered in iodine, went back the next day and started again.

'Come on, yer buggers. Let's be having you!'

All over South Yorkshire, people were beating the crap out of each other. It was marvellous!

Anyway, back then all the big champion heavyweight boxers seemed to come from America, as did the majority of the champion middleweights and all the other divisions, so when I was first made aware of a British heavyweight who was tipped for big things, I was more than a little suspicious. In fact I was incredulous! For a start, there was his name:

Woodcock, Bruce Woodcock. Wooden Cock! To a seven-year-old, this was the height of sophisticated comedy.

It was my friend Geoff Green who'd first told me about him.

'Dad says he's the best heavyweight we've got,' he enthused. 'He thinks he can beat Joe Louis one day!'

Now, this in fact turned me against Woodcock for a time, because in my eyes Joe Louis was the greatest boxer in the world.

'Nobody can beat the Brown Bomber,' I argued. 'He'd make mincemeat of your Wooden Cock!'

Joe Louis was one of the true great heavyweight champions. He could hit from any angle and was truly magnificent to watch. Highlights from his fights were shown on the Gaumont-British News and I remember watching him with Geoff, Colin Picton and all our other pals. We just sat there and dribbled. He was invincible!

'Honestly, Brian,' said Colin, after a game of football one day. 'This Bruce Woodcock is bloody brilliant. He trains above the Plough Inn in Doncaster. Some of my dad's friends have been over to watch him. They said he makes the whole room shake!'

Ah, now this was a game-changer for me, you see. It brought it all closer to home. Suddenly, Bruce Woodcock went from being yet another intangible heavyweight we'd see fighting on the cinema screen each Saturday morning to being as good as family. He was local – born and bred in Doncaster – and came from good mining stock. I now felt a loyalty towards Bruce Woodcock that I could never have felt towards Louis or any of the other Americans. He was one of us!

Over the following weeks, all my Joe Louis photographs and newspaper cuttings were gradually replaced by ones of Bruce. I still admired Louis enormously and knew deep down that if Bruce ever were to fight him, he probably wouldn't last five rounds, but that didn't matter one jot. Bruce was real. He was tangible. After all, he only lived seven miles away.

The first photo I ever procured of Bruce cost me exactly six glass marbles and had written beneath his name, 'Mr Dynamite'. *Wow*, I thought. *Imagine answering to the nickname 'Mr Dynamite'! I've got to have some of this.* And so, from that day forth, I began referring to myself as 'The Dynamite Kid'. In my mind, I was already Robin to Bruce's Batman.

On informing my mother of my change of identity, I received short shrift.

'Mr Dynamite, you say?' she said, looking disapprovingly at my photograph of Bruce. 'And you want to be just like him, do you? The Dynamite Kid?'

'But I am just like him, Mum,' I said, punching the living daylights out of the back of our settee. 'I'm going to meet him one day and he's going to train me.'

Now, if I ever had to choose one word to describe myself, in addition to virile, sensual, intriguing, dainty, elegant and of course sensitive, it would have to be tenacious. Once I set my mind on something, that's it. I'm like a big hairy dog with a dinosaur bone. I wanted to become an actor, so I became an actor. I wanted to explore lost worlds and climb mountains, so I did. Nothing can stop me!

Anyway, one Saturday morning my gang and I trotted out of the cinema after soaking up the usual assortment of science fiction, cartoons and sports reports. It had been a good one this week. The episode of *Flash Gordon* had been tremendously exciting; starting with Flash heroically escaping certain death and finishing with him facing – you guessed it – certain death! Straight after that, the Pathé newsreel crowed into action, telling us all about England's now fabled 8-0 drubbing of Scotland. What a day to be a seven-year-old boy! Except if you were from Scotland.

I came out of that cinema pumped. I felt like an amalgamation of Flash Gordon, Bruce Woodcock and the entire England football team. I could do anything! As is my wont, as opposed to just letting it pass, I decided to act on this feeling of invincibility.

Bugger it, I thought. *I'm going to go and watch Bruce Woodcock train.*

And so, with a determination the size of Jupiter and all its moons, I ran home, threw myself onto my Mickey Mouse bike and set off in the direction of Doncaster, which as I said was about seven miles away. I knew what I was doing would get me into trouble, but I was helpless, possessed by an irresistible mixture of enthusiasm and adrenalin. I'd been to Doncaster before by bus, and it had only taken twenty-five minutes or so. I could reach tremendous speeds on my bike, so how long could it take? An hour at most, I assured myself. Hickleton was the furthest I'd ever ventured on my own, but that was only two miles away. This was my mini Everest!

Nobody batted an eyelid as I flew out of Probert Avenue. It was just young Brian on his bike; nothing unusual about that. Past the cinema in Goldthorpe I flew.

'Where you off to, Brian?'

It was some lads from school.

'Just for a ride.'

Try and keep calm, I thought. I didn't want anyone getting in the way of me completing my mission.

'See you later then.'

'Yep, see you.'

Next, I had to negotiate the police station. *This should be OK*, I thought. *Middle of the day? They'll all either be asleep or patrolling the shopping areas.*

No such luck! As I approached, I saw Sergeant Gruber and PC Hawksworth standing outside having a chat. *Oh bloody hell!* There was no other way. *OK, just keep your head down and go like the bloody wind.*

Yes! I was past the police station. Now to Hickleton. But it's all hills to Hickleton: this was going to be painful. *You can do it, though, Blessed*, I encouraged myself in my mind. *Come on, just think about Bruce. Bruce, Bruce, Bruce! You're going to watch him train. The most promising heavyweight in the world! Just do it, Brian!*

God, the agony of those terrible hills! It was murder. Have you ever ridden a Mickey Mouse bike, dear reader? I'd had it since I was about four and so it was by then far too small for me. It was perfect for bombing round the back yard a few thousand times, but climbing over hill and dale? Not really.

I arrived in Hickleton exhausted. That said, I was still on familiar ground. *Only five miles to go*, I thought. *I know the way*. Just then it dawned on me. *Oh bloody hell!* I thought. I did indeed know the way; to the centre of Doncaster! But I hadn't a clue where the Plough Inn was. *Never mind. Just listen for the sound of punchbags being beaten to smithereens and follow that.*

Actually, that's complete bollocks. I was terrified.

As I was catching my breath in Hickleton, I suddenly heard a very friendly but unfamiliar voice.

'Where's tha goin', lad?'

It was a miner on his way to work.

'I'm going to the Plough Inn in Doncaster to watch Bruce Woodcock train.'

'But that's five miles away, lad! Where on earth have you come from?'

'Goldthorpe. I'm Bill Blessed's son.'

'Bill Blessed's lad, eh? He's told me all about you and your baby brother. Does he know you're out?'

'No, but I've told my mum,' I lied.

'Well, you're two miles into your journey, lad, and I'll tell yer what: it shows. Look at your face. You're as red as a tomato. Here, lad, drink this.' And with that, he took a small tin bottle from his bag, what miners called a Dudley, and handed it to me.

'Aw, thanks very much,' I said, before taking a huge and very welcome swig of water.

'You do know the way to the Plough Inn, don't you, lad?'

'Nope.'

'Well, if you follow this road for about three miles, you'll get to the outskirts of Doncaster. When you see the first house, ask there and they'll direct you to the Plough. I've got to get to work now, but take care of yourself, and if you get too tired, promise me you'll turn back.'

'I promise. Anyway, I'd best be off too. Thanks for the drink. I must be off!'

We waved at each other and within a few seconds Hickleton was behind me. A drink and a friendly voice had been exactly what I'd needed. Now it was only a matter of time!

When I reached the outskirts of Doncaster, I rewarded myself by relieving myself, if you see what I mean. Not many people know this, but I was Highgate school piddling champion four years running. There wasn't a wall in the school that I hadn't peed over. Anyway, with my 'spadge', as we used to call it, safely tucked back in my shorts, I rode on in search of directions.

Obviously I must have looked a strange sight: a seven-year-old boy on a Mickey Mouse bike looking lost and slightly dishevelled; and so after not very long I began to attract a small but nevertheless very interested crowd.

'What are yer doin' 'ere, lad?' asked one old gentleman. 'Where's yer mum and dad?'

'They're at home,' I replied. 'I'm on my way to see Bruce Woodcock.'

This amused my audience no end. 'What's tha want to see 'im for?'

'I'm going to watch him train. He's going to beat Joe Louis and win the World Championship!'

This had them all in fits.

'He may well do, lad, but you ought to be at home! Where are you from?'

'Goldthorpe. Can anyone tell me where the Plough Inn is, please?'

Yet more hoots of incredulous laughter. 'Yer a rum lad!'

'By 'eck, lad,' said the old chap who had been first to express his concern. 'You've got some brass neck. I'll tell you what. If I tell you where the Plough Inn is, you promise me you'll set off home well before the sun sets. How does that sound?'

'Yes, I promise.'

Anyway, after getting lost and being fed some bread and butter by a couple who took pity on me, I was eventually delivered (they showed me there themselves) to the Plough Inn. At last, El Dorado!

Woodcock, by the way, had started his career two years previously in 1942 and had won his first twenty bouts by stoppage. In just a few months he was due to fight Jack London for the British heavyweight title and after that was tipped for a shot at Louis. He was the great British hope, no doubt about it. He looked like a giant Jimmy Cagney with a rather handsome, heroic face, and the British press were all over him like a rash. 'At last,' they said, 'Britain's got a future World Champion!' He was unbeatable. Everybody was talking about him.

The room where Bruce trained was actually a stable behind the main building, and I could hear the punching about fifty yards away. I arrived at the door to his makeshift gym, exhausted by my endeavours, and there, with his back to me, was Woodcock. What an extraordinary physique! His waist was absolutely tiny, yet his shoulders must have been about a metre across. He was an absolute bull of a man. He looked like Hector at the gates of Troy.

Bruce was working a heavy bag at the time, and he was hitting it with such ferocity and speed that it was being pinned against the wall. Suddenly, I heard what must have been his trainer.

'Last ten seconds, Bruce!' he shouted.

At which point he seemed to take it to another bloody level. Colin Picton had been right. The whole room did shake!

Then, when he stopped, all I could hear was the sound of him breathing. It was slow and heavy, and had a kind of growl underneath it. I was petrified! Slowly, he turned round and, on seeing me standing there by the door, smiled suddenly.

'Who's this, then? Who are you, lad?'

Most children in my position wouldn't have known what to say, but I'm afraid that, although momentarily petrified, I was full of it.

'I've come to watch you train, Bruce. I've come to watch you train before you beat Jack London at White Hart Lane, and then when you've beaten Jack London you're going to go to America and beat Joe Louis, and then you'll be World Champion, Bruce.'

And I said all that in what must have been a little under three seconds. I was so thrilled!

Bruce's smile widened further still.

'What do you reckon, Tom?' he said, calling to his trainer, Tom Hurst. 'This young lad reckons I'm going to beat Jack London then jump on a boat to America and flatten Joe Louis.'

'One step at a time, young 'un,' said Tom. 'He's got a long way to go yet. Where have you come from, lad?'

'I've come all the way from Goldthorpe. I got here on my bike. It's taken me almost all day.'

'Is that right, lad?' said Bruce. 'You've come all the way from Goldthorpe on your own just to watch me train?'

'I have, Bruce, yes I have. You're going to beat Joe Louis!'

'He's off again, Tom!'

'Can you box, lad?' asked Tom.

'I'm learning,' I said. 'I watch all the reports at the cinema and I listen to all the matches on the radio with my dad. He's teaching me. I'm called the Dynamite Kid!'

This made the two of them howl with laughter.

'Did you hear that, Bruce?' said Tom. 'You've got yourself a young pretender.

'I'll tell you what, lad,' he then said, turning to me, 'how would you like to fight Bruce here and now?'

It's a wonder I didn't spontaneously combust!

I gulped nervously and then muttered in disbelief, 'Yes, I'd love to! Oh thank you thank you thank you!'

Bruce then took off his sparring gloves and put them on my hands. Each one was about as big as my bloody head! Anyway, I assumed the orthodox stance and waited for Bruce to make the first move. In he came, his shoulders arched, fists high. *Oh heck*, I thought. *What do I do now?*

'Hit him on the knee, lad,' yelled Tom. 'That's his weak spot!'

So I did. When Bruce got to me, I let go a great right hook which hit him right on the kneecap. Bruce dropped to his knees in front of me.

'Now hit him in the jaw, lad,' shouted Tom.

So once again I let go a punch and hit him right on the chin. Bruce fell flat on his back and Tom counted him out.

'. . . Eight, nine, ten, YOU'RE OUT!'

I'd won!

Bruce got up, ruffled my hair and said, 'Bye 'eck, lad, you can't half punch! That's the first time I've ever been knocked out. Somebody should tell Joe Louis and Jack London about thee!'

What an absolutely marvellous time I'd had. I was in heaven!

Suddenly, Tom looked at his watch. 'Where did you say you'd come from, lad? Goldthorpe?'

'Yes, that's right.'

'Well, it's getting dark. We can't have you going back on that bike of yours.'

And so, in the end, they got a farmer friend of theirs to give me a lift home on his tractor. I remember Bruce lifted me onto the trailer, ruffled my hair again, said, 'Goldthorpe please, Reg,' smiled at me, and with that disappeared back inside.

When I arrived back at Probert Avenue, it didn't take me long to realize that half the bloody street had been out looking for me. In fact, the first person I saw as I made my way towards our front door was Sergeant Gruber. He was a hard man, Sergeant Gruber, and ruled the streets with a rod of iron.

'It's alright, Hilda,' he shouted into the house. 'It's alright, he's here. Look at the state of you, lad! Where the hell have you been?'

The house was full of people. There was my granddad, two of my uncles, my parents, of course, and young Alan. Poor Mother's face was swollen she'd been crying so much.

'Look what you've done to your mother, lad,' said Dad. 'She's been crying since three o'clock!'

'Don't shout at him, Billy,' she said, taking me in her arms. 'Don't shout at him, love. Let's just be thankful he's safe.'

Sergeant Gruber wasn't quite so understanding, I'm afraid. He wanted answers!

'Where's tha been, lad? Come on, out with it! Where's tha been?'

Once again, I was almost overcome with excitement.

'I've been to see Bruce Woodcock. I went all the way to Doncaster on my bike and after watching him train, he put his gloves on me and I boxed him. I knocked him out!'

'I'll tell you what, lad,' said Gruber, 'the next time you go off like that without telling your mum and dad, I'll put thee in the ring with me, and you won't be so bloody lucky with me as you were with Woodcock!'

After a little while, everyone started to drift away and so normality ruled once again. Following a smashing tea, I kissed my parents goodnight, sang them a little song (which I sometimes did if Mum was upset), and made my way up to bed. As I lay between the sheets, basking in the glory of what had gone on and rehearsing how I'd tell my friends, it all of a sudden dawned on me.

Oh bloody hell! I thought. *I forgot to get his autograph!*

Bruce became British, Empire and European heavyweight champion and was number three in the world ratings. In September 1946 he fought the American Gus Lesnevich at the Harringay Arena, winning by a knockout in round eight – at which point the whole of Britain stood up as one in hope and adulation. He ended up suffering some horrific injuries later on in his career; the worst taking place during the fight which, had he won, would have given him a crack at Louis. His opponent was an American named Joe Baksi, who, before taking up boxing, had been a coal miner, and Woodcock was tipped to thrash him within five rounds. Only Baksi stood in the way of Woodcock and Louis.

I won't give you chapter and verse, but Bruce could be a slow starter – that was his only flaw, really – and in the first round Baksi caught him with a huge left hook, right on the jaw. Bruce fell forwards, which is always a bad sign during a fight. It's actually a bad sign during any bloody fight, but in boxing if you fall forwards it means you're in trouble, and let me tell you: Bruce was in trouble.

I couldn't believe it. Until that point, Woodcock had hit Baksi several times with his left, but then Baksi got him into a corner, let go a couple of body blows, which slowed Woodcock down, and then threw this deadly left hook.

Bruce's jaw was broken instantly, but then, as he got up after the count of eight, Baksi began free-hitting him. He knocked him all over the bloody ring! Woodcock tried to fight back, but he was obviously hurt and in great pain. Baksi then let go a right hook, which almost made Bruce do a somersault. Once again, he was down. When the count got to nine, the bell went for the end of the round. Bruce had to be carried to his corner by Tom and the rest of his training team. Stupidly, Bruce pleaded with the referee and Tom to let him fight on, and – stupider still – the referee and Tom allowed him. He didn't know where he was! So as the next round began, Baksi, who was a really big puncher, kind of like a white George Foreman, began free-hitting him again. Bruce went down three times in that round.

We were all in bits on Probert Avenue. I'd never been so worried and nervous in all my life!

I later found out that Baksi had hit Bruce's cheek so hard that bits of his cheekbone had actually gone into his eye. Nothing in the history of boxing has ever been as bestial as the Woodcock vs Baksi fight. Some dreadful refereeing. Utter madness! You see, they just couldn't believe that Bruce could be beaten.

By the fifth round, Bruce, now blinded in one eye, actually fought Baksi off and won the bloody round. Unbelievable! Eventually, the referee stopped the fight in the seventh round, by which time Bruce was smashed to smithereens. It wouldn't be allowed to happen today.

Bruce was rushed straight to hospital, where he actually spent the next fifteen months receiving treatment. FIFTEEN MONTHS! The boxing world reported they had never seen such courage.

I remember that, after the fight, the entire street congregated outside. We just stood there in shock.

'What happened, Dad?' I asked. 'Bruce is better than Baksi. What happened?'

'I don't know, lad,' he replied.

'He will come back, though, won't he, Dad?'

'After tonight, lad, I don't know.'

Our neighbour, Mrs Simmons, who for some reason didn't like Woodcock, was cheered by his defeat.

'I told you all he wouldn't last against one of those big Americans. I told you! He's not good enough.'

My dad had to hold me back when she said that. It's a wonder she wasn't lynched!

I wept and wept and wept. I was inconsolable. I have never, to this day, got over it. You see, heroes were important to us back then. During World War Two we had of course relied on heroes to see us through those dark, dark days. We had all the wonderful men and women of the Allied forces, of course, and then we had people like Churchill, Eisenhower and Zhukov. Each and every one of them was a champion of the free world. But it was the boxing heroes who really captured our hearts and imaginations, especially the ones who also fought in the war.

Joe Louis, the man credited as being America's first ever national hero and one of the greatest heavyweights of all time, volunteered to enlist in the army the day after he'd fought a charity bout for the Naval Relief Fund. Pathé newsreel recorded his inclusion and when asked by the army clerk what his occupation was, Louis said, 'I'm a fighter! Now let me at them Japs!' After that, he fought bout after bout after bout, and every single cent he earned was donated by Louis to the war effort. Hundreds of thousands of dollars! That's what a hero looks like, boys and girls. He was ruthless in the ring, but totally selfless out of it. And, my word, could he fight. He never wasted a punch, Louis, and he successfully defended his world title twenty-five times over eleven years;

a feat which has never been matched or beaten by a heavy-weight – nor will it be.

So Bruce Woodcock was our Joe Louis and was considered one of the greatest heavyweights we'd ever produced. This was our Achilles! He had everything. He had punching power, good looks, personality and physique. And he had been destroyed by somebody who was considered a no-hoper. Imagine what that did to morale. We were going to conquer the world with Bruce . . . but no more. It was a tragedy.

Because Baksi was a former coal miner – and even despite the fact he'd beaten firm favourite Woodcock – he was sent on a tour of some of the British coal mines. It was a publicity stunt, I suppose. When he came to Hickleton Main, which was my dad's pit, I ran there from school as fast as I could. I was going to beat this Yank to a pulp! When I arrived, I saw Baksi standing head and shoulders above everyone at the pit gates, signing autographs. I rushed over, pushed everyone else out of the way, grabbed hold of one of his hands and I pinched him as hard as I bloody well could! His hands were bigger than me, so it's a wonder he noticed me.

'You got lucky, Baksi,' I shouted, incandescent with rage. 'You put everything into the first round and everybody knows Woodcock's a slow starter. Next time, he'll bloody murder you!'

Baksi, who really was a giant of a man, bent down and picked me up.

'What's your name, boy?'

'Brian Blessed.'

'You're right, Brian, I was a bit lucky,' he said. 'Bruce is a great fighter and he's dangerous. I couldn't take any risks. I had to give him all I had early on. Next time, he'll beat me.'

Then he put me down and ruffled my hair.

My dad was introduced to Baksi shortly after me, and

when he got home that evening he handed me a photograph. It was of Baksi.

'He's signed it for you, Brian,' he said. 'Have a look.'

And he had. It read: 'To Brian, Sorry! Best wishes, Joe Baksi.'

I looked at it and thought, *Ah well, he can't be all that bad.*

So obsessed was I with Woodcock, Louis and all things pugilistic that I very nearly trained to become a professional boxer myself. This was when I was in my early teens. In the nearby town of Thurnscoe lived a chap named Billy Thompson, a friend of the family, who was the British and European lightweight champion, and he, believe it or not, used to train me. Fancy being trained by a British and European champion! He had it all planned out for me, Billy, and was adamant I had what it took to succeed.

'You could become another Woodcock, you know, Brian lad,' he said. 'We'll make you a middleweight first. That'll take about two years. Then we'll move you up to light heavyweight and see how it goes. You move well, you've got a good defence and a great right hook. Yes, lad, I reckon we could mould you into a good pro, and a heavyweight.'

Naturally, I was excited by the prospect of following in my hero's footsteps, but I'm afraid that my mother was horrified.

'No, Brian!' she said. 'I won't have it. I'm fine with you wanting to become an actor, but I will not support you as a boxer. Look what happened to Woodcock!'

She was absolutely adamant, and was probably right to put her foot down. After all, I couldn't do both. I had to make a choice.

Now, you can say what you like about boxing, but it is a sport which requires great courage. It's no use criticizing it. Have you ever been in a red corner? Have you ever been in a blue corner? Do you know what it feels like to face somebody? Life itself is a fight. You have to face enemies! But boxing is honest: just two men, a referee and a boxing ring. It is without any doubt the noble art; providing it's done properly, of course. I've seen wonderful things happen in the ring: examples of friendship and camaraderie you never see anywhere else. The friendships that develop between boxers and their opponents are fascinating to watch.

Can boxing be dangerous? Well, yes, of course it bloody can; the same as Formula One can be, and the same as motorcycle racing can be (Isle of Man TT, anyone?), and horse racing, and skiing, and rugby. Darts is potentially the most dangerous sport on the planet! And what about mountaineering?

But I digress.

Years later, when I was working on *Z Cars*, myself and some of the other cast members were invited to go to New York by the New York City Police Department. It was organized by the BBC – as a publicity stunt – but as far as we were concerned it was a free holiday, and so over the pond we all went. We stayed for about ten days if memory serves, and in that time had lots and lots of photos taken with our transatlantic pseudo colleagues. We were just actors, remember! They treated us like absolute royalty, though. In fact, the day we arrived we were asked by the Chief Commissioner if there was anything in particular we'd like to do while we were there. My hand went up immediately. I thought, *If you're going to put in a request, make sure it's a whopper!*

'I'd like to have lunch with Joe Louis, Rocky Marciano, Jack Dempsey, and as many of the great American heavyweights as you can muster.'

Two days later, I was taken to Jack Dempsey's restaurant on Eighth Avenue and 50th Street, the one that featured in the film *The Godfather* a few years later. Anyway, as I walked in, there's Jack Dempsey waiting to greet me. The Manassa Mauler: my father's favourite boxer and winner of sixty-five bouts; fifty-one by a knockout. I was almost overcome. A fantastic world champion!

'Good afternoon, Mr Blessed,' he said, 'and welcome to my restaurant. Would you step this way please? I've got some friends I'd like you to meet.'

With that, he led me to the back of the restaurant and into a private room. As the door opened, I saw a table in the room, and sitting at the table were some middle-aged men.

'No!' I said to Jack Dempsey. 'It can't be? I recognize all of them! I don't believe it.'

This was, ladies and gentlemen, a roll call of the greatest heavyweight boxers of the 1920s, 1930s, 1940s and 1950s. There was Ezzard Charles, the Cincinnati Cobra; Gene Tunney, the Fighting Marine; Rocky Marciano, the Brockton Block-buster; Jersey Joe Walcott; and there, sitting at the very end of the table, was Joe Louis himself, the Brown Bomber!

I was gobsmacked! 'I don't believe it,' I cried. 'Look at you all! Dempsey, Charles, Tunney, Marciano, Walcott, Louis: six of the greatest heavyweights of all time!' And they were such gentlemen. It was an honour to meet them all.

For the next two or three hours, I basically entertained them. I knew more about their careers than they did, including all their statistics. I took them through fights they'd forgotten they'd had and could tell them exactly when they'd knocked people out. Breaking bread with these colossi and making them all laugh was one of the most joyous experiences of my life.

When they could get a word in edgeways, I was astonished by the generosity they all showed to one another. First, I asked Joe Louis how he'd have got on against Jack Dempsey, but Dempsey interjected.

'I'll answer that, Brian,' he said. 'Over a fifteen-round fight, Joe would have outpointed me. He wouldn't have knocked me out, though. Nobody could knock me out.'

Then Joe Louis said, 'Yeah, maybe Jack's right; maybe I

would have outpointed him. But I'll tell you what; he'd have beaten me in a phone booth. You wouldn't want to get too close to Dempsey in his prime.'

Obviously I asked them who among them was the best, and when I did they all cried out, 'Rocky Marciano!' – except for Rocky himself, of course, who then smiled and shook his head in disbelief. When I asked them why, they all said, 'He never got beat and he retired with lots of money. We all got beat and retired with next to nothing! That makes him better than us!'

Ezzard Charles, who had lost to Marciano twice in his career, then said, 'The only time I have ever sworn in my life is when I fought Rocky. I said to the referee, "Get that motherfucker off me!"'

What remarkable generosity and friendship. These were warriors – some of the best there's ever been – but when all's said and done, they were just human beings. Decent men.

What a privilege it was being in the company of such true gladiators.

Incidentally, Joe Louis told me that he watched Woodcock knock out Lesnevich at the Harringay Arena on film and thought Bruce was the most dangerous fighter he'd ever set eyes on. And it was not long after my New York trip that the subject of Bruce came up in a conversation with David Rose, who'd been my boss on *Z Cars*. David had asked me if there was anything I'd like to do, and so I'd told him that my big ambition was to make a film about this great champion boxer who, for a time, was second only to the great Brown Bomber.

David thought this was a marvellous idea. We'd been developing the project for the BBC and were actually due to start filming in March 1971. David was going to be the director, Alan Plater the writer, and I would be playing Bruce Woodcock. Bruce was slightly taller than me but I could box, of course, and so with a few special effects and a following wind we were sure we could pull it off. What a production it was going to be! In preparation for the role, I'd been training with the great Henry Cooper, who was also a pal of mine, and so I was in amazing shape. He'd really put me through my paces and we'd had a marvellous time together. I tell you, we'd got all kinds of amazing people on board, including Joe Louis himself. The Brown Bomber had agreed to take part in my film. Unbelievable!

Anyway, to cut a long story short, Bruce, who by this time had become a great friend of mine and had been all set to act as a consultant on the film, suddenly decided that he'd rather we didn't go ahead. I was devastated, but he had good reason. You see, Bruce had endured some absolutely horrific injuries during his career, including in the fight against Baksi. Apparently, these injuries had left a far bigger mark on Bruce than either he or his family had originally thought, and our trip down memory lane was beginning to affect him mentally.

'The closer we get to making it, the closer I get to the pain,' he said. 'I can't stand it, Brian. And there's the fame. I don't want that again.'

When word had got out about the film, Bruce had been approached by all kinds of people. Publishers wanted to re-issue his autobiography and the taxman was already on at him, asking how much he was going to make out of it all.

'I play golf in the afternoon with my friends and I come home to a wonderful family. I don't want anything else, Brian; money or fame.'

By this time, we could have made the film without Bruce's permission, but there was no way I was ever going to let that happen. Bruce had cooperated in good faith and had been flattered and thrilled when I'd originally approached him. But the closer the film came to becoming a reality, the more distressed he became, and so with heavy hearts we decided to close down the production and move on. Would you like to be responsible for sending a friend over the edge? Well, of course you bloody wouldn't.

The BBC was furious with me. You see, they would have been happy to carry on without Bruce's permission. They'd already invested a great deal of time and money in the film – taxpayer's money that could have been spent elsewhere – but because by now I'd also dropped out, they were up shit creek without a paddle.

What an enormous bugger! I'd got within a gnat's chuff of making a huge film about my favourite sportsman; and the BBC thinks I'm a charlatan. Not one of my better weeks, it has to be said.

So back I went to TV. Now, don't get me wrong, I was eternally grateful for my roles on TV – in fact, I still am, and am offered lots to this day – but I couldn't help feeling that I'd missed out on the big one! Do you know what I mean? Helpfully, of course, *The Trojan Women* film was in my stars, but I didn't know that at the time and I was in an awful grump about it for quite some time.

Funnily enough, the next time I spoke publicly about boxing was indeed on the small screen. It was a few years ago now, but I was to take part in a television debate on the future of boxing. Several politicians wanted to ban the sport at the time, and had been waffling on about it in the press for weeks. Anyway, in the end one of the television companies put on a debate about the sport. One of the said politicians was captain of the 'Against' team, while I was captain of the 'For's, together with Henry Cooper.

Although I firmly believe the politicians' opposition to boxing was born from a genuine desire to keep people from harm, they were terribly ill-informed and had obviously never spoken to anybody associated with the sport. Bad move! They were simply going by statistics they'd no doubt read in some anti-boxing report, but let's be fair here: if we all obeyed every bit of research we ever read about in the newspapers, we'd never eat butter or red meat or drink alcohol ever again. You cannot and should not make decisions based on statistics alone. It's madness!

Boxing has been in existence since about 3,000BC, and has been an Olympic sport since 639BC. It also does a tremendous amount of good in the world. You may think it's a bit of a cliché, but it genuinely does take people off the streets; people who've had no chance of a decent education, and certainly no further education. There are millions of these people all over the world, and quite a lot of the time boxing is their only hope. It offers them friendship, fitness and a future that does not involve drugs or crime.

Anyway, these politicians were reading out statistic after statistic after statistic during this debate, and I'm afraid to say that for the first twenty minutes or so, they made mincemeat of us. My team were all boxers, you see, not talkers, and I'm afraid that I was so annoyed that I couldn't really think straight.

In the end, it was the Brown Bomber who came to my rescue, or at least some of his experiences.

'Would you mind if I introduced a bit of reality into proceedings?' I began. 'It's all been quite one-dimensional thus far. When the great Joe Louis, who I had the pleasure of having lunch with some years ago, had retired, the American government hounded him and eventually forced him out of retirement to pay a tax bill. This was the man who'd handed over every single one of his five wartime purses to the government. Every single one! He was also the one who made it possible for the black man to walk from Harlem into downtown Manhattan. He was a war hero who changed history! But no: they claimed he owed them tax and so they forced him out of retirement. Louis fought nine bouts in all, lost seven, and ended up later in a wheelchair.'

'Exactly,' interjected one of the Againsts. 'That's what I'm talking about. You see, your argument's flawed. He ended up in a wheelchair!'

'But why did he end up in a wheelchair?' I responded. 'He ended up in a wheelchair because he was forced to fight by the US government. Politicians! He didn't want to fight. You mark my words: the real villains of the piece are lawyers, the politicians and the promotors. Not all of them, of course, but there are still people within the sport who exploit these men time after time after time. If it's regulated and executed properly and within the law, boxing is quite, quite safe. There's danger, of course – just as there is with horse racing, rugby, skiing and all kinds of other sports – but managed properly it can be one of the most enjoyable and exciting spectacles on earth.

'And by the way, do you know who paid for Joe Louis' funeral? He didn't. He died with nothing. And it wasn't the US government or one of his lawyers or promoters. It was Max Schmeling, the German boxer who had fought Louis twice, beating him the first time and then losing the next. He paid for Louis' funeral, and he even settled one of Louis' tax bills. For about $50,000! Now you work that one out. That is what boxing is really all about.'

They said nothing, of course, and there the debate ended. I didn't enjoy the experience, though, not one little bit. You see, believe it or not, I actually dislike that kind of verbal confrontation. Physical confrontation's fine, as long as it's part of a controlled sport, but I'm afraid that verbal to-ing and fro-ing simply bores, annoys and frustrates me. I'd far sooner be reading a script or writing in my little hut, as I am now.

I've been quite lucky, though. As well as all my exploits in the wonderful world of boxing, I've also done a tremendous amount of judo over the years (I'm a black belt) and have been on the mat with some of the greats: the legendary Robinson brothers and the wonderful Brian Jacks. He tried forever to throw me – but he couldn't. Said it was like trying to throw a tank! A few years ago, I even commentated at the Sumo Wrestling Championships. I did it four years running. How about that?

So, to all the warriors in the world, I SALUTE YOU!

Continue, you young men and women, to follow your star.

6

BLESSED ARE THE ROMANTICS

I know this will come as a shock to you all, but there are people in this world today who have difficulty comprehending the notion of Brian Blessed the romantic.

'I just can't imagine it, Brian,' they say. 'You're a rough, tough action man, always climbing up mountains and fighting people. It just isn't you!'

So, when they find out that actually I am thirty-six years into a blissfully happy marriage, their initial incredulity tends to proliferate somewhat.

'No? Really, Brian?' they exclaim. 'You, married? I always imagined you living alone somewhere, like a hermit.'

The general consensus – that I wouldn't know romance if it jumped up and smacked me in the bollocks, and that I also live alone in a cave like some giant bearded amoeba – are somewhat wide of the mark. I may not have the experience of a Clark Gable or a Rudolph Valentino, but old Brian can turn on the charm when needs be, and is indeed married to the most beautiful, warm and talented human being. It's fair to say, though, that the path to our love was not an especially smooth one, and to tell you the full story I'm going to have to jump in my time machine and whiz back a few years.

When I left *Z Cars*, I had a string of wonderful television roles, the first really big one being Porthos in the BBC series *The Three Musketeers*. And it was on *The Three Musketeers* that I met the director Peter Hammond, who is probably the most talented television director I have ever worked with. He was a wonderfully eccentric fellow, and could turn his hand to just about anything. Anyway, we got on like a house on fire, Peter and I, and he ended up casting me in all manner of things; most interestingly, perhaps, as Reuben Starkadder in *Cold Comfort Farm*. That was made in 1968 and starred the likes of Alastair Sim, Fay Compton, Rosalie Crutchley, Sarah Badel and a very young Peter Egan. It was a real A-list production.

But Peter Hammond knew exactly what he was doing in casting me as Reuben – as the WILD Reuben Starkadder who lived on a strange farm. He'd growl at anyone who came within a hundred yards of the place, young Reuben, which had me delivering some very strange lines from time to time, none more so than when I greeted my cousin, Flora Poste, played by the beautiful Sarah Badel.

'Grrrrrrrrrrrrrrr, what you doin' 'ere?'

'I've come to see you, Reuben.'

'Grrrrrrrrrrrr, I scranletted three hundred furrows before dawn. Could you do that?'

'Erm, no, I don't think I could.'

'Grrrrrrrrrrrrr, I don't like you!'

Completely bizarre! It really was the most wonderful production. A thousand times better than that other one they made in the 1990s. Who was in that? Ah yes, Lord McKellen of Actor-shire and Baron Stephen Fry. Rubbish! Both of them!

Anyway, it was during this production that I met and befriended a chap called John Jacobs, the brother of the late disc jockey, David Jacobs. He was directing a very successful series at the time called *ITV Playhouse* and asked me if I'd be interested in playing the lead in one of these productions. Being a jobbing actor, I quite naturally snapped his bloody hand off and so the moment I finished filming *Cold Comfort Farm* I began learning my lines. They were pretty hot stuff,

these *ITV Playhouse* plays, and boasted writers such as
Dennis Potter and Jack Rosenthal, not to mention actors like
Edward Woodward and Ian Hendry. The play that John had
in mind for me was called *Double Agent* and would also star
Leonard Rossiter, Bernard Archard, Timothy Carlton and
Edward Judd.

Leonard Rossiter and I both had a swagger about us at the
time. We'd been quite successful in the 1960s and had never,
ever been out of work. That made for a bit of healthy com-
petition, I suppose, and when we all turned up for rehearsals,
which took place in the West End, the atmosphere was definitely a little charged.

Poor old Edward Judd was having a few problems with
the booze at the time, which I think probably dampened
mine and Leonard's brashness somewhat. It's such a pity as
Edward was a very warm person and a truly formidable actor.
He had played the lead in some of my favourite-ever science-
fiction films, such as *The Day the Earth Caught Fire* and *The
First Men in the Moon*. If you haven't yet seen *The Day the
Earth Caught Fire*, make sure you do. It's a masterpiece!
Somehow, though, Edward had got onto the drink, and so
always seemed to be sweating a bit and forgetting his lines.

Anyway, I played Reg Sugden, a Yorkshire cloth salesman
who is sent to Russia as an industrial spy. Unfortunately,
things go wrong for him over there and I'm imprisoned by
the KGB. Leonard played my interrogator, Nikolai Krob-
nevsky, and I remember we had some absolutely marvellous
scenes together. If you can find it on DVD, it's top stuff!

I remember there were only two female roles in *Double
Agent*, and one of these was to be played by a young up-
coming actress named Hildegard Neil. Now Hildegard is and
always has been a very, very stylish dresser, and I remember being distracted by this all throughout rehearsals. Until
then, I'd always been sartorially impotent, if you like, and
had never in my life taken any notice of what I or anybody

else was wearing, so this was like an awakening, really. I'm not going to make an arse of myself by trying to describe Hildegard's clothes – usually dresses or blousey things, that's all I know – but suffice to say they had an effect on me.

Then, as we began rehearsing, I started to become familiar with Hildegard's voice – and, oh my God, *what* a voice! Like a younger, sexier Katharine Hepburn. Good heavens, I was becoming fascinated! But as I sat there and really began studying Hildegard, I once again underwent what could actually only be described as an epiphany.

You see, until then, as far as I had been concerned, a pretty face was just that, a pretty face, and I had never once been seduced by the beauty of a woman. Hard to believe, I know, but I assure you that was the case. I had found women attractive, of course, but I had never once been either distracted or disturbed by their beauty. Yet Hildegard was different; she was pensive, thoughtful, startlingly beautiful and radiated an allure, the like of which I only thought existed in works of fiction by Emily Brontë and Thomas Hardy.

You see, you're somewhat taken aback by Romantic Blessed, aren't you? Never thought I had it in me.

Anyhow, Hildegard had come from a two-year stint at the Liverpool Everyman Theatre, where they'd been producing all kinds of exciting new stuff, and so she was artistically very sharp and could challenge the director and challenge the script quite boldly. I think John Jacobs, the director, was quite knocked for six by this, but at places like the Everyman you were encouraged to do it, just as I had been at the Bristol Old Vic. So you had to be on your toes with Hildegard a little bit. She wasn't stern at all, in fact she had the most radiant of smiles, but she definitely had a bit of clout about her; something the establishment were not used to.

She thought bugger all of me at first, I can tell you that for nothing. As I said, Leonard and I had this swagger about us and were quite possibly on the verge of being a bit cocky. To be fair to us, we were quite young, relatively famous and had been successful for a number of years. It wasn't the biggest crime in the world. Or so I thought! Hildegard didn't like this at all. All the *Z Cars* and *Three Musketeers* nonsense meant nothing to her; and as for my swagger? Well, as far as she was concerned, I could take a running jump.

'You're very fond of yourselves, aren't you?' she once said to Leonard and me after rehearsals one day. 'You may have talent, both of you, but then so do countless others. I know at least ten actors who could act you two off the stage. If anything, you should consider yourselves lucky.'

Well, we were speechless. Stunned and speechless. Nobody had ever said anything like that to us before, and mark my words she meant it. It certainly quietened us down a little. She was right, of course: to a certain extent, we had been lucky. Perhaps we should exchange our swaggers for something a bit more humble?

Once Hildegard had put us in our place, we all relaxed a little bit and began to get along famously, and as rehearsals progressed I was able to continue my study of her, each day noticing something new and wonderful. I remember one day being struck by the height of her cheekbones, and the next day noticing that her eyes seemed to change from grey to green. It was a continuous round of discovery and admiration. Later on, it came up in conversation that she had been born and brought up in South Africa. *That's it*, I said to myself. *That's the crux of the attraction. She's African. AFRICAN!*

I'd never really been a fan of what they call the 'English Rose' type, and I'd also never really gone in for the more busty Hollywood sorts. Perhaps it was the explorer or the mountaineer in me, but the moment I found out that Hildegard was from South Africa, it all fell into place. The more I got to know Hildegard, the more African she became to me;

and that drew me in and increased my admiration of her. Her English was perfect and she spoke the language beautifully, yet there was something very fresh in her timbre. Her tone was somewhat unique.

Now, I keep on talking about Hildegard in the past tense. This is simply to avoid me having to insert the words 'and still is' everywhere. But let me just put down on paper that whatever I tell you about my dear, dear wife is as true today as it was in 1968. OK? Right then. Onwards and upwards!

So, I very quickly became immensely attracted to this South African queen. Mildly obsessed, even. She liked me a bit I think (although only in a platonic fashion) and we began to develop a very close yet gentle relationship. Thoughtful, frank and honest at times, but nonetheless gentle. Another element to our growing friendship was that we were both working-class and loved the classics.

After a week or two, we completed the rehearsals and made the move down to Anglia Television to begin filming. They were based down in Norwich, of course, and so being the gallant gentleman that I was and am, I offered to give Hildegard a lift in my *Z Cars* Zephyr. I forgot to mention this in the *Z Cars* chapter, but one day during filming all the main cast members were given a car by Ford. It was just a publicity stunt, of course, and received a ridiculous amount of press coverage, but we all got a new car! Not bad, eh? Anyway, I still had mine and so offered its services to Hildegard.

This wasn't a ploy so I could make a pass at her, by the way. I was far too honourable for anything like that; a true gentleman. She was hard up for cash so I thought it was the right thing to do. I'd make a pass at her at the hotel.

Only joking! It did turn out to be an awful mistake, though, as I almost ended up killing us both. Travelling down to Norfolk by car in the 1960s right in the middle of winter probably wasn't a very good idea. In fact, it was a bloody awful idea. Stupid! The roads were hardly ever salted back then, and as wonderful as the Ford Zephyr looked on TV, it was absolutely awful in the snow. The engine was heavy and the rear light. Bloody dreadful! The tyres were also totally inferior to the ones we have today.

It happened about ten miles outside of Norwich. Everything had been going swimmingly thus far. I had been regaling Hildegard with tales of my antics in Yorkshire, and she had been reciprocating with stories about her life in South Africa. It was all good and I had a feeling that she might even be warming to me. Then, all of a sudden, I remember this enormous humpback bridge hoving into view, and just as we drove over the top of the wretched thing I totally lost control of the steering. I admit that I might have been going a little too fast on our approach, but there was bugger all I could do about it at the time and so we just clung on for dear life. We went careering all over the bloody road, though. It was absolute turmoil! We almost turned a somersault twice and missed a huge articulated lorry by what must have been millimetres. I have to say, Hildegard remained very calm. Probably just a mixture of shock and fear!

That was the first of many times I have almost killed Hildegard. I must obviously have a talent for it.

Anyway, I'm pleased to report that on this occasion we arrived safe and sound at our destination, all ready to begin the first day's filming the following morning. Although nothing at all happened between us there, we still spent the majority of our spare time together. At dinner, Hildegard would smile at me provocatively, as if to say, 'You haven't got the confidence to make a move, have you, Brian?' She was dead right.

After the second day of filming, I met Hildegard in the bar at the hotel. The place was full of our fellow cast members such as Leonard and Edward, and there must also have been at least twenty businessmen there, all drinking cocktails in their suits and talking bollocks.

Hildegard was wearing a light brown sleeveless dress and she looked absolutely stunning. The trouble was that everyone else in the bar thought the same, and so they all made a beeline for her. She had actors falling at her feet and businessmen trying to buy her drinks. It was a ginormous fiesta of fools and flattery, and poor Hildegard quite obviously hated it. In the end, they even began asking to have their photos taken with her, something I'm ashamed to admit I encouraged as a way to relieve the tense atmosphere.

'Oh go on, Hildegard,' I said. 'It's just a bit of fun! There's no harm in it.'

The next look I received from Hildegard was not so much provocative, more vehement, as if to say, 'You stupid bastard, you wait!'

Anyway, in an attempt to get rid of the idiots, Hildegard agreed, and so running from our table to the door was a great line of suited and booted businessmen, all waiting to have their photos taken with the ravishing Ms Neil. I believe the modern parlance for this kind of thing is a 'selfie'.

When things eventually quietened down, we decided to call it a night and so made our way back to our respective rooms. As we got into the lift, a bellboy asked us which floor we'd like to go to.

'The second floor, please,' I said.

'And you, madam?' asked the bellboy.

'Yes, same for me please.'

'Ah, same room then,' said the bellboy, being not only wrong but ever so slightly presumptuous.

'NO, WE ARE NOT IN THE SAME ROOM!' yelled Hildegard. 'CERTAINLY NOT. I AM IN A ROOM ON MY OWN.' And, with that, she stormed out of the lift and took the stairs.

I think she'd had enough of men for one night. The look on that bellboy's face though! Poor little mite. The next morning, Hildegard set off back to London. She'd finished her scenes in the studios and so there was no point in her staying. Believe it or not, I didn't see her in person again for the best part of six years. We'd left on fairly bad terms, you see, and, not being the most confident of suitors, I'm afraid I couldn't pluck up the courage to call her. I did have a feeling, though, that our relationship wasn't quite done. It's a difficult thing to describe, but I just had this feeling that fate might take a hand one day.

Who am I kidding? I was clutching at straws.

Although I didn't see Hildegard in person, I never stopped seeing her on the bloody television. Now I was quite a popular actor in the late 1960s and early 1970s – I did plays galore on both stage and TV and was just starting to break into films at the time – but Hildegard was matching me pound for pound. She was never off the TV! One day she'd be in an episode of *Jason King*, and the next a *Play for Today* with Joss Ackland. Then she too started breaking into films. A leading role in *The Man Who Haunted Himself* with Roger Moore came first in 1970, quickly followed by the lead role in *Antony and Cleopatra* alongside Charlton Heston. Then, in 1973, she had leading roles in two hugely popular films: *England Made Me*, alongside Peter Finch and Michael York, and then the Oscar-winning *A Touch of Class*, with Glenda Jackson and George Segal. Not bad for your first four films, is it? Every man in the country wanted to go out with Hildegard Neil after seeing *England Made Me*. She looks, and is, stunning in the film. My God! I've never seen a woman as mysterious and beautiful as that!

Actually, I told a porky: I *did* see Hildegard in person before we met again, but I didn't speak to her. I'd just finished filming *The Trojan Women* and my agent, John Miller, had taken me out for dinner at a restaurant called the White Elephant. And that's where I saw Hildegard – with a heavy bald man. I remember John even tried to persuade me to go over to her and congratulate her on her success.

'You've worked with Hildegard, Brian. Go over and say hello to her.'

'No, John, I couldn't. She probably won't remember me.'

'Of course she will. Go over and say well done.'

'I can't, John, honestly.'

'She's looked over here twice now. Go on!'

And so it went on. Do you know, I couldn't even make eye contact with her. I was so consumed with jealousy to see her with another man. She was now considered one of the great beauties of the film world. A sex siren! What on earth would she want with me? Somebody who had made her have her photo taken against her will with hordes of lecherous businessmen. I just wanted to dig a big hole and jump right in.

Anyway, not long after that, the strangest thing happened. You honestly won't believe this, but I swear to you it's true.

I was having a relationship at the time with a beautiful actress. We were lying on the sofa one night – she fast asleep and I dozing off – when all of a sudden she sat bolt upright.

'Christ, Brian!' she yelled. 'You're going to marry Hildegard Neil!'

To say I was taken aback would be the understatement to end all bloody understatements.

'What on earth are you talking about?' I said. 'I've only worked with Hildegard once. I don't even know her. Where did this come from?'

'It was in my dream. Mark my words, Brian. You will marry Hildegard Neil.'

I thought, *You're off your bloody rocker, love. If I believed every dream I'd ever had, I'd have climbed Everest a hundred times and would have holidayed on Mars every year since I was six.*

Anyway, forward on two years to 1974, and there I am one day, minding my own business in my little house in

Richmond: Number 2, The Vineyard. I'd been renovating the place for a number of years and it really was a dear, sweet cottage. Swallowed up all of my money, of course, but I had bugger all else to spend it on at the time. So one day I was sitting outside in the courtyard when all of a sudden I heard these voices approaching; quite rowdy ones at that.

Drunks in Richmond? I thought. *But there's no rugby on . . .* Whoever it was had certainly had a few, though. Anyway, when the voices eventually turned into actual human beings I realized straight away that they were friends of mine: a producer, a director and a casting director from Yorkshire Television.

'BRIIIIIAAAAAAAN!' they screamed. They really were in an advanced state of refreshment. 'I hope you don't mind us popping round. We've been out for a lunch and have just been given the go-ahead on a new series we're making called *Boy Dominic*. Richard Todd's agreed to one of the three adult leads and we want you to take one of the others.'

Although they were sozzled, I knew them all well enough to know they weren't messing me about.

'Sounds wonderful,' I said. 'I've always liked Richard Todd. It'll be a pleasure to appear alongside him.'

'Yes, yes, he's great, old Richard,' Rodriguez, the casting lady, slurred. 'We've got a wonderful actress too. She plays Dominic's mother. A very beautiful, dark-haired lady. Actually, Brian, you'll have heard of her. She's called—'

'Hildegard Neil!' I shouted. 'You were going to say Hildegard Neil, weren't you?'

The three of them just stood there aghast.

'How the bloody hell did you know? We only offered it to her yesterday . . . *hic*.'

'Oh, honestly, it was just a wild guess,' I said, desperately trying not to appear like some kind of mystic stalker.

I bloody well knew it, though. The moment they started the sentence I *knew* they were going to say Hildegard Neil. It just clicked with what my former girlfriend had said. Don't ask me why, I have absolutely no idea. It's the strangest thing, don't you think?

Anyway, the offer duly arrived the following week and within a month I was on my way to Yorkshire Television in Leeds, and who was the first person I saw when I arrived at the studios, fresh off the train? Hildegard, of course.

'Oh hello,' she said. 'How are you, Brian? Long time no see.'

'Hello Hildegard!' I replied, battling to remain as cool, calm and collected as possible. 'How lovely to see you again.'

'Yes, you too,' said the radiant Ms Neil. And, my word, she was just that.

'Have you seen the script?' she said, in an almost haughty manner. 'It's very good, isn't it? I think this is going to be an excellent series.'

It was all very formal and a little bit uncomfortable from where I was standing, but at least it seemed like we'd be able to start with a clean slate. She'd obviously wiped me from her memory, which I have to admit upset me ever so slightly. *Never mind*, I thought, *perhaps we can still become friends?*

Rehearsals for *Boy Dominic* took place in Shepherd's Bush, and once we'd started it didn't take me long to discover that Hildegard lived but a mile or so away from me in Twickenham. She still had no car at the time and so I gallantly offered to give her another lift, each morning into rehearsals. Was there an ulterior motive hidden within my chivalry? Well, yes, of course there bloody was. I was potty about her. But I assure you that my intentions were still halfway to being honourable in that I simply wanted to be *with* Hildegard. I wanted to be in her presence. Does that make sense to any of you?

So I duly began collecting Hildegard from her flat in Twickenham and driving her and myself to rehearsals each morning. And what a way to begin a day! Each and every morning I was greeted by a smile that would soften even the most dedicated and hardened curmudgeon, and it was all wrapped up in a body that would make a bloody eunuch grow his bollocks back. I'll tell you now, I – WAS – IN – HEAVEN! Rejoice!

This was the start of what very soon became a fulfilling and quite mesmerizing friendship. I also drove Hildegard home, you see, and so we had oodles of time together. And we left no subject unturned, let me tell you. That said, we did gravitate towards the classics somewhat, which is where our conversations usually ended up after not very long. It was the big thing we both had in common. This was intoxicating, though, melding our two brains together.

Hildegard used to humour me when I started talking about boxing and judo and the like. During one journey, I remember telling her all about Rocky Marciano. I must have gone on for at least an hour, and then, when I eventually stopped, she just looked at me and said, 'You're very primitive, aren't you, Brian?'

'Yes, I suppose I am really,' I said.

'There is actually great subtlety and imagination to be found in the primitive,' she continued. 'You yourself are primitive, but you also have a great love of what is primitive.'

And so began one of the most interesting conversations I think I've ever had. We discussed that people in general are primitive. Forget the Wild Man of Borneo and just look at people today. They've got metal in their stomachs and through their ears and their bloody penises. They've got jewellery everywhere. And we all wear bloody make-up for heaven's sake. You see, the primitive will always come out in people. It's very healthy!

These journeys to and from rehearsals were, while they lasted, the highlight of my life. They were what I lived for. It was still a purely platonic relationship at this time, and it was totally natural. Sometimes there was silence, which was

Yours truly as the WILD Reuben Starkadder growling at his cousin Flora Poste (played by the gifted Sarah Badel) in the BBC's 1968 production of *Cold Comfort Farm*.

When I first met Hildegard she struck me as pensive, thoughtful and startlingly beautiful.

Filming *Double Agent* for ITV Playhouse with Hildegard
in 1968. Once she'd put me in my place, we got along famously.
(Bernard Archard is the chap on the left.)

I met Hildegard again in 1974 on the set of the series
Boy Dominic. The entire cast and crew were wondering
when we were going to get together.

Our daughter, Rosalind, aged two.

Hildegard and I got married in 1976 and,
four decades later, she still hasn't managed to divorce me,
poison me or lose me in a forest somewhere.

Prince Vultan holding the fabled ice jewel of Frigia! *Flash Gordon* is now a cult classic.

With Chaim Topol, who played Dr Zarkov.

Max von Sydow, also known as Ming the Merciless, with the beautiful Ornella Muti, who played Princess Aura.

Rosalind, aged fourteen.

Henry V at the RSC.
I'm playing the Duke
of Exeter, while my
old friend Kenneth
Branagh plays
the king.

Dad at the Japanese
reception for *Henry V*,
at home amongst all
the dignitaries.

Playing Spiro in the
strangely ill-fated *My Family
and Other Animals*.

Sitting on young
Max Beesley's lap on the
set of *Tom Jones*.

As I've often
said to the
Prime Minister,
'GORDON'S
ALIIIIVE!'

The effects of climbing without oxygen.

The Khumbu icefall, or the
White Dragon as it is more
poetically known.

A Sherpa child,
praying to us for help.

Always follow your dreams. Mine have taken me from
a small mining town in South Yorkshire to some of the
remotest places on Earth. What's next? Mars!

fine, and then I'd talk her head off or she'd talk my head off. We just seemed to spark off each other. Visually, I was spoiled rotten on a daily basis. Not only has Hildegard always been extremely attractive, but she also has the most astonishing sense of style, and every time I arrived to pick her up she would leave her flat wearing something stunning; all bought from a shop called the Richmond Bazaar, so I later found out. Do you know, I sometimes had difficulty breathing; such was my love for this South African queen. That had never happened to me before. Looking back, it was easier taking a breath on Everest than it sometimes was on those journeys.

When rehearsals finished, we all moved back up to Leeds to begin filming. There were to be thirteen episodes in all and the first director assigned to the series was a chap named John Davies, who a year or two later would direct me in a marvellous episode of *Tales of the Unexpected*. Do you remember it? It was called 'Lamb to the Slaughter' and has to be the most perfect of all mystery stories. A policeman announces to his wife that he's leaving her, after which she hits him over the head with a frozen leg of lamb, killing him stone dead. Poor bastard! Thinking on her feet, she then calls his colleagues at the station claiming that she found him dead after returning from the shops. I played the inspector, by the way. Then, whilst they speculate over who and what killed the poor man, she invites them all to stay for a roast lamb dinner, so we all eat the murder weapon. Perfect! Anyway, John directed that. He was a wonderful tall gangly fellow.

Boy Dominic was a very enjoyable series to work on. For those of you who've never seen it, here's a quick synopsis. A merchant ship is wrecked off the North African coast and its owner, Charles Bulman (Richard Todd), is believed to have perished. Subsequently, Bulman's wife Emma (Hildegard) and her twelve-year-old son Dominic are left destitute in London. Forced to sell the family home, they travel to Yorkshire, where they eventually open a guest house with me, the kind-hearted, if frequently inebriated, William Woodcock. Unbeknown to Emma and Dominic, Bulman is still alive, and while they struggle to make ends meet living with me, he tries to find a way back to them, enduring slavery, villainous bandits, musket fights and all manner of tropical adventures.

But, fabulous story aside, *Boy Dominic* was enjoyable to work on for several reasons. For starters I was with Hildegard, of course, but in addition we had scripts written by Penelope Lively, who went on to win the Booker Prize, and we had guest actors like Julian Glover and Maxine Audley – big, big names. But the icing on the cake, for me at least, is that the series was being produced by Terence Williams, who had directed me on *Z Cars* for a time. What a warm and wonderful atmosphere *Boy Dominic* had. Bloody good series too!

During all this time, I had never once enquired about Hildegard's private life. Our relationship was still platonic and I felt that asking her whether she was married or had a boyfriend would almost be a declaration of intent. And then what if she rejected me? I was desperate to make a move – to let her know just how much I loved her – but there was too much at stake. I could just about stand not being able to hold and kiss Hildegard, but not being able to talk to her? That particular scenario was downright apocalyptic. I did feel that she was warming to me, but certainly not enough for the relationship to move in my desired direction. I thought she found some of what I said tiresome, you see. Zoroastrianism and the Buddha were subjects that fascinated me, but I have to admit that I probably did go on a bit. She must have considered me a dreadful bore, I was sure of it.

So the more I thought about it, the more I convinced myself that Hildegard could, and would, never love me as I did her. Paranoia had set in, and a paranoid Brian is not a happy Brian!

Although she is three years younger than I am, Hildegard has always had a mature head on her shoulders. She is also terribly perceptive and can spot a dilemma at a thousand paces.

'Why have you never asked me about my love life, Brian?' she enquired in a break during filming one day. 'Aren't you interested?'

'Erm, well,' I stuttered. 'I, erm, yes, I am interested. Probably should have asked before. Anyway, erm . . .'

I rambled on like that for ages. Hildegard just sat there and laughed. It turned out Hildegard was married – but unhappily so – to a man named John. They got on OK as friends but the marriage itself was dead. To me, this was almost like a licence to come clean. I was still uncertain as to whether she actually fancied me, but I'd reached the point where I had to say something. I was desperate to tell her that I loved her. It was all I wanted to do!

A few days later, I was pulling into the car park at Yorkshire Television when I saw Hildegard. *Right*, I thought, *this is it. Come on, Blessed. Make her yours. MAKE HER YOURS!* I got out of my car and walked over to her.

'Excuse me, Hildegard,' I began, a little too formally perhaps. 'I wanted to . . . I wanted to . . . Erm . . .'

I didn't know what to say. Everything had gone: my mettle, my confidence, everything!

'I wanted to ask how you are,' I finally whispered.

So ensued a vacuous conversation that went nowhere. *Don't mess this up, Blessed*, I said to myself. *What's the matter with you?* Anyway, eventually I managed to pull myself together – and spoke from the heart.

'I went to see my dad two weeks ago. I don't see him often enough and he's only twenty miles from here. I don't confide in him enough. He's a wise, delightful fellow. Anyway, while I was down there, I informed him that I'd found the woman of my dreams. The woman I want to spend the rest of my life with.'

Hildegard looked genuinely quite surprised.

'Have you really, Brian?'

'Actually, you know her. You know her quite well, I think. She is also an actress.'

This obviously threw her a bit. She didn't like it at all.

'Who is it, Brian, if you don't mind me asking?'

I paused for a moment and stared at my feet. *This is it, Blessed*, I thought. *Come on, son. See it through!* 'It's you, of course!'

'What?' she muttered. 'What?'

Hildegard then moved towards me.

'No, no. Please don't,' I said. 'Please stay where you are. Sleep on it, OK? Think about it over the weekend and we'll talk again on Monday.'

Then we both started laughing, held hands and walked into the studio.

Anyway, the following week we were filming in Masham in North Yorkshire, home to the famous Theakstons and Black Sheep breweries. Hildegard and I barely spoke when we met that morning; neither of us daring to mention the conversation we'd had the previous Friday.

Not being needed for filming that day, I took myself off for a walk on the moors, where I watched all the Gloster Javelins flying in and out of nearby RAF Leeming. Once again, I had to try and find my courage!

When I returned to the hotel, I went straight to Hildegard's room and knocked on her door. The door opened and there she stood, wearing an emerald-green dress and looking more beautiful than I had ever seen her before. What I did next was quite possibly the bravest thing I have ever done in my life — and I've climbed mountains, done forty-six parachute jumps, and even worked with Sooty, for heaven's sake.

'I have missed you, Hildegard,' I said. 'I have missed you so very much.'

As the last word left my mouth, I saw her smile at me, a

smile that melted my very being. I was SO in love with this woman. I then leant forward and kissed her very gently on the lips.

'Let's go out for dinner,' I said. 'Come on.'

I took her by the hand and drove us to the Forum Hotel in nearby Harrogate. I remember I ordered a bloody great steak with greens and roast potatoes, my favourite meal. Hildegard ordered something equally enormous – yet do you know, neither of us could eat even a single mouthful. We just drank coffee. They knew us at the hotel and had gone to great lengths in preparing this wonderful meal, yet to us it was inedible. Eventually, the chef and the head waiter came to the table.

'Is there anything wrong with the food, Mr Blessed?' one of them asked.

I just looked at them both, half in a daze.

'We're too in love to eat,' I whispered. 'We can't eat.'

The chef and the head waiter nodded in understanding.

With that, I looked back at Hildegard and we stared at each other for what seemed like hours. Our lives had become entwined. We were now one.

We went back to the hotel that night and just held each other. For the first time in my life, I experienced total oneness with another human being. It was absolute perfection. I've never known perfection like it. I'd known one or two women in my time – not that many (I've never been a womanizer) – but this was perfection beyond my wildest dreams.

Do you know, I'm actually in tears myself writing this; such beautiful, cherished memories. Hildegard Neil was and still is my reason for living.

I actually found out later that the entire cast and crew of *Boy Dominic* had been wondering when we were going to get together, right from day one apparently. Everyone in the world knew that it was only a matter of time, except me.

'Why doesn't he just kiss her and get it over with?' they'd asked.

Now we were together, I was desperate to get over to South Africa. I wanted to do things properly, meet her family and friends. Luckily, Hildegard was about to go on tour there. I had an advert to make in America, but we agreed I would join her the moment I'd finished.

When I met Hildegard at Johannesburg airport, I immediately began to notice a transformation in her.

'Bri, Bri, Bri!' she shouted, while wearing the most beautiful dress.

She didn't change personality exactly: she became more herself. You see, in England she was always acting; always having to conduct herself with a certain dignity and stillness, and that obviously wasn't the real her. But in South Africa that had gone. She was free of the mask she'd been wearing for so long.

I watched her with children for the first time and was fascinated. It was as though her hips had opened up. She would pick up a Zulu baby on one hip and a five-year-old Zulu boy on the other, and she would hold them and walk around and play with them. She spoke Afrikaans perfectly, and she also spoke Zulu and Ndebele. I saw this white African. I saw Cleopatra the Queen. Amazing!

She showed me things; taught me things. She took me to a kraal in KwaZulu. Not one of the commercial ones, but a *real* one. I saw dancing like I'd never seen before. Zulu women leapt over our heads, their bodies gyrating frenziedly yet perfectly in time to the music; all except for their bellies, that is. The whole body moved but the belly. It was fascinating!

Here she was, at home with the Africans. We'd sit in Kruger National Park watching the sun set, a great orange ball that disappeared so rapidly, and then she'd wake at four o'clock in the morning so she could watch it rise again. Everything about Hildegard broadened: her voice, her speech, her confidence, her culture, her entire personality. She was a new woman and yet the same woman I had fallen deeply in love with. For me, it was a total African experience. I felt drumbeats, I felt sun, I felt an entire continent. It was staggering.

Eventually, we travelled up to Cape Town, where we were to meet her family. Her parents picked us up from the airport and from the moment I met them, all I felt was love. Her mother, her father and her two brothers quite literally showered me with affection and kindness. I might be getting a bit soppy now, but I honestly couldn't give a fig. I was having the time of my life with quite possibly the happiest family on earth, and I was accepted by them! There was no bitching and no sniping; just fun, happiness and love.

The day after we arrived, Hildegard took me to a place she'd often talked about called Fish Hoek. She'd always said that it was her favourite place on earth – a beach town on the Cape Peninsula – and that one day she'd like to take me there. And I wasn't disappointed. The beach was stunning, and I couldn't wait to get in the sea. We frolicked together, kissing and holding one another, and all the Africans watched. They could tell we were desperately in love. We then walked hand in hand the length of the entire beach, which seemed to go on for miles and miles. I'd never known such happiness. Such bliss!

Every other day, I'd climb Table Mountain, which is a flat-topped mountain near Cape Town; about 3,500 feet. I did all these different routes, and there were pythons up there, and cobras and so forth. And I went round the crags and up, before coming down by cable car. I did Africa Face, which is the front face of Table Mountain. Deadly!

One day, Hildegard and I climbed the famous Nursery

Buttress route on Table Mountain. Breathtaking! Then, about halfway up, I heard somebody shouting for help. I told Hildegard what I'd heard and went off to see if I could find where they were. I only had a small rope with me, but I had to do something.

'Stay where you are,' I shouted. 'I'll come and get you. Keep shouting!'

'Help, help, help,' they cried again.

I got to where the cries were coming from – and came face to face with a bloody great King Baboon! It wasn't a human being, it was a baboon.

'Hyyyelp, hyyyelp, hyyyelp,' it cried.

In addition to feeling like a tit for mistaking a baboon for a climber in distress, I was in a precarious position. HE – WAS – ENORMOUS! And he didn't know what to think of me. I just watched him eye me up and down, but I could almost tell what he was thinking. 'This is a strange bloody ape!' To him, I must have looked like a gorilla or something, so he was baffled. I decided to make conversation.

'Hello,' I said. 'I've just come to help you. I heard somebody shouting so decided to investigate. I mean you no harm.'

He was obviously mystified, and as I carried on talking he began to move away, very, very slowly. *That must be some kind of record*, I thought. *I've bored the arse off a baboon in under a minute.*

Seriously, though, I've come into contact with all manner of apes over the years, usually at very close quarters, and have never, ever been attacked by one – never in my life. They like me, you see. They think I'm one of them. We're back to the primitive thing!

Looking back, it was like a dream, my first visit to South Africa. It was a truly magical world, it really was. Almost mythical, if that makes sense. Not quite real. It was as if I was in the 1950s – always a happy time for me.

I remember one of Hildegard's brothers, Carl, was a big fan of Rugby Union. One day, he said to me, 'Brian, who do you think is the greatest rugby player of all time?'

'Well,' I said. 'It could be Meads, Colin Meads, or then again Gareth Edwards. Yes, I'd go for either Meads or Edwards.'

'No, you're wrong, Brian,' said Carl. 'The greatest player of all time is Frik du Preez.'

'OK, Carl,' I said, 'I shan't oppose you on this. Let's go for Frik de Preez.'

Rugby was Carl's life, so I thought it best to go with the flow on this occasion. He knew more than me! Anyway, about a week later, Hildegard and I were back in Johannesburg for a few days and I was in the gymnasium which was underneath her flat. Now, at the time I could bench-press over 400 pounds, even at altitude. I was a strong lad! So I was in the gymnasium, and it was a lovely place, full of mod-cons and masseurs and stuff, when in walked this grey-haired chap who looked about my age. He was a bit taller than me, about six foot, and he had big shoulders and veins like hosepipes sticking out of his arms. They put 1,700 pounds on his shoulders and he squatted a dozen times with it. The bar was almost bent in bloody half, and he's squatting up and down with it like a flaming kangaroo! I went over to him.

'Excuse me,' I said. 'I have never seen anything like that before in all my life. I have never seen a human being do that. Who are you?'

'My name is Frik du Preez,' came the reply.

'Really?' I said. 'So you're Frik du Preez. Well, according to my friend Carl you're the greatest rugby player the world has ever seen.'

'Carl's a bright man,' he said. 'And what do you think, my friend?'

'Exactly the same as Carl,' I replied, and with that I shook his hand and cleared off.

A few years later, I was talking with the legendary Gareth Edwards and I asked him about Frik du Preez.

'Bloody hell, Brian! Whenever I found out that I was going to have to play against Frik du Preez, I didn't sleep for a bloody month. Five men couldn't hold him down. He was a monster! He could run a hundred metres in ten seconds and he could jump higher than anybody. He's a friend of mine now and the greatest rugby player ever.'

Suddenly, it made sense. So there you are: Frik du Preez.

Anyway, let's finish this chapter off and move on, shall we?

So after a couple of weeks of this amazing dream holiday in South Africa, I went back to the UK. I had to get back for a job, but if truth be known I also wanted to sort out a flat for myself and Hildegard, which is precisely what I did. I wanted us to have a new home that was our own. She had another month out there, and so by the time I picked her up at the airport I'd already rented what would become our very first home together in Twickenham. And from then on, it's all been an absolute dream. For me, anyway! Hildegard became pregnant with our delightful daughter Rosalind, very quickly, and we became a small but perfectly formed family living in our ark with hundreds of animals.

We got married in 1976; and, the best part of four decades on, Hildegard still hasn't managed to divorce me, poison me or lose me in a forest somewhere. And, believe me, I've often given her reason to, what with climbing up mountains every five minutes, disappearing off to the North Pole for months on end and subjecting my body to the rigours of space training in Moscow.

Blessed indeed are the romantics, but most of all, blessed is my wife: my beautiful, talented and incredibly patient Hildegard.

7

GORDON'S ALIVE!

Before I start this chapter, I must ask you a question: have you seen the film *Flash Gordon*?

If you haven't, I strongly suggest that you pop off and watch it now before continuing. In fact, I must insist. You see, if you haven't seen the film, you won't understand a flaming word of it, love. Not a word. All the jokes will be lost on you. It'd be like me turning up for a rehearsal without having read the script, or climbing a mountain without any boots. Pointless! Trust me: you'll thank me for it afterwards.

OK? All ready?

I have to say that my childhood was marvellous, and although it took place during the war years, they were, to me at least, very exciting years. When it came to entertainment, radio – or, as we then called it, the wireless – was where I cut my teeth. We owned various models over the years: crystal sets and those big wooden Bush things. You could hide a small child in some of them. But with regard to output we were really quite spoiled, and the BBC in particular served us marvellously. I was intoxicated from about the age of three, addicted to it all. But the setting itself – at home with my parents – made it even more special; completely idyllic. Allow me to set the scene.

Early evening before tea (or dinner to you posh buggers),

after my dad had arrived home from the mine, the radio would be switched on and we'd all sit down and wait for it to warm up. The tablecloth would have been freshly laid, and the huge black kettle would be resting over the blazing fire. Waiting for the wireless to warm up was an event in itself, as it could take anything from one to about three minutes. I remember staring at it, full of expectation. What delights would it offer us tonight?

Early evening was always a time of great joy in our house. You see, my dad arriving home free from injury always put my mother at ease, and she could truly relax and enjoy what remained of the day. And let me tell you, that relief was palpable, even to a three-year-old. Every working day, roughly ten minutes before my dad was due home, my mother and I would take it in turns to pop our heads round the front door, silently praying that the reassuring and familiar silhouette of his person would appear on the dimly lit cobbles. Anyway, there we all were, safe, smiling and sitting round our radio.

The news was usually first up, after which there'd be all kinds of magnificent programmes: *Dick Barton – Special Agent*; Paul Temple and *Saturday Night Theatre*. *Saturday Night Theatre* was a favourite of mine as it produced things like H. G. Wells's *The War of the Worlds*. My God, I remember listening to that, totally transfixed and absolutely terrified! It was all so wonderfully real. I was sure we were all goners. Even when the Martians began to die, I wasn't convinced we were safe. *Perhaps there are more of them? Who will they send next?* I wasn't aware of it at the time, of course, but this was my introduction to science fiction and, I'll tell you what, it swelled my imagination like you would not believe. It had a profound effect on me and has, as you will soon discover, provided me with one of my favourite roles.

We had, nearby to where I lived in Probert Avenue, a disused railway embankment that my friends and I used as a playground. Every Saturday it was compulsory for us all to go there after we had visited the Empire Picture House. There we'd watch the Gaumont-British News followed by an episode of *Flash Gordon*. Magical!

For the benefit of those who are not in the know (or those under the age of seventy-five), *Flash Gordon* first hit the big screens way back in the early 1930s, in a self-titled film serial made by Universal Pictures. At the time, it was the most expensive film serial ever made, costing a rumoured $1 million. A fortune in those days! It wasn't some kind of cheap rubbish. Everything about it oozed quality: the sets, the costumes, the special effects. They'd look ridiculous today, but back then we were all amazed by them.

A man called Buster Crabbe played Flash. He, among many other things, was an Olympic swimmer and had won the Olympic gold medal for freestyle swimming back in 1932. He had a fabulous personality and a slight touch of Laurence Olivier about him – brooding eyes and a rich tenor voice. The similarities didn't stop there, however, as Crabbe was also a very good actor, extremely believable. Whenever he got into trouble on *Flash Gordon* he almost wept as he struggled, and we felt every wound and blow. Such effort! Such talent! As children we were gobsmacked.

I remember that first there'd be *Tom & Jerry*, then the news, and then, at last, it was time. The screen would go black, with only tiny shards of light illuminating the vast auditorium. Then suddenly, out of nowhere, came the music, from Franz Liszt's *Les Preludes*: *Dum – Dum – Duuuum – dum dum dum dum dum Duuuum*! Evoking tension and danger in spades, the opening titles always put the fear of God into us. And then, as the music played on, you would see a rocket ship going round and round this great mountain. *Voom, voom, voom*. But there was something sinister about this rocket, because this was from Ming's fleet. The Imperial Fleet! After this, you went straight into the episode.

There were several series made, I think, including *Flash Gordon Space Soldiers*, *Flash Gordon's Trip to Mars* and *Flash Gordon Conquers the Universe*, and each episode had a hugely evocative title, something that was meant to get a seven-year-old's imagination racing, not to mention their heart. I even remember a few of them. How about that? There was 'Tunnel of Terror', 'The Destroying Ray', 'Shattering Doom', 'Fighting the Fire Dragon' and 'The Living Dead'.

I remember the 'Destroying Ray' episode vividly, because in it Ming and his scientists put the Destroying Ray on Dr Zarkov. He's chained to a chair and ever so slowly the ray approaches his face, threatening to burn him alive. All of a sudden, Flash enters the arena and starts to unchain him — only for the ray to envelope him as well as Zarkov. There's no escape! The ray is now upon them and they're about to be burned alive. They're going to die, THEY'RE GOING TO DIE! And that was the end of the episode. That was it. It left us all completely terrified. Naturally, we were hooked.

But what really sealed the deal for us boys in terms of terror was the constant groaning sound which seemed to loom in the background of each and every episode. You see, the planet Mongo had noise in its atmosphere, a horribly threatening sound which was meant to spell just one thing — imminent death! What memories! But even though the atmospheric noise haunted us a great deal, we were galvanized by this fantastic superhero. A superhero, by the way, without superhuman powers. He was one of us.

Week after week he got into terrible scrapes, and every time we'd sit there thinking, *He can't get out of this, surely he's going to die?* After which we'd spend all the following week debating how he might escape and save himself. 'Couldn't he wrestle a ray gun from one of the guards? Perhaps Prince Barin might cut him loose before the dragon eats him?' Each week a new and more exciting cliffhanger.

When we eventually left the cinema, imaginations firing

off like jet engines, we always headed straight for the disused railway embankment in order to play the whole thing out again. Once there, I would immediately become Vultan. I *wanted* to be Vultan. Everyone else played different parts – Ming, Prince Barin and Zarkov, and so on – but I was always Vultan. I completely lost control when this happened. You see, because I believed I was Vultan (and I bloody did!), I thought nothing at all of leaping off disused coal trailers and suchlike. I also wanted to impress the leader of our gang, a wonderful lad called Caldeon Williams.

'Follow me, Hawkmen. Watch this, Caldeon. DIIIIIIIIIIIIVE!'

THUD.

I smashed my back, scraped my legs till they were red raw, and twisted my right ankle so badly it turned dark blue. I just couldn't resist, though. I believed. I BELIEVED I COULD FLY!

In the end, my mother and our local doctor had to sit me down and try and persuade me that I couldn't fly and that I was actually nothing more than a simple mortal. I took no notice, of course. Me, mortal? As if. You see, as well as having a supercharged imagination, I was also outrageously daring. I'd do anything. Any bloody thing! Back then, we challenged each other to what we called 'dasties', or dares as they're called these days, and I was always the one willing to take on something dangerous. Or, as my mother would say, bloody barmy!

My poor mother and our doctor didn't stand a cat in hell's chance, really. They just had to carry on bandaging me up and applying iodine.

Although Vultan had been a part of me from about the age of seven, never in my wildest dreams did I think I'd ever play him. Good heavens, no. It was just a childhood fantasy. But then, in 1978, I found myself in the company of the celebrated film director Mike Hodges, a medium-sized chap who'd directed that most seminal of gangster films, *Get*

Carter. He had a ruddy face, not unlike a farmer's, and a huge and infectious grin.

'Brian,' he announced, 'I'm about to make a rather bold science-fiction film and I'd like you to be in it. Dino De Laurentiis is producing and it will be made at Brooklands, Elstree and various other venues. The film in question is *Flash Gordon* and the part I'd like you to play is Prince Vultan.'

'Jesus Christ, Mike,' I said, almost dying of excitement. 'I'd walk a million miles and eat a thousand bloody dinosaurs to play that part. This is too good to be true! You're not pulling my plonker, are you?'

'No, it's all real, Brian, I promise. No plonkers are being pulled, least of all yours. If you're interested in the part, we can arrange for you to meet Dino as soon as possible.'

A couple of days later, I was sitting with Mike in his office at Elstree when all of a sudden I heard this strange noise. It was human, or at least I thought it was, but it was guttural, like something you'd find in the Lost World. Then, as it came closer, I realized that whatever was approaching had a thick Italian accent. It could only be – DINO! Dino De Laurentiis, one of the most ruthless and feared film producers in the business. He was Italian, about sixty years of age at the time, and had been producing films since 1940 – anything from Ingmar Bergman to *King Kong*. In he walked then, like a diminutive, but nonetheless dangerous-looking Godfather, flanked by three enormous henchmen; all black suits and white faces. And you could see the bloody guns! In fact, all three of his henchmen were armed, and by the looks of things extremely dangerous. I'm not sure what they thought might happen to him. Get goosed by an extra, perhaps? Dino, on the other hand, simply carried a satchel full of cash – and I mean full! There must have been tens of thousands of pounds in there. Petty cash, probably.

He greeted me warmly, like a long-lost son.

'Who the hell are you and wada-you-want-a?'

'This is Brian Blessed, Dino,' said Mike pleadingly. 'The chap I told you about. I want him to play Prince Vultan.'

I'm not altogether sure what Dino said next. 'Bluuuuu-urgh,' or something.

Now, Dino wasn't sure I was right for this role; his argument being that there were so many big film stars around, why should they hire somebody who, well, wasn't one? He wanted a big name. The industry suffers with this, as do we actors. Always have. Producers want a safe bet, regardless of whether the actor is right for the part or not. So at the start of the process, Dino was against Mike hiring me, and I went away from that meeting feeling somewhat annoyed and dejected. Actually, no, I was bloody furious! I thought, *Give me a chance and I'll show you. I've been playing Vultan for over thirty years!*

Anyway, about a week later, I was invited to visit one of the sets they were building back at Elstree. I still had no idea whether I'd actually got the part or not. Mike said he'd been working on Dino, but I was still none the wiser.

When I arrived and walked into Mike's office, I couldn't help noticing that the walls were covered in huge blown-up pictures from the *Flash Gordon* comic strip, and every single one featured Vultan. I turned to Dino, who was glaring at me.

'See!' I boomed. 'It's me, it's bloody well me! A thick-set chap with a beard and bloody great wings. Me to a tee! Now, you don't want to die, do you, Dino? Because if you deny me this role, I promise you, you won't last till sodding lunch-time!'

Dino began to laugh.

'No, I don't want to die, Brian. You're right: he does look like you; which is why I can tell you now that you're playing Vultan. You'll get £30,000. Take it easy, kid [he called every-body kid], and I'll see you on set.'

From then on, Dino and I had this wonderful relation-ship. A very honest relationship, and at times slightly raucous and profane, but we always had enormous fun. What a character! He made some great films.

Apart from learning the lines, my first job on *Flash Gordon* was to make myself known to the wardrobe department, whose job it was to turn me into this huge flying Viking. I was still bench-pressing over 400 pounds at the time and doing a lot of judo, so was in great physical condition. Tremendous! Just right for Vultan.

I'd already had a bit of a set-to with Dino with regards to the costume. He wanted Vultan to carry a great sword, or maybe a gun, whereas I was against this.

'In terms of strength, Dino, Vultan should be the most powerful man in the film, and the best way to convey this is to have him fight with his bare hands, not with a gun or a huge sword. He should use only his fists, Dino!'

In the end we compromised and I carried a kind of club, which at one end was shaped like a beak. A pretty formidable weapon, as it turned out. So all through the film – apart from in one scene, which I'll come to later – you see me belting aliens with either my fists, like John Wayne, or with this enormous beaked club. Anyway, back to wardrobe.

After covering me from head to toe in brown make-up, they started putting the costume on. It was only once the wings were screwed in that I suddenly realized I couldn't sit down anywhere. It didn't matter what kind of chair I tried to back on to, it didn't work: the wings got in the way. In the end, they had to make me a perch! Vultan, King of the bloody Hawkmen, had to park his arse on a perch. How about that? The camera crew loved this, of course, and used to shout 'Pretty Polly, Pretty Polly' every time I 'perched'.

Sam Jones, the chap who played Flash, has come in for a lot of criticism over the years, and I'll tell you why I believe this to be unfair. You see, it's quite easy to cast Vultans (although I'm the best), or Ming the Mercilesses, but it's very, very hard to cast a Flash Gordon. Take Tom Cruise, for instance. His smile is perfect, and not many people have perfect smiles. Nevertheless, you can put a camera on him at a certain angle and he looks sinister. Now, with Sam Jones, you could put a camera on him from any angle and he looks pure. When Ming asks who he is and he replies, 'Flash Gordon, quarterback, New York Jets,' that's so wholesome and honest, and it completely confuses Ming, of course.

But I'll tell you something else about that boy, something that really impressed me. I remember coming in to film one day, only to find that everything had ground to a halt. The whole place was like a bloody morgue.

'What the hell's going on?' I asked Mike. 'Why aren't we filming?'

'It's Sam,' said Mike. 'He won't carry on. He won't film.'

Now Sam wasn't at all temperamental, so I was intrigued.

'What's the matter with him?' I asked.

'You go and ask him, Brian. I'm fed up,' said Mike.

So along I went to Sam's dressing room. 'What's the matter, Sam? Why won't you film?'

'Brian, there's a scene they want me to film where I walk up behind a guard and knock him out. But that's all wrong. Flash Gordon wouldn't do that. It's deceitful. He just wouldn't do it. You've seen the serials with Buster Crabbe, Brian. Flash Gordon wouldn't steal up on someone who couldn't defend themselves. He would only fight if it was fair.'

Well, I have to say that I was in complete agreement with young Mr Jones. Flash Gordon would not have hit somebody without them knowing.

'I'll tell you what,' I said. 'Just whistle at him. Then, when he turns round, hit the bugger!'

Sam smiled with relief and did just that.

There we go, job done. But I had to explain to Mike and Dino that what Sam had done was the right thing to do. That he was merely being respectful to the character. Mike seemed to get it, but Dino most certainly did not. To him it was all about the money. Typical bloody producer. To be fair, though, it is their job to be all about the money, God bless them.

So, as far as I'm concerned, Sam Jones was perfectly cast as Flash Gordon and did a marvellous job. When Mike and his team were ready to start filming the opening scenes, we all made our way down to Brooklands, where they had built one of the main sets. Ming's palace was the set in question, which is where most of the main characters in the film are introduced. Apparently, this had taken around ten weeks to build. Ginormous, it was!

In addition to the main characters and the crew, there were also around ten dwarfs shuffling about. I say shuffling because, given the costumes they had to wear, that's about all they could manage to do. The poor little buggers were totally concealed by fabric, and let me tell you, those costumes weighed a ton, at least as much as the man inside them. They could hardly breathe, let alone move.

Sympathetic to their predicament, I naturally set about having fun with them as they wheezed like brightly coloured asthmatic power balls. Rusty Goffe, who had played one of the Oompa-Loompas in the original Willy Wonka film, was there, as was the wonderful Kenny Baker, who played R2-D2 in *Star Wars*. Gave them hell, I did. I was a law unto myself, really. 'You alright under there?' I'd enquire, giving them a friendly kick up the arse. Poor buggers didn't have the oxygen to answer.

I remember filming the first take of my entrance as if it were yesterday. What was my line again? Ah yes . . .

'THE FABLED ICE JEWEL OF FRIGIA! WE SEIZED IT IN BATTLE FROM THE ROYAL PRINCE!'

I delivered it, but then, before I could go any further, old Dino piped up, like some cigar-chomping Italian bear.

'Aaah, that's just how I see it, kid. That's just how I see Vultan. That's great, kid. That's great!'

Now, people were terrified of Dino and his comments, and because they were terrified of him they'd already started making mistakes – but I didn't have that terror. In fact, I used to bollock him from arsehole to breakfast time. So when he interrupted the scene, I thought, *I'm not having this*, and I gave him what for.

'Get off the set, Dino! We can't fucking work because everyone's fucking scared of you, love. Fuck off. Fuck off, Dino!'

He found this hilarious.

'Hey kid! Don't you say-a fuck-off-a to-me-a. You cannot-a say-a fuck-off-a to-me-a!'

But I did, I said: 'Fuck off, Dino! You're putting everyone off. You're costing YOU money!'

That did it. 'Ah, okay, kid, I-a fuck-off-a.'

Once I'd got rid of Dino, it was time for my first close-up. The second assistant director, Terry Needham, was arranging the shot. He was a lovely Cockney chap with a wicked sense of humour.

'Alright then, Brian, we're ready for your close-up. Is there anything you need? Anything you'd like me to do?'

'Actually, love, yes there is,' I said. 'I'd like you to announce me to the cast and crew and tell them how great I am. Tell them that I am without doubt the finest actor the universe has ever seen and that I demand absolute silence. Would you tell them that, love? Would you?'

'Yes, of course, Brian.' He cleared his throat and turned to address the cast and crew.

'Now then, ladies and gentlemen, now then, let's 'av a bit of 'ush. We are about to film the first close-up of Mr Brian Blessed, otherwise known as Prince Vultan or, to some, as Pretty Polly. I can say without fear of contradiction that he is without doubt the greatest living actor the universe has ever known, so let's show a bit of respect. He's cost the producers a lot of money. Millions, some say, and we're very lucky to 'ave 'im. I want absolute quiet. Is that quite clear?'

Of course, there's the great Max von Sydow looking on, as well as Timothy Dalton. God knows what they must have thought. Terry turned back to me.

'Anything else you want, Brian, before we begin?'

'Yes, love, keep those fucking dwarfs out of my fucking eyeline!'

'Of course, Brian. Dwarfs, fuck off!' To which there followed a wheezy chorus of 'Pretty Polly, Pretty Polly!'

This became a running joke, and whenever I saw a dwarf I'd go absolutely berserk. To put it mildly, they suffered in their costumes, and it was a way of keeping their spirits up.

'I can see a dwarf, Terry! I can see a dwarf! Push him out of the way, love, push him out of the way!'

Even Dino got involved. He'd lean over one of them and growl, 'Who's in there? Who is it? Have you been upsetting my bird man?'

'Leave off! I can hardly breathe!'

All joking aside, it really must have been hell for those lads. Week after week without oxygen or daylight. It's not good for you. Next time you watch the film, just you have a look. Poor lads. We all became great chums!

Although there are many superb performances in *Flash Gordon*, for me, Max von Sydow as Ming the Merciless is simply sensational. I'd seen Max in all those marvellous Ingmar Bergman films, *The Seventh Seal* and *The Virgin Spring*; great films and a remarkable actor. I was incredibly honoured to be working with him.

Despite being an immense talent, Max could be a nervous soul, and I remember speaking to him shortly before they were due to film his entrance (entrances everywhere in this chapter!). A scene, incidentally, that for my money is one of the most dramatic character entrances ever committed to celluloid. Anyway, there I was, happily sitting on my perch shouting at the dwarfs, when all of a sudden I felt a tap on my shoulder.

'Hello, Brian,' Max said, in a brogue not too dissimilar to that of the late Clement Freud. 'You know, Brian, I still don't know how I'm going to play Ming. I always get like this. My first scene is due to start filming and I'm at a loss. What am I going to do, Brian?'

Talk about leaving it till the last minute! In roughly five minutes' time, he'd have to turn himself from Max von Sydow into Ming the Merciless, ruler of the bloody universe!

I took a good look at him. Ruler of the universe? He couldn't rule a small village in the state he was in. I had to think on my feet. Suddenly, I had a brainwave.

'Max,' I began, 'I remember seeing you in *The Quiller Memorandum* torturing George Segal.'

The Quiller Memorandum was a spy film from the mid-1960s. As well as Max and George Segal, it also starred Alec Guinness and was based on a marvellous book called *The Berlin Memorandum*. Max had played the chief baddie in the film, a character called Oktober, and I'd been impressed by his performance. Amazingly sinister!

'Max,' I continued, 'when George Segal woke up at the beginning of that scene, you leant over and began to interrogate him, but as you were doing this, you kept on cracking your fingers, which made the audience believe you were about to hurt him. A terrifying scene!

'Max, Ming the Merciless is basically a wizard, a terrifying wizard, and his power is in his hands. You can't harm him; he'll stop you in your tracks. There's your answer, Max, my old son: play Ming through your hands.'

'Oh my God, Brian, you're right. That's it. That's it! That is how I will play Ming. How can I ever thank you, Brian?'

'Don't you worry, old son, you can owe me one. A pleasure to be of service.'

And, sure enough, Max took my advice and played Ming

almost like an evil Fagin, always playing with and cracking his fingers. A brilliant performance. Best in the film – next to ME of course!

As I said, though, old Max was a nervous soul. Everything fazed him, everything – including women, which reminds me of another story. I'll bring Max back in in a minute, but first a bit of a preamble.

Anyone who's seen *Flash Gordon* will know that there's no shortage of pretty girls in the film. The set was overrun with them. Top of the pile, though, was the Italian actress Ornella Muti. What a stunner! Has to be one of the most beautiful women who ever drew breath, and a bloody good actress too. She played Ming's daughter, Princess Aura, and I remember Chaim Topol, who played Dr Zarkov, pretending to faint whenever he clapped eyes on her. 'There she is again, Brian. I can't stand it! What a beauty!'

In the film, Princess Aura had a pet called Fellini, which she used to pull around on a leash. I'm not sure what species Fellini was supposed to be, but he was played by a rather small chap called Deep Roy. What a marvellous name. DEEP ROY. Terrific! I'll never forget my mate Terry, the second unit director, announcing Deep Roy to the crew before he came out for a scene.

'We've got Deep Roy coming on set, ladies and gentlemen. That's right, you heard me correctly, Mr Deep Roy. He's a very big star so once again can we 'av a bit of 'ush please – thank you very much.'

From Terry's build-up, we thought we were going to see somebody at least seven foot tall, with muscles sticking out of their sodding ears. We were expecting Geronimo at the very least. And then on came Deep Roy, who, according to Wikiwotsit, is about four foot three.

'Hello,' he said.

'Hello, young man,' I replied.

'I'm not a dwarf, you know, or a midget.'

A little left-of-centre for an opening line, but I was game.

'Wouldn't matter if you were, love,' I replied, throwing my helmet at Kenny Baker. 'So, if you're not a dwarf or a midget, what are you?'

'I'm perfectly formed, that's what.'

I was about to ask how big his cock was when he was called on set. So it's still a mystery to this day. If you're reading, Deep, write in and let me know!

I'll tell you something, though, Deep was more than just a perfectly formed non-midget. He turned up to the studios in a white Rolls-Royce and apparently produced films or something. Worth a bloody fortune. Good for him! Anyway, this lucky little perfectly formed producer was playing Ornella Muti's pet. Think how many men would give their right arm to be on the end of that bloody leash!

We didn't do too badly on the good-looking actor front either, of course. In addition to my good self, we had Timothy Dalton, who played my rival Prince Barin. Tim's an incredibly handsome man and looked just like Errol Flynn in the film. A bit of rough compared to me, of course, but he definitely has something.

I've flown off, haven't I? I told you this would happen. Here, there and bloody everywhere. Anyway, in the midst of all this beauty there was one girl, apart from Ornella, who seemed to have caught everybody's eye. She played one of the Ardentian women and for the sake of this book will be referred to as Mary.

Now, I'm not normally a boob man, but in addition to her beautiful Renaissance shape, good old Mary had a pair of boobs which would have sent Isaac Newton himself into a spin. Seeing her sideways on was like watching a dead heat in a Zeppelin race. Every time Mary came on the set, conversations would immediately come to a halt and heads would swivel in her delectable direction. Well, a lot of the men's would. Not even old Dino had that kind of effect!

After a while, some of the girls playing the Ardentian women actually became quite friendly with me. This was a purely platonic love, you understand; I was a father figure, shall we say. Anyway, in between takes one day, one of these girls sidled up to my perch.

'Brian,' she whispered, looking round to make sure no one else could hear.

'Yes, my dear,' I said, swinging away quite merrily. 'What can I do for you?'

'You know Mary?'

'Yes!' I said. 'We all know Mary.'

'Well, the thing is, Brian, Mary's got a thing about you. She thinks you're lovely. She says she can see you as a cave-man, and that really turns her on. She wants to know if you'd like to meet her at lunch.'

Well, you could have knocked me off my perch with a feather! After all, it's not often old birds like me get offers like that. *What should I do?* I thought. *Hit her over the head with my beaked club and drag her off to my dressing room?* As soon as I'd caught my breath, I spoke.

'I can't, love,' I said. 'It'll take me at least an hour to get my bloody wings off. She'd have to unscrew them. Then there's the paint. I'm covered head to toe in brown bloody paint. She's all pale and beautiful. It'd be a disaster, love! What about Timothy Dalton? He looks like Errol Flynn!'

'Ooh no, she doesn't like him. He's far too handsome. She doesn't go for good-looking men. She likes rough men like you.'

I didn't know whether to kiss her on both cheeks or blast her into space. 'Rough men like me'? I'm not bloody rough. I'm gentle and sweet!

I thanked her for the offer but decided to decline the invitation. Right, time to bring in old Max! I told you he'd arrive eventually.

A few days after I was propositioned, I received another tap on the shoulder. I looked round and there was Max.

'Excuse me, Brian, there's a young woman in my bath-room.'

'Really, Max? Can't you just ask her to leave?'

'Well, not really, Brian. You see, she's in my bath.'

'You mean she's *having* a bath?'

'Yes, she's *having* a bath.'

'Naked?'

'Not a stitch, Brian. What am I going to do?'

Poor old Max. He was a very happily married man and so the sight of a nubile young lady in his bath must have played havoc with his anxieties.

'Brian, I don't know what I'm going to do,' he lugubri-ated. (Is 'lugubriated' a real word? I think it's rather splendid. Anyway, I'm sure you know what I mean.) 'Could you get rid of her for me, Brian? I don't know what to say to her, or where to look. It's making me feel ill, Brian, please go and talk to her.'

'Alright, love, leave it to me. You sit on my perch and I'll go and have a word with her. Sit down, love. There you go.'

Well, it appeared that Mary wasn't the only one who was after something 'a bit different'. According to the lady of the lake, she wanted to make love to Ming the Merciless, not Max von Sydow. She wanted the costume, the voice, the character – everything!

'I want him to ravish me!' she said. 'I love a baddie. I've never been ravished by an alien baddie before.'

'Nor are you likely to be,' I parried. 'Not a bloody chance. Look, he's just turned fifty and he has a wife and two sons. Now get yourself out and dried, and we'll say no more about it, OK, love?'

With that, I returned to Max and gave him the good news.

'All sorted, Max. Give her ten minutes and I promise she'll be out of your bath for good.'

'Oooh, Brian, I don't know how to thank you.'

'That's two you owe me now.'

Talking of Peter Wyngarde . . . (which I wasn't) he played Klytus in *Flash Gordon*, Ming's right-hand man, and was one of the biggest stars on TV in the late 1960s and early 1970s. He starred in all manner of shows such as *The Prisoner* and *The Saint* and suchlike, but he's probably best remembered for being the star of a wonderful show called *Jason King*. Bags of style and the most delightful voice you've ever heard. Great presence, too, and perfectly cast in the role of Klytus.

There is no doubt at all that the film had the most wonderful atmosphere to it. Best fun I've ever had as an actor. I know you hear it a lot in our business, 'Oh, we were just like a family . . .' Well, let me tell you now, most of that's nonsense. People say it because they feel they have to. *Flash Gordon* was different, though. For a start, there were no, what you might call, 'superstars' in the cast. To use a footballing analogy, we were all fairly mid-table. It genuinely didn't matter if you were a chippy, a boom boy, a runner or a member of the cast – everybody was treated the same. Even Dino!

One of the great joys during filming was the weekly lottery that we set up. Oh yes, *Flash Gordon* had its own lottery! There must have been at least 400 people attached to the film and each week we all put in a pound. So, if you won, you stood to pocket £400, which is about £2,000 in today's money.

I'll tell you who won more than once, though: Dino De Laurentiis. AND he took the money. I just couldn't believe it.

'Dino, you can't take it,' I said. 'You can't take the money. You're rich. Put it back, you thieving Italian shyster!'

'Why the hell should I, kid? It's my money. I won it fair and square. You drew my name out!'

And, with that, he waddled off, chuckling to himself. Cheeky sod!

I remember this as being one of the happiest times in my life. I was appearing in my biggest film to date and had the most beautiful family a man could ever wish for. At the time we were living in a delightful little place in Chobham, which is not too far from Elstree, called Primrose Cottage. Rosalind was about two-and-a-half years old and every night, while I was filming, Hildegard would bathe her in the kitchen sink. This meant she could see me – and I her – as soon as I walked through the door. But as opposed to a 'Hello Dad', or 'Look, Mum, Daddy's home,' Rosalind just looked at me each night and said, 'Evening, Vultan.' Unbelievable!

One of my favourite parts of *Flash Gordon* is where Flash, the Hawkmen and I make our attack on the War Rocket Ajax. That was a proper 'blood and thunder' battle. 'SECOND WAVE – DIIIIIIIIIIIIIIIIIIIIIVE!' Tremendous part of the film.

We did have one or two problems with the explosives, though. I remember during one scene Mike said to me, 'OK, Brian, there's going to be an explosion which will blow the door off. I want you to get down till you hear the bang, then stand up, look back at Sam and shout, "Flash, follow me," OK?'

Well, of course they put far too much bloody powder in the explosive and when I got up and turned round, there was a black Flash Gordon.

'Mike,' I said. 'I'm looking at a black Flash Gordon here, love. Black Gordon! That's not in the script, is it, love?'

The splendid actor John Hallam played Luro, my right-hand man. Then there was a guy called Ted Carroll, who played Biro, the Hawkman with the broken nose. Now, Ted wasn't really an actor, in fact as far as I know he used to be a Rugby League player and in his time had turned out for teams like Hunslet, as well as for England. He had a little pub up in Ilkley, so I've no idea how he came to be in the film.

Anyway, I always used to say to Ted, 'Keep close to me, love. If you keep close to me, you'll be in every shot. Here, you carry my whip.'

So he used to carry my trusty whip everywhere!

'I'll make you a bloody star, Ted,' I used to tell him. 'Bigger than Garbo!'

After the film came out on video, I think he played it on a loop in his pub. Lovely man.

Anyway, at one point during this huge battle, old Biro gets hit by a laser gun, after which Flash dives down on his Rocket Cycle to help him. Now, in the original script, Flash was supposed to say, 'Biro, are you alright?' to which Ted would reply something like, 'Yeah, I'll be fine.' But just before they were due to begin filming, I said to him, 'Now look Ted, as opposed to saying, "Yeah, I'll be fine," why don't you say, "Yeah, they just winged me"? That'll bring the house down!'

Poor old Ted almost pissed himself. 'I can't say that, Brian. Don't be ridiculous! It's not in the script.'

'Don't be ridiculous? DON'T BE RIDICULOUS? We're sitting here on bloody perches with four-foot wings screwed onto our backs, and you're telling me not to be ridiculous?'

'You've got a point there.'

Ted delivered my line in the end and everyone fell about laughing – and in the cinemas too! It worked perfectly, and in my opinion completely sums up the spirit of the film: a superb piece of 'tongue-in-cheek' family entertainment.

Just prior to us filming the attack on Ajax, we shot all the flying sequences. In films like *Superman* and suchlike, you only ever see one person flying – two at the very most. But in *Flash Gordon* we had hundreds. The skies were swarming with bloody Hawkmen! This wasn't computer-generated, by the way. All that was still several years away. This was all done the old-fashioned way, using wires, a blue screen and dozens of stunt artists!

First of all, we had to lie down on our fronts while the wires were attached to us. All at the same time, by the way. Unfortunately, because I was so bloody heavy I had to have an extra wire strapped round my privates. That tickled more than somewhat, I can tell you! After that was done, we were all hoisted up into the heavens in front of a huge blue screen. We must have looked like some kind of giant human nursery mobile. Ridiculous! But while all the other Hawkmen just had to hang there, I had to act! Acted my backside off, I did, delivering all these Henry V-type lines.

'Onward, my brave Hawkmen! Let this be known forever as Flash Gordon's Day!'

But there's no freedom up there, of course, and no luxuries such as lunch. When we wanted something to eat, they just lowered us down for five minutes and fed us a bit of bread and soup. Straight after that, we were back up.

The biggest problem the crew faced was getting all the wings to flap at the right time. You see, not only did we have wires attached to our shoulders (and, in my case, my privates), but we also had them attached to our wings. But for some reason, no matter how hard they tried, they couldn't get our wings to flap at the same time. Not *all* at the same time, you understand. I mean, they couldn't get each of our two wings to flap simultaneously. My left wing would be going like the bloody clappers while my right one was lying limp.

Then we had a problem with vomiting and fainting. Nosher Powell, who was a powerful stuntman, was the Hawkman in question. During one of our rare flights down to Mother Earth, Nosher – despite being told not to overdo it – had overindulged on the bread and soup one day. Then, ten minutes after being hoisted back up, I suddenly heard a groan from above.

'I feel sick. Gawd, I feel faint too. Gordon Bennett, I think I'm going to throw up. Bluuuaaaagh!'

'We've lost one, Mike,' I shouted. 'Nosher's gone.'

You'd never seen such a huge pile of puke in your life. I looked up and there he was, six foot five inches of Hawkman suspended thirty feet in the air, looking like the last of the pterodactyls. Poor old Terry Needham nearly had a heart attack.

'I told him not to overdo it on the bloody soup. Lower him down, somebody, then get some water into him and sit 'im on Brian's perch for a bit.'

Just then, old Dino wandered in. That was enough for me.

'Fuck off Dino!' I said. 'The Hawkmen are fainting, the wings aren't flapping and I've got a huge wire strapped to my bollocks. Every time you walk in, something goes wrong. Now fuck off!'

'Hey kid! You cannot-a talk-a to me like a-this. Remember, I am the producer!'

'Exactly, now fuck off, love!'

'The kid keeps telling me to fuck off! I love this kid. OK, kid, I fuck off.'

When it came to filming the actual battle on Ajax, we suffered all kinds of bloody disasters. It took about five days to get everything ready: the Hawkmen, the rocket, the explosives, the lights, Ming's soldiers, etc., and must have cost old Dino an absolute fortune. The first shot was me in flight, sending in Squadron 40 to attack.

'Squadron 40, DIIIIIIIIIIIIIIIIVE!'

Straight after which, they filmed my second line.

'Oh well, who wants to live forever? Ha ha ha ha ha! DIIIIIIIIIIIIIIIIVE!'

As soon as that was done, we got stuck into the fighting. Enormous fun!

Later on in the sequence, I'm carrying this gigantic bazooka gun made out of cardboard. Mike had persuaded me that Vultan had to have something more than a beaked club, as he was supposed to blow up doors and suchlike. 'Fair enough,' I said. It was a huge great bloody thing, though, and could have blown up an entire planet if it was real. And therein lay the problem. You see, in my mind, or in my imagination at least, that bazooka *was* real, and to compensate for the lack of sound, I started making all these bang noises with my mouth every time I pulled the trigger.

'There's a guard, BANG! There's another two, BANG, BANG!'

I'm not afraid to admit that I got completely carried away. For a few moments, I was back on the old railway embankment in Yorkshire, running round like a lunatic.

'BANG, BANG, BANG!'

After a while, a voice began cutting across my rampaging. 'Cut,' it said. 'Cut!'

At first, it didn't register. Then I heard it again, louder still.

'CUT, CUT, CUT!'

Finally, I woke up.

'FOR CHRIST'S SAKE, BRIAN, CUUUUUUUUT!'

Poor old Mike Hodges. He'd first shouted 'cut' about five minutes ago, at which point everyone else had downed fire-arms and agreed to a temporary armistice. Not me, however. I had continued the carnage; totally in character, apparently.

'Brian,' he sighed. 'WE put in the special effects, OK? For heaven's sake, no more bangs!'

My 'BANG's and overexuberance had ruined the entire shot.

'I'm so sorry, Mike, please forgive me. I got carried away!'

'Don't worry, Brian, it's a great outtake. OK, everyone, from the top.'

Alas, I'm afraid that the next shot went equally 'to pot', as when the last lot of Hawkmen duly dived at War Rocket Ajax they all missed their spot to land and ended up either slamming into the side of the rocket or flying over the top. Thing is, they took all of Ming's men with them. It was carnage! There were wires, helmets, wings and cardboard guns everywhere. Last man standing was me. There I was, on the wing of this enormous rocket, with nobody to fight.

'They've all buggered off, love,' I shouted to Mike. 'There's nobody for me to kill!'

Suddenly, I saw a hand fly up. It was one of Ming's guards who'd been knocked off the wing by a stray Hawkman.

'Half a mo, Brian. I'll be right with you. You can kill me if you like.'

'CUT!'

Another great scene, although with far fewer takes if memory serves, was Ming's death scene, where the spike at the front of Ajax goes straight through his stomach. Gruesome stuff! They filmed this on a Friday night and, because they were going to put in the sound effects later, they filmed it without any sound. I was behind the camera on my perch and all the dwarfs were there sitting at my feet. Lord knows what it must have looked like. Some kind of bizarre alien nest, probably. Anyway, unfortunately for Max, we were all in his eyeline, so as he's trying to pull this huge great spike out of his stomach and die the most horrible death imaginable, he's got ten dwarfs and the King of the Hawkmen sitting in front of him doing a running commentary.

'Oooh, oooooooh! That must be painful. What do you think, Rusty? That'd make you wince a bit?'

'Wouldn't it just, Brian? He's got green blood too. Fancy!'

'Poor old Mr Ming, he's not enjoying it, is he?'

'Come on, Max, put your back into it, love!'

And all through this, Max had to act out the death of the most evil man in the universe. Poor sod! In between cuts, he'd stare at us all, as if to say, 'If I really was Ming, I'd blast the lot of you into bloody space,' but he managed to keep his cool. When Mike eventually shouted 'Cut!' for the final time, Max got up off his knees – and chased us all out of the studio.

'Make sure you check the bath, love!' I shouted.

When the film eventually came out, we all had enormous expectations, as everybody was thrilled with the finished product. *Star Trek: The Motion Picture* had come out the previous year and had grossed over $100 million. Old Dino was chomping at the bit! Unfortunately, it didn't happen for *Flash*. It just about wiped its face as far as I know – it cost about £25 million to make and grossed about £27 million – but that was far from being considered a financial success.

It got marvellous write-ups and did extremely well in Europe, but for some reason it just didn't take off in America. Dino was always separate from Hollywood – from Paramount and all the other big American companies – and they never really accepted him. Perhaps that was it. Who knows?

I almost forgot the fantastic music. Now, in my opinion, the soundtrack to *Flash Gordon* is a work of absolute genius. Queen did one hell of a job and it should have won them an Oscar, or at the very least a BAFTA. No doubt about it. If you don't agree with me, go and kick yourself up the bloody arse. You're wrong!

My favourite part in the film is when Flash, Dale and Zarkov make their journey through space to the kingdom of Mongo. Soon after breaching the earth's atmosphere, the ship's boosters fall away, and for a moment silence reigns. Then, as our three heroes fall into a deep sleep, we hear two simple guitar chords, signalling the start of the main theme. I remember watching it for the first time. I'd never heard such an hypnotic piece of music, and it augments the scene perfectly. Go and have a listen now. It's called 'In the Space Capsule'.

Incidentally – you see, I told you I go back and forth all the bloody time – that American football fight towards the start was all ad-libbed, you know. Mike just told us to do what the bloody hell we liked.

'Your job's to try and sabotage the fight and mess it up for Ming's guards, OK?' he said.

'Fine, leave it to us!'

So while Ming's guards are all running round trying to get to grips with what Flash is doing, we're all tripping them up or, in my case, belting them over the head with a huge beaked club!

Anyway, what of *Flash Gordon*'s legacy? Well, thirty-five years on, it's become one of the most popular science-fiction films of all time − a cult classic, apparently − and far more popular than *Star Trek: The Motion Picture*. And it's a much better film, of course. Even in America, *Flash Gordon* is now enormously popular. I think it has a comic-strip quality and in my opinion it could never be bettered. For God's sake, don't remake it!

No matter where I go, someone will ask me to say, 'Gordon's alive!', which is undoubtedly my most famous line from the movie. I get out of the car when I'm going to the doctors: 'Say, "Gordon's alive!"' I'm walking down bloody Oxford Street: 'Say, "Gordon's alive!"' I go to talk about *Star Wars*: 'Say, "Gordon's alive!"'

In 2013, I attended the Metal Hammer Awards at the O2 Arena in London. They're like the Oscars for heavy-metal bands and I'd been invited along to collect the Metal Hammer Spirit of Hammer Award. How about that? I believe it's something they give out to non-musicians whom they believe encapsulate the spirit of heavy metal − which is me to a tee. Anyway, after being introduced, I walked out on stage and there before me were 20,000 people all shouting, 'Brian, Brian, Brian!' I'll tell you what, in all my born years I'd never experienced anything quite like it. When they eventually quietened down a bit, I raised my hands, took a deep breath and shouted, 'GORDON'S ALIVE!' − thus prompting a twenty-minute standing ovation. Try picking the bones out of that!

This simple line in a film script suddenly turned into this kind of powerful maxim after my friends Queen used it in their single 'Flash'. Ever since then, it has become ever more popular. It's almost like a battle cry for freedom. When people hear it, they cheer! Like in *Braveheart*, but an awful lot better.

I was halfway up Kilimanjaro once, taking some tourists trekking, when all of a sudden we came face to face with some Maasai. The moment they clapped eyes on me, one of them shouted, 'Aaaaah, it is you! Would you please say, "Gordon's alive"?'

So there I was, halfway up the highest free-standing mountain in Africa, and I'm shouting Gordon's a-fucking live! Could have caused a bloody avalanche of loose rocks or something!

About sixteen years ago, at the age of sixty-one, I became the oldest man on earth to reach the North Magnetic Pole on foot. Is there no end to my talents? Quite a bloody achievement, I can tell you – almost killed me. Anyway, as you get nearer to the Pole and the magnetic field starts to strengthen, all your hair stands on end and everything starts to vibrate. It's natural, when you think about it, but the experience itself is really quite bizarre.

When I was close to the Pole, I suddenly began to hear a rumbling sound. At first, I thought it was the magnetic field, but then it became louder and heavier. *Christ*, I thought, *I'm under attack!* A few seconds later, a couple of hundred yards away, this enormous Russian Typhoon submarine appeared, breaking straight through the ice. *Bugger me sideways*, I thought, *I'd better go and say hello*. So off I trotted. I got as close as I could without putting myself in danger and waited for someone to appear.

Five minutes later, there's a horde of Russians all patting me on the back. 'Is Mister Vultans, King of Hawkmens on *Flash Gordons*. You say, "Gordon's alive!"'

'GORDON'S ALIVE!' I boomed, very nearly taking us through the ice.

'You come onboard and say this again to comrades, *da*?'

'Of course, my old chum. Anything you say.'

'Hello comrades, "GORDON'S ALIVE!"'

After that, I sang them 'The Song of the Volga Boatmen', a traditional Russian folk song. They weren't expecting that, I can tell you. Anyway, I went down a storm. Bloody loved me, they did.

But there you go, you see: it doesn't matter where I am – up a mountain in Africa or at the North Magnetic Pole – if there are people and Brian Blessed, one question will be asked, and a reply duly boomed! People even record me doing it now on their phones.

'Hello Brian, could you shout, "Gordon's alive!" into this for me, please? My mates will go spare!'

'Of course, my old love. Into here? Ready? "GORDON'S ALIVE!"'

I've even been asked to record answer-machine messages for people in the street.

'I'm sorry, but Keith can't take your call at the moment. Please leave a message after the beep and remember – "GORDON'S ALIVE!"'

I went to Number 10 Downing Street a while ago for an event that was meant to encourage people to take part in expeditions. Ranulph Fiennes and David Hempleman-Adams were there, along with a few others. There were around thirty of us in all. I got there about half an hour early. I thought, *I don't want to miss this, love.* So towards the famous black door I skipped, wrestling with the police and calling them plebs along the way. 'You're all bleeding plebs, you are!' We had a right time together. Loads of fun. And loads of photographs.

Anyway, when I got there, I was told I had to wait outside. 'You're too early, I'm afraid. You can't come in until after the Prime Minister's here. Just wait out there.'

It was a nice enough day, so I went and sat on a windowsill opposite. Fifteen minutes later, the gates opened and David Cameron zooms up, just like Flash Gordon – or Ming, depending on where you sit. He got out of the car quick as a flash and was just walking into Number 10 when he froze and turned around.

'Is that you, Brian? What are you doing here?'

'Well, I've come for a meeting with all these explorers, Prime Minister.'

'Yes, of course you have, I'm so sorry.'

'Don't you mention it, me old love.'

'Brian, would you mind doing me a favour?'

'Ah, Prime Minister, I know what you're going to say!'

'Yes, would you mind?'

'No, of course not.'

'Oh, thank you. Ready, Brian? One, two, three . . .'

'GORDON'S ALIIIIIIVE!'

This is the Prime Minister of Great Britain. He wasn't finished though. There was one more request.

'I've got a cabinet meeting soon, Brian. Would you mind shouting it to them? That'll wake them up.'

So off I popped with my mate Dave to wake his minions up.

'GORDON'S ALIVE, YOU BUGGERS, WAKE UP!'

Anyway, that's enough of all that. We've still much to get through.

Onward, my brave Hawkmen!

8

THE SCOURGE OF THE ORIENT

Did you know that I'm actually quite big in the Far East? That's not a smutty euphemism, by the way. What were you thinking? No, there are in fact several reasons why I and the good people of Eastern Asia have bonded over the years. Our affair started as long ago as the 1970s, whilst I was trying to garner support for a documentary I wanted to make about George Mallory's ill-fated 1924 expedition to Mount Everest. I met several Sherpas, some of whom were in fact related to those who had accompanied Mallory's expedition, and between them they regaled me with a cornucopia of classic Himalayan legends and tales. Marvellous!

In 1991 we eventually got to make our film, *Galahad of Everest*, by which time I considered all Tibetans to be family. They still talk about that film over there – as they also do in China and Japan – and it has been the catalyst for some truly beautiful friendships, not least the one I share with the Dalai Lama.

Then you have good old *Flash Gordon* of course. They have marvellous taste for films in the Far East and *Flash* is still shown all over the continent on a regular basis. I've even attended the odd science-fiction event over there, and let me tell you they know their onions. They went bonkers for me – and I them. But the culture! Oh, don't get me started. I could go on for millennia. You should see my log cabin; it's chock-a-block with Asian artefacts.

But as opposed to rabbiting on about artefacts in my log cabin, why don't I tell you about two of my favourite Asian adventures? That would be far more exciting, wouldn't it? The first takes place in Japan, the second in Hong Kong, and between them they feature a cast that includes (in no particular order) Kenneth Branagh, my old dad, Princess Anne, a Yorkshire paint magnate, the Emperor and Empress of Japan and a bunch of VIP, penny-pinching Hooray Henrys.

Are you intrigued? Well, let me begin.

At the end of 1988, I appeared in the film *Henry V*, directed by my old friend and father figure, Kenneth Branagh. We'd already been friends for a number of years, Ken and I, and were basically reprising the roles we'd played together at the Royal Shakespeare Company about a year or two previously: Ken as Henry V, and me as the Duke of Exeter.

When Ken told me that he intended to make a film adaptation of *Henry V*, I was absolutely cock-a-hoop. Olivier's version was a work of undoubted genius, but at the time had nothing to compare itself to. No, it was definitely the right time for a new adaptation – a fresh approach.

But, despite my fervour for the film, I'm afraid that beneath all the enthusiasm lay the rather tragic actuality that it might never even go into production. It was all well and good coming up with an idea, but getting a film made in Britain in the late 1980s was nigh on bloody impossible, and throughout the decade the entire industry had been on the brink of extinction. The Americans still made films over here, like the Indiana Jones trilogy, and the studios themselves such as Pinewood and Shepperton had seldom been busier, but British films made by British production companies featuring British talent were very rare indeed. It was all the more tragic because the decade had started so well! There'd been *Chariots of Fire* in 1981, written by Colin 'Oh Fuck Off' Welland, the fellow I told you about earlier, and a year later there'd been *Gandhi*, of course. What a platform!

With films like that as a starting point, the 1980s should have become the best decade we'd ever had. Anyway, I'm digressing slightly.

Now, ever since I was a child, I've always been a great optimist. And I remember thinking to myself, *If anyone can pull this off, Branagh can. He has tenacity, great ability and immense courage.* And, sure enough, a few months later, he did it: he got the money, or at least enough to put the film into production.

And do you remember the cast he assembled? Wow! We had Paul Scofield, Derek Jacobi, Judi Dench, Ian Holm, ME, Richard Briers, Robbie Coltrane, Geraldine McEwan, Alec McCowen, Emma Thompson . . . There was great excitement surrounding the film. The biggest British-made film to be made in years, and with one of the finest casts ever assembled. It created a real buzz!

For the first couple of weeks or so, everything went marvellously. Rehearsals began in earnest and the production office was a hive of activity. It was all good stuff. *Well done, Ken*, I thought. Then, all of a sudden, a rumour started going round that they were about to pull the plug on the film. One of the backers had backed out, so to speak, and had left Ken in limbo. Anyway, there was nothing we actors could do about it, so we simply carried on and hoped for the best.

After another week or so of waiting, worrying and rehearsing, we were then told that a Yorkshire businessman might be interested in investing. *That's impossible*, I thought, *we all squeak when we walk and have short arms and long pockets!* Once again, I was on the wrong side of being right. A Yorkshire businessman *did* appear one day, and with a view to helping finance the film. If memory serves, he owned some paint factories. How Branagh had come to find this chap I've absolutely no idea, nor can I, for the life of me, figure out how he managed to talk him into becoming a potential investor on a Shakespearean film. The words 'Yorkshire', 'money', 'Shakespeare' and 'paint' were not known to mix well together.

This cove was our last hope – but he'd need convincing. He certainly wasn't going to just hand over the cash. Ken was worried.

'He's very hesitant,' commented the executive producer Stephen Evans to me. 'He hasn't heard of any of the cast, Brian. He's not even that keen on Shakespeare! How are we going to sell it to him? What if he says no?'

Anyway, when this fellow eventually arrived at the studios he was exactly how I'd imagined him to be: broad of frame, ruddy of face and quite obviously teeming with cash. A typical Yorkshireman, you might say! He was very charming, though, and instantly likeable. And, as far as I could make out, all was going well. Stephen had been showing this fellow round and introducing him to everybody. Eventually, they got to me, at which point I smiled, reached out my hand and readied myself to deliver the greeting.

'This is Brian Blessed,' started Stephen. 'He's going to be playing the Duke of Exeter.'

The emperor of emulsion took a step back.

'No!' he shouted. 'It can't be! Bloody Nora, it is. It's Fancy Smith! You played Fancy Smith in *Z Cars*!'

Stephen looked like he'd lost a quid and found a fiver. I shot him a quick glance as if to say, 'We're in here, love. This is our chance!'

'HELLO, MY FINE FELLOW!' I bellowed, before throwing a friendly but non-theatrical arm around him. 'Yes, I certainly did play Fancy Smith, in more than a hundred episodes. I'll tell you what, let's you and I get a cup of tea and I can tell you all about Victor Division. How is the paint world, by the way? Tartan paint still selling well?'

We must have spent a good two hours chatting, this chap and I. He told me all about his life and his business, and I told him all about *Z Cars* and the BBC; after which I began my appeal as to why he should invest in the film. And, as appeals go, it was first class.

'Kenneth Branagh's the biggest talent to have appeared on earth since Jesus Christ himself,' I began. A bold statement, perhaps, but these were desperate times. Branagh would have endorsed the description wholeheartedly, of course.

'He is currently attempting to resuscitate the British film industry almost single-handedly, and is but a few English pounds from realizing his ambition. It is a goal, a common goal; something that should be shared by each and every one of us.

'If we allow him to fail now, we allow the hopes and dreams of an entire nation to be cast into the abyss.' A little fanciful, perhaps, but he seemed to be enjoying it.

'We must not turn our backs on him, nor must we allow this once-great industry to die. It is our responsibility to come to the fore and bear arms.' Or, in his case, cash. 'Why? Because we have the opportunity! We must embrace both the talent and the ambition. I beg you, sir, collaborate with this man. Say yes to the film, and the dream can be completed!'

And the award for best pleader goes to . . . Brian Blessed. Do you know, he stumped up the money there and then – and all in cash! I've no idea how much, but he brought in two bloody suitcases from his car, both full! He only dealt in cash, apparently. It wasn't all down to Fancy Smith, of course. Stephen Evans spent several hours with him after I'd finished rabbiting, but once he'd seen somebody he recognized – somebody he was familiar with – that put him at ease a bit. It also made him feel better about parting with his money. Let's just say Fancy Smith oiled the wheels.

I have no idea whether this chap is still alive or not, but it's difficult to put into words just how important his investment was. After all, he saved what is now widely considered to be one of the greatest Shakespearean film adaptations of all time – a piece of genius. Even the great Marlon Brando said it was his favourite film. Isn't it funny how things turn out? Anyway, good for him!

When the film eventually came out, it was a great success and won awards all over the world. The critics adored it, as did the public. Everything about *Henry V* worked: the music, the costumes, the cinematography. It was all first class. But it also had a very *organic* feel to it. It was all very natural. Take the battle of Agincourt, for instance. People who've seen the film always assume that it was shot in France. Why? Well, because to them it feels genuine. If truth be known, the battle of Agincourt was filmed in a field behind some council houses in the south of England, but therein lies the beauty of Kenneth Branagh's *Henry V*; the secret of its success. This realism wasn't achieved using millions of pounds; it was achieved using galaxies full of talent and imagination. The direction of Agincourt oozes virtuosity, as does every single costume, set and performance. Even the horses were wonderful!

So there we are. We've made *Henry V* and it's doing great business all over the world.

Another of the executive producers on *Henry V* was a chap called Gary Kurtz, who was the original producer of the first two *Star Wars* films. He was helping to arrange one or two of the premieres for *Henry V* and one day asked me if I'd like to help out.

'We're planning a huge world premiere in Tokyo, Brian. Princess Anne and the Emperor and Empress of Japan will be the guests of honour, and after the film there'll be a trade reception. Would you mind being the Master of Ceremonies? You'd also have to look after Princess Anne on the night and introduce her to the Emperor and Empress.'

'Why can't Ken do it?' I asked.

'He's busy doing the same thing somewhere else, although he will be sending a video message that they'll run before the film. What do you say?'

Herbie Wise immediately sprang to mind: 'Nobody shoots crap like Brian Blessed!'

I have to say, though, that I was hesitant. You see, I was a war baby and, even then, the very mention of Japan evoked all kinds of memories, none of which was especially pleasant. I remembered them as a terrifying power; one that wreaked havoc in Asia during the war, its soldiers often displaying barbaric cruelty. Some of the stories we heard were beyond imagination. But then I had to remind myself that this was over forty years ago, and that the generals, admirals and politicians were not necessarily representative of the people. In fact, they rarely are.

'Yes, alright,' I said eventually. 'One thing, though, would you mind if I took my dad with me?'

'That won't be a problem, Brian,' said Gary. 'We'll send you both first class and you'll stay at a top hotel. Thanks for saying yes!'

Great, I thought, *a free holiday with my dad and all for the price of a couple of hours of schmoozing.*

Wrong again, Blessed! This wasn't, as I'd hoped, just a film followed by some drinks with a princess, an emperor and a few oriental luvvies. In addition to Princess Anne and the Emperor and Empress of Japan, the entire Japanese government was going to be there, as was just about every Japanese dignitary this side of Mount Fuji. *Bloody marvellous*, I thought, *and I'm supposed to look after these people and make sure they all get on. It's going to be like running a diplomatic crèche!*

Now, in the late 1980s, Japan was still considered to be, financially at least, the major power in the world. They will be again, in my opinion, but back then they could have bought and sold anyone else a hundred times over. This was the land of the Rising Sun! And here's me, a coal hewer's son from South Yorkshire, about to fly out to meet the Emperor and Empress of Japan, representing both my country and my profession.

My old dad was thrilled to bits when I told him he was coming with me. He even went out and bought a new second-hand suit! I offered to buy him a brand new one, but he wouldn't hear of it.

'I'll only be wearing it once, Brian. Maybe twice if I've a funeral to go to.'

Yorkshire logic, you see – sensible and sparing.

Anyway, so off Dad and I went to Heathrow, where we boarded our flight to Tokyo – but what they'd laid on for us wasn't simply your common or garden first class (whatever that is). I'd never experienced such opulence and luxury first hand, all courtesy of the Japanese government, and as for my old man! Bloody hell, he was in seventh heaven. But it didn't faze him at all, as you'd be forgiven for assuming. You see, although he was a simple coal hewer from South Yorkshire, my father was a very confident man, and had also experienced much in his life. He'd been to Vienna after the war to represent the miners and he'd lived with Emil Zátopek, the great Olympic runner, for several weeks. He'd even met King George VI and Winston Churchill several times. He was good with everybody, my dad; kings, queens, miners, it didn't matter. And he was also a very natural raconteur. I flatter myself that I too can tell a story when the mood takes me, but my father was a master of the art. He could keep hordes of people spellbound for hours – which is precisely what he did on this flight. There were only a few people with us in first class but, after just a few minutes of being in the air, he was regaling all of them, stewards and stewardesses included, with all manner of tales. The old boy was in his element and they were all absolutely transfixed! I simply sat there admiringly, filming his antics on my video camera. It was so good to have him there. I was proud!

I remember that as we flew over the Soviet Union, shutters came down over the windows, which prevented us from taking photographs. There was much suspicion back then. I'm not sure what they thought we might see from 30,000 feet. A Russian yeti, perhaps?

We eventually landed at Tokyo airport and there it was – Japan, the land of the Rising Sun! Its people tended to rise less so, of course, which meant my father and I walked around feeling like giants. After hopping off the plane, we completely bypassed passport control and were taken instead to our waiting cars. Sorry, to our enormous bloody limousines! There was an entire fleet of them, each about twenty-five foot long. I almost lost Dad in ours. After about a twenty-minute drive, the car stopped and we got out, expecting to see our hotel.

'My God, Brian,' said Dad. 'This isn't a hotel. This is a castle!'

And he was right. This *was* a flaming castle! It had turrets, a drawbridge; all sorts of things. And the inside was just as impressive. We honestly felt like kings; or like queens once we'd put on our kimonos. They gave us those to wear in the evenings. I remember the first night we were there, which was the night before the premiere. A geisha, who it has to be said was stunningly attractive, knocked on our door and asked us if we'd like to follow her to the spa. Dad was out of the room like a bloody whippet!

'Lead on, my dear,' he cried, walking about a step behind her with an energy that belied his eighty-eight years.

When we arrived at the spa, she sat us both down and proceeded to explain what she had planned.

'We like to give you a full body massage,' said the geisha.

At first Dad looked thrilled by the news, as though all of his Christmases had come at once!

'But first you take off your clothes,' she continued.

The look of joy and expectation that had until now infused my father's weathered face was very quickly replaced by pure, unadulterated terror!

'You mean we have to take *everything* off?' he asked.

'You're only wearing a kimono, Dad,' I countered.

'Yes, you will have to be naked,' said the geisha. 'But please do not worry about nudity. There is no need for embarrassment.'

'No need for embarrassment?' he protested. 'They'll be able to see me "you-know-what", Brian! Your mother would have a fit.'

'Rubbish!' I said. 'Anyway, when was the last time she saw your you-know-what? Look, they're not going to massage your cock, Dad; they just need to get to the other bits. That's why you have to be naked.'

I managed to calm him down eventually and, not surprisingly, he enjoyed the experience immensely, as did I.

I'm going to go round to the other side now, physically I mean, because while we were there in the spa, I decided I'd try and seek clarification on something I'd been told, namely that all Japanese babies are born with a blue birthmark on their bottoms. The marks usually remain for about two years and are known as either Blue Butt, Mongolian Spots or, rather more imaginatively, the Mark of Genghis Khan! Anyway, while we were lying there in the spa, I thought I'd ask these geishas whether it was true.

'Yes!' one cried. 'How do you know this? We all have the mark when we are babies.'

Obviously there was no point them showing me their bottoms, more's the pity, as the blue spots disappear after childhood. So there you are: the Mark of Genghis Khan! How marvellous. You see, you've learned something new today.

Anyway, these geishas were fascinated by my dad. They found his shyness quite endearing, I think, but it was in fact his chest hair that they found most interesting.

'Men in Japan do not have hair on chest,' they said. 'You have lot of chest hair, like monkey.'

'Ay, steady on!' he said, laughing. 'A monkey, indeed. Did you hear that, our Brian? They said I look like a monkey!'

The full body massages were followed by head massages, which were then followed by hot and cold baths. After that, they covered us in bloody perfumes. Once again, Dad didn't know what had hit him.

'Oh my God!' he yelped. 'They're covering me in perfume, Brian, they're covering me in perfume! Yer mother would have a fit!'

After explaining to my father that the perfumes were all part of the procedure, we donned our kimonos again and went to have some dinner. Sushi, to be exact. Dad, perhaps not surprisingly, was at a loss, bless him.

'Yer can't eat fish raw, Brian. No no no no no. Yer mother would . . . !'

'Yes, yes, I know,' I interjected. 'She'd have a fit. Just try a bit. It's good stuff.'

The following morning, I received a telephone call asking me if I'd like to come down and meet Princess Anne's equerry. I was going to be looking after the princess that evening, so the equerry probably had lots of 'do's and 'do not's to pass on. To be honest with you, I was half expecting him to be a stuffy old official in a black suit. I was wrong, though. This particular equerry was young, bright and full of fun!

'Her Royal Highness is rather looking forward to this, Mr Blessed,' he began.

'Call me, Brian; the name's Brian.'

'Oh, yes, of course. *Brian*. And she's also looking forward to meeting you, of course.'

'Naturally,' I concurred. 'Now, what's all this about etiquette? I know that you're not supposed to goose them on a Tuesday afternoon and that you're not allowed to use certain words, and so on. What's it all about? Come on, what are the rules? Can I say, "fuck"?'

This threw him a bit.

'But I'm going to be with her all night,' I said. 'One's bound to slip out!'

'I'm not sure about that particular word, but you can be quite natural,' he reassured me. 'Don't worry too much about P's and Q's.'

'It's the F's and the C's I'm worried about, love! Can I take her by the arm?'

He looked worried. 'In what way?'

'Like this,' I said, linking my arm in his.

'Oh, I see!' he declared, looking ever so relieved. 'Yes, of course.'

'So, basically, you want me to be her boyfriend for the evening? OK, will do.'

As it turned out, there was a great deal riding on the premiere, but in particular on the reception. In fact, the film itself was almost peripheral. All manner of business deals and whatnot were being planned and this was a chance to oil some of the wheels, so to speak, which is why Princess Anne had been brought in. They love our Royal Family, the Japanese, so it was a good move. And what a flirt she was! A marvellous woman, and I flirted with her *all* the time. I'll get on to all that later.

Anyway, after I'd said cheerio to the equerry, I was taken to the cinema to begin rehearsing the premiere. I was the Master of Ceremonies, of course, holding it all together. As I've mentioned, before the film was shown we were due to play a video message from Ken, which would then be followed by a short speech from one of the line producers present.

'Now, whatever you do,' I said to the producer, 'whatever you do, don't try and make a gag. They won't understand a word of it, and those that do won't laugh. They don't understand British humour. OK?'

I wasn't being disparaging about the Japanese, by the way. Over the years I have spent a great deal of time with many Japanese people, some of whom speak very good English. I can never get a bloody squeak out of them, though. Not a sausage! They have *a* sense of humour, the Japanese, but it is not like ours. If you pinch yourself in front of a Japanese person and say the word '*itai*', which is Japanese for 'ouch', you'll have them rolling round on the ground laughing their little socks off. You can do it anywhere. But beyond that – no!

Anyway, that evening, this line producer took absolutely no notice of what I said, told a load of jokes and went down like a suet pudding at a Weight Watchers meeting.

My own performance wasn't without incident either, however, and when it came to introducing our distinguished guests, I'm afraid I didn't know my dress circles from my front stalls. When everyone else was seated, I was given my cue to step forward and introduce our three royal guests. And what a build-up! Music! Clarions and gongs playing like you've never known! Musical pandemonium! Then the house lights were dimmed; now just one solitary spotlight shining upon yours truly as I faced the auditorium.

'Ladies and gentlemen,' I boomed. 'Would you please welcome Her Royal Highness Princess Anne, and their Imperial Majesties, the Emperor and Empress of Japan.'

With that, I lifted my hand and beckoned to the right-hand side of the dress circle – only for the Three bloody Degrees to appear at the left-hand side of the stalls. I was pointing in the wrong bloody direction! Every single person in that auditorium was looking away from the royals as they walked in, as if they were pooh-poohing them!

Good start, Blessed, I thought. To be fair, it wasn't actually my fault, as it was the director who'd told me where to point.

I still felt like a tit though. One or two people even thought I'd done it as a joke! Me?

The film seemed to go down very well indeed. The Japanese might not get our humour quite so much, but they love their Shakespeare. It's big in Japan, so lots of brownie points to them! Afterwards, we were all taken round the corner to where the reception was being held. As we walked through the enormous doors, there they were: the entire Japanese government and their Imperial Majesties the Emperor and Empress of Japan. The Power of Japan all in one room.

'I don't know who these people are,' I said to Princess Anne. 'Which one's the Prime Minister?'

'I'm afraid I've no idea, Brian,' said her royal loveliness.

So there we were, me, myself and Anne, all ready to meet the most powerful people from the most powerful nation on earth, but without having an earthly idea of who was who! They were all quite small, had dark hair, dark suits, and were grinning like Cheshire cats.

'I'll tell you what,' she whispered. 'There's only one way to find out. Let's just ask them. Come on!'

And, with that, we linked arms and made our way towards the line-up. Thank God we had a translator with us. As we went down the line, every single one of them was trembling with excitement. They couldn't wait to shake her hand! Now, I appreciate the value of politics and politicians, but don't you ever get rid of the Royal Family. This was the whole hierarchy of Japan. They could have bought us in the blink of an eye and there they were, almost fainting because they were about to meet the only daughter of Queen Elizabeth II, the greatest monarch the world has ever known. Can you imagine that happening if they were about to meet a politician? Ridiculous! I've seen royals at work and I know the value of them.

So off we went along the line. I'd say, 'Could you tell me your name, please? Ah, you're the Minister of Defence.' Then

I'd turn to Princess Anne. 'Your Royal Highness, allow me to introduce you to the Minister of Defence,' and so it went on.

When we were about three ministers in, I suddenly felt something tugging on my backside. Whatever it was had hold of my trousers and was tugging away like nobody's business. I looked round and there, behind me, was the smallest man I'd seen since my dwarfs on *Flash Gordon*. He looked terribly sweet standing there with his wife, but I still had absolutely no idea who he was.

Suddenly, it clicked.

Oh Christ all-bloody-mighty, it's their Imperial Majesties! I've forgotten to include the Emperor and Empress. They're supposed to be with us on our walk!

'Excuse me, excuse me,' said the Emperor, in what was actually pretty good English. 'I'm sorry to disturb you, Mr Blessed, but I think that my wife and I should be with you and the Princess.'

This was the Emperor of Japan! I'd forgotten him and there he was, tugging at my backside! Pulling myself together, I began to make amends.

'Oh, my dear fellow!' I cried, putting my arms around his and his wife's shoulders. 'I'm so sorry, I didn't see you there! Come up here with the Princess, both of you. There, that's better, isn't it?'

You're not supposed to touch their Imperial Majesties, but as he'd grabbed my trousers I thought they were fair game. Once they were alongside the Princess, I just bowed a few times and carried on. I still had a job to do. I had to try and pronounce all these bloody Japanese names, and there were dozens of them.

'Allow me to introduce Mr Yakomoto, the Minister of Health.'

'Allow me to introduce Mr Toroyama, the Secretary of State.'

'Allow me to introduce Mr Takataniwani, the Minister for Soft Furnishings,' etc., etc., etc.

It seemed to be never-ending! After about an hour, we eventually came to the end of the line.

'Hang on, somebody's taking photographs,' said the equerry in a panic. 'He's actually standing on a chair! Security will go mad.'

And he was right. The only rule we'd been given for the evening, apart from not touching either Princess Anne or their Imperial Majesties inappropriately, both of which I'd violated, was not to take any photographs. It was strictly forbidden and anyone caught doing so would first have their camera confiscated, before being removed from the venue. *Bloody hell*, I thought. *Who on earth's been stupid enough to bring a camera?* Then, when I looked round to try and see who the idiot was, the only person I could see who seemed to be standing on a chair was my old dad. Dad was the phantom photographer!

There he was, eighty-eight-year-old Bill Blessed, a retired coal hewer from Bolton-on-Dearne, standing on a chair at an official Japanese reception clutching his old 1936 Nikon rangefinder, and he was taking photographs of the most revered people in the whole country! Rather ironically, the most effective way for me to attract everyone's attention before it all got out of hand was to stand on a chair and shout.

'Don't worry, loves,' I said. 'It's just my old dad! He's eighty-eight and doesn't know where he is or what he's doing, bless him. No idea about etiquette.'

The Emperor thought this was marvellous.

'Oh, please do not worry, Mr Blessed. He is your papa, yes? He is your papa? It is OK. He can come and take photographs. We make special concession for him. Please, we bring him forward.'

As soon as the Emperor spoke, the whole room stopped dead and my father, this octogenarian Yorkshireman, was slowly brought to the front of the room by the Emperor's own security guards.

'Sorry, I hope I didn't upset anybody. I just wanted something to show the wife. If I don't take any photographs, she'll be very disappointed,' my old dad muttered as he was ushered forward.

'Please go ahead, Mr Blessed,' said his Imperial Majesty. 'Take as many photographs as you wish.'

So there's Dad, standing in front of half the Japanese government, the Emperor and Empress and Princess bloody Anne, and he's asking them all to 'move in a little bit' so he can get his shot! I have to say, my old dad could get where water couldn't go. Anyway, just then – and this is all true, by the way – his camera breaks down! Unbelievable!

'Brian! It's stopped working. It's stopped working, Brian!'

But before I even had time to think about a reply, the Japanese Prime Minister stepped forward.

'Haaaah, this camera number XMC67542 [or something like that]. My company make this camera many, many years ago. This one of oldest camera in world, and it still work. IT STILL WORK!'

The man was out of his mind with excitement! He obviously hadn't seen one in years, let alone one that actually worked – or, at least, had worked until just recently. Everyone broke down with laughter, after which they descended on my bloody father. *He*, at this most austere occasion, was now the centre of attention!

The next half-hour or so was absolute pandemonium. It was bedlam! The Prime Minister was borrowing pencils and pens trying to adjust the camera, people were running off looking for screwdrivers and whatnot. In the end, the Prime Minister managed to take the whole thing apart, found out what was wrong with it and then put the whole thing back together again! After that, he handed the camera back to my dad and they all lined up to have their photos taken.

The government, the Emperor, Princess Anne, the lot of them. And there's my dad, who had them all eating out of the palm of his hand, and he's telling the whole congregation where to stand. He was the centre of attention – the guest of honour!

When he'd finished snapping, they all gathered round him and he started telling them all coal-mining stories. The whole of the Japanese government, half of whom couldn't speak a word of bloody English, were sitting round a table listening to stories about coal mining in South Yorkshire circa 1940! In all my life, I have never seen anything like it. And do you know, he probably encouraged more trade between Britain and Japan than any politician could have done. In fact, I think between him, *Henry V* and the Princess Royal they just about cleaned up. The next day my father was the toast of Tokyo!

Rather unbelievably, given what happened the first time I was asked to MC a high-powered diplomatic event in the Far East, my services as an oriental-based host were now very much in demand. But I wasn't just big in Japan. Oh no. I was big in China and Hong Kong too!

You see, at midnight on 1 July 1997, I, Brian Blessed, handed Hong Kong back over to the People's Republic of China. Many people believe that it was Prince Charles who did the deed, or that Chris Patten bloke, but I can assure you now that it wasn't either of them; it was me. I was the Master of Ceremonies for the occasion and I ran the whole bloody show. I opened it, closed it, introduced the dignitaries and announced the handover. Not bad, eh? A working-class boy from Yorkshire presiding over one of the most significant geopolitical ceremonies of the twentieth century.

The story starts the day I knocked out Peter Capaldi.

That's right, I floored Doctor bloody Who! Complete accident, by the way. Allow me to put some meat on the bones.

In 1997, I appeared in *The History of Tom Jones* for the BBC. Now, I'd always wanted to play Squire Western in *Tom Jones*, and the director, a very clever chap called Metin Hüseyin, cast me as him in this new adaptation. I thought, *Great, I'm in!*

The BBC so often gets it just right with these classic adaptations. We had Frances de la Tour playing my sister, and Samantha Morton playing my daughter. Young Max Beesley played Tom Jones, and then after him we had all manner of stars: Lindsay Duncan, John Sessions, Celia Imrie, Kathy Burke, Peter Capaldi. An absolutely stellar cast!

Now, as I said, I'd always wanted to play Squire Western – though not for the reason you might imagine. Oddly enough, I'm actually at my best and most comfortable as an actor when I'm playing quieter roles. Quiet and still. It's hard to believe, I know, but Kenneth Branagh cast me as the two dukes in *As You Like It* for that very reason; they both have to be static and quite quiet, and he knew that was the kind of role I enjoyed playing. So, when it came to playing more mobile, loud and eccentric characters, such as King Richard IV in *The Black Adder*, I always found it a challenge. It all felt very, very unnatural. And, believe me, there is no character on earth that is more eccentric, loud and mobile than Squire Western, so for me as an actor it was the ultimate challenge. He's completely feral, of course, and has the broadest of West Country accents. He also has about twenty dogs with him at all times. I had to cover my face and neck in chicken fat so that, when I was supposed to be asleep, all the dogs would leap on me and lick my face. It was the wildest of parts!

In one scene, I had to destroy the entire set. It's my daughter's wedding day and she doesn't turn up, and I go absolutely bloody bananas. If you go onto YouTube and put in the words 'Squire Western Loses His Temper', you'll be able to watch the scene in full. I destroy tables, chairs – and people! I throw chickens and food everywhere, and scream all kinds of foul oaths. Wonderful fun!

This may sound slightly egotistical, but this role was a huge success for me as an actor, and it is a performance of which I am very, very proud. Probably the best I've ever given, in fact. A few days after that scene was televised, an MP tried to bring a motion in the House of Commons to have me presented with a BAFTA immediately! I promise you, that's absolutely true. It was in all the papers.

So, anyway, lovely Peter Capaldi was cast in the role of Lord Fellamar, a rather foppish aristocrat who conspires to rape my daughter so as to force her into marriage. What a bastard! I remember he wore a lot of make-up for the part and had wigs, beauty spots and God knows what else – a real floozy – and he was marvellous in the role. I admire Peter a lot; he's an outstanding actor. My cup of tea, as you might say. Very versatile and completely believable.

As it happens, there's a scene in *Tom Jones* where Squire Western has to protect his daughter from Lord Fellamar. Smarting at the impertinence of this simpleton, Lord Fellamar then proceeds to call the Squire a few names – an 'oaf' and suchlike – before slapping his face with one of his gloves and then threatening to kill him if he doesn't hand over his daughter. The Squire's reaction to this is a left hook to the jaw, after which the Lord drops like a sack of potatoes. What a scene!

Now, Peter Capaldi and I had rehearsed this scene God knows how many times over. We had a lovely fight arranger on set with us and I, of course, was already quite experienced in this sort of thing. Stuntmen used to love me on films and TV because I was always prepared to get stuck in and help wherever I could, and because I spent so much time with these people they showed me time and time again exactly how to throw or take a punch. All actors are taught how to fake a fight, of course, but they're not supposed to get involved in the really rough stuff. So, anyway, I threw this left hook at Peter about four or five different times before the take and of course missed him completely – as is intended in a stage fight.

'OK, let's go for a take,' said the director. 'Ready, ACTION!'

At this moment, I swear to God, Peter put his head forward – just as the director said 'action'. My left fist was already over halfway to his head when I realized, and by the time I managed to pull the punch it had already hit him and knocked him clean out. I hit him right across the eye and the cheekbone – BANG! He went flat on his back.

'Peter's down,' I shouted. 'Somebody fetch the nurse!'

What a mess, though. There was blood pouring out of his eyebrow and his legs were doing the death quiver! Peter was in a bad way, and I felt absolutely dreadful. Medics were onto him like a shot and I remember one of them trying to persuade me to drink some bloody whisky.

'I don't drink. It's Peter who needs a Scotch, love, not me!'

Eventually, the quivering calmed down and he started to come round a bit, at which point they strapped him onto a stretcher and took him off to hospital. All kinds of horrible scenarios were going through my head at the time. *What if he has brain damage? His head hit the floor with one hell of a thud. He may never act again! Oh my God, I've ruined a career. I've ruined a life!* I felt for poor Peter, I really did.

I later learned that when he arrived at the hospital, nobody wanted to treat him. He was covered in all kinds of make-up and beauty spots, and they thought he was a transvestite! Fortunately, apart from a few cuts, bruises and mild concussion, Peter was OK and he made a full recovery very quickly. I couldn't call him, though. I wanted to, believe me I did, but I was just too ashamed. Every time I went to pick up the phone, I saw him lying there doing the death quiver. We'd got on so well together and I just didn't know what to say to him. In hindsight, I should have just bloody well called him and said sorry. Anyway, a day or two after he'd been released from hospital, Peter actually called *me* to see if I was OK. I was out and my daughter Rosalind answered the phone.

'How's Brian?' he enquired. 'Somebody told me that he'd been worried about what happened, but he mustn't be. Please tell him I'm fine. These things happen.'

Rosalind has always been a huge fan of Peter and so was delighted to take the call. She thanked him and later gave me the message. And that was about it, really – all forgotten about. Except for my guilty conscience.

Later on in the series, Lord Fellamar challenges Squire Western again, this time using a sword as opposed to a glove, and I end up shooting him! It reminded me of that scene from the Indiana Jones film, where Harrison Ford kills the Arabian swordsman. Fellamar approaches the Squire doing all these fancy things with his sword, and the Squire, looking terribly unimpressed, simply takes out his gun and shoots the bastard. Bang! So I almost killed him twice in one series.

A few days after Peter had finished filming his scenes, I was sitting having a cup of tea with the delightful Samantha Morton. What a beauty she is, and a fine, fine actress. Anyway, we were both sitting there quite happily when, all of a sudden, I noticed two chaps in dark suits standing by the doorway. They were looking very furtive, both of them; their expressions flatter than a kipper's cock. Once they'd caught my eye, they began beckoning me over to them.

Good heavens, I thought, *Capaldi's sent the lawyers in. How could he?*

'Mr Blessed?' enquired one of the Men in Black.

'Yes,' I replied.

'I wondered if we could have a word with you in private. Our car's just outside.'

And then I saw it. Ye gods! This wasn't a car, it was a

twenty-five-foot limousine, just like the one that had picked up me and my dad in Tokyo.

'Just step into the back, would you, Mr Blessed?'

'Yes, of course. Now look,' I said, sitting down on a seat closest to the door, 'if this is about the incident involving Peter Capaldi, I honestly don't know what else I can say.'

They looked perplexed.

'Er, we don't know what you're talking about.'

'Ah.'

'Look, Mr Blessed, apologies for all the covert nonsense, but we've been sent on behalf of the British and Chinese governments to ask you if you'd like to be Master of Ceremonies at the official handover of Hong Kong.'

The sense of relief hit me like a bloody freight train. What had I been thinking?

'I see. Well, yes, I'd be delighted. Tell me more, my dear fellow.'

'As I said, we'd like you to be the Master of Ceremonies when Britain hands Hong Kong over to China. We've already taken the liberty of asking the BBC if you can be spared and they say they're prepared to juggle the schedule for you.'

I was absolutely gobsmacked.

'You'll be paid £15,000 for three days' work and we'll fly you out first class with Tony Blair, Robin Cook and all the other dignitaries.'

The second part of the sentence made me want to throw up, but the first part made me want to jump for bloody joy. Fifteen grand for three days' work. In Yorkshire money that's around three-quarters of a million!

'Count me in,' I said. 'When do we start?'

'The ceremony will begin at about 6 p.m. on 30 June and will finish in the early hours of 1 July. The estimated global audience will be over 2 billion and you will be responsible for linking the entire event, which, we have to warn you, Mr

Blessed, will be vast. All three military services from both countries will be involved, as will just about every politician.'

Visions of a repeat of my carefree Japanese escapade were fading fast, and understandably so. The magnitude of handing over an entire administrative region from one country to another was significant and would affect millions upon millions of people. No, this was Responsibility with a capital R! Poor old dad would have to stay at home this time, I'm afraid, and there'd be no tickling or flirting. For once, I'd have to be on my best behaviour.

Kenneth Branagh thought the whole thing was marvellous and rang me up to wish me luck.

'Brian, you're the only person I know who could host an event featuring a cast of thousands and an audience of billions without blinking an eye!'

'Rubbish,' I said, desperately trying to lay my hands on some self-effacement.

'You could do it with your eyes closed, you know you could!' he told me.

Bizarrely enough, almost fifteen years to the day later, Ken rang me up again; except this time it was because *he* was about to perform at the opening ceremony of the London 2012 Olympics. Do you remember? He played Isambard Kingdom Brunel, and what an absolutely outstanding job he did. Seriously, though, when he actually puts his mind to it and applies himself, that great man is second to none.

Anyway, back to the handover. The day eventually arrived for me to fly to Hong Kong and at around 7 a.m. on 29 June 1997 yet another enormous car pulled up outside my house. I said goodbye to my wife and my daughter and the animals and away we went. Once again, this knocked the whole Japanese experience into the sidelines, as not only did we bypass both passport control and security, but when we arrived at the airport we drove straight onto the bloody tarmac. I was dropped off right next to the plane! *I could get used to this*, I thought.

It all went belly up when I boarded, of course. The entire plane seemed to be teeming with either Hooray bloody Henrys or politicians. There was Tony Blair, Robin Cook and all manner of other governmental types. *This is going to be interminable*, I thought. *Twelve hours of smug self-congratulatory nonsense!*

And, Lord, was I right. The politicians were bad enough, but it was the hooray Henrys who were the biggest pain. About twenty minutes into the flight, a couple of them started complaining that they hadn't received their per diem (daily expenses!). 'We were promised our per diem *before* we flew! This is a disgrace, where is it?'

They were all rich, of course: filthy rich. That didn't stop them, though. Then, after that, a couple more joined in, all whinging that they hadn't received their spending money for their free trip to Hong Kong.

Incidentally, about a week before the ceremony, two of the officials had visited my house to talk about the ceremony itself and what I was going to wear and so on. When I showed them what was in my wardrobe, they almost bloody died.

'Ah . . . You don't really do suits, do you, Mr Blessed?' they said.

'Not really. If I'm not on stage or in front of a camera, I'm either up a mountain or buggering about at home.'

'I think we'd better get you something slightly more appropriate.'

'Fair enough, love,' I said. 'Shall I pop down to Debenhams or something?'

'NO! We'll take your measurements now and have something made.'

So they ended up getting me this suit, and apparently it cost them over £2,000! I admit that you need a lot of material to cover my frame, but two grand?! Anyway, it was very nice and fit me like a glove.

After twelve hours in the air, we arrived in Hong Kong – a staggering place. When I eventually got to my apartment, I opened the curtains and looked out over the sprawling metropolis. *In twenty-four hours' time, I will be helping to hand all this back to China*, I thought. *Well I never!*

But the tension between the Chinese and the British, even then, was palpable. Britain didn't want to go and China couldn't wait to get in. You could have cut the atmosphere with a knife. What's more, there were thousands upon thousands of Chinese troops everywhere. There must have been at least 50,000 of them. And this, amongst other things, was making the British contingent nervous. Little Robin Cook was the Chinese's most vociferous critic, and seemed to be falling out with just about everyone.

The next morning, I went off for a rehearsal and the first person I was introduced to was Cook's Chinese counterpart, the Chinese Foreign Minister, Qian Qichen; and what a charming fellow he was. Apparently, he'd seen *Galahad of Everest* and was a big fan. He'd also spoken to some of the Chinese climbers who'd been on that first climb with me, so I was told, and had been instrumental in making the decision to hire me. Good for old Qian! When I met him, he was cock-a-hoop.

'I want to meet the man with the voice!' he shouted. 'I want to meet the mountaineer, where is he? Here he is! The man with the voice!'

'How the devil are you?' I said. 'It's always nice to meet a fan!'

'I have seen your film on Mallory many times, Mr Blessed. It is one of the best. Let me say that I am very happy you are hosting this ceremony.'

'Couldn't be happier being here,' I replied.

He then leant forward and whispered in my ear.

'You know, Mr Blessed, that Mr Cook of yours. He says many strong things. His manner is almost threatening. Do you know, Mr Blessed, you must tell him I don't think we are frightened.'

'I'm sure you're not,' I smiled. Never in a million years would you have pegged me for a diplomat in foreign affairs, eh? Life is full of surprises.

Later on that day, I was taken to the square where the ceremony would take place – and that's where the magnitude of the event hit me. It was absolutely enormous! There were warships, tanks, soldiers, cannon, lights, stands, flags; it was un-bloody-believable. Anyway, I had my own lectern, lucky old me, and of course a microphone. Well, when it came to testing that, I almost bloody died. Everything was quiet and still, and then:

> 'ONE, ONE, ONE, ONE.
> 'TWO, TWO, TWO, TWO.
> 'THREE, THREE, THREE, THREE.'

I could hear my voice reverberating all over Hong Kong. It was the most bizarre experience. Speakers had been placed throughout the city and it was as though I could hear every single one of them. Remembering it now still raises the hair on the back of my neck, you know.

As the ceremony opening time drew nearer, the crowds began to gather: hundreds of thousands lining the streets, which were still permeated with an overwhelming air of caution and distrust. Then the politicians, the military and the dignitaries began arriving. Wow! All of a sudden, everything was becoming very, very real.

When everybody had eventually taken their place, I was given the two-minute warning. It was then that I suddenly experienced an almost overwhelming pang of vulnerability. I stood behind my lectern, fenced in by hundreds of thousands of people; some of whom could lay a genuine claim to being among the most powerful on earth. Dozens of cameras were pointing at me, as were God knows how many lights. Then there were the 2 billion plus watching at home of course! And that's what I mean about feeling vulnerable. In a few seconds' time, I would have the full attention of almost a third of the world's population, yet I was completely and utterly alone. What if I introduced the wrong section at the wrong time, or the wrong dignitary? This was live. *Z Cars* times a million. I was seconds away from becoming the scourge of the Orient! To make things worse, it rained profusely, hot rain that washed the text away on my lectern. No worry, being an actor I had learned my lines and I held my nerve. I still remember the opening lines word for word.

'Ladies and gentlemen, today the eyes of the world are upon us. Will you please welcome the Chinese Premier and His Royal Highness, Prince Charles?'

The ceremony, which resembled something out of a Cecil B. DeMille movie, went off without a hitch. What was really impressive was the performance of the British army, navy and air force – what terrific drilling. The sergeant roared the commands and the forces responded in unison with absolute precision, and I should know as I was awarded best airman of my flight after completing my square bashing at RAF Bridgnorth in 1954. From my vantage point, I could see the Chinese government were shaken and impressed. We weren't leaving Hong Kong with a whimper. (Incidentally, in 1996 I made my way across Tibet and, on arriving at the garrison town of Tingri, witnessed the Chinese soldiers doing their drill. It reminded me of a bad rehearsal of *Cats*.)

Back to Hong Kong. On the evening of that day I stood on top of a skyscraper overlooking the harbour and watched Patten and all the representatives of the British government sailing away in the distance. It was over and Hong Kong belonged to the Chinese. I felt rather sad. And I never found out if those toffs got their per diem or not. If they did, it should have been shoved up their arses for safekeeping.

So there you have it. I, Brian Blessed – officially endorsed and approved by the Communist Party of China – handed over Hong Kong, with, it has to be said, just a little help from Prince Charles. That's got to be better than a bloody BAFTA, hasn't it?

9

EPISODE I –
THE PHANTOM BLESSED

As much as I have enjoyed, and am indeed grateful for the vast majority of my film roles, there aren't many that I'd put into the 'Dream Come True' category. *Peppa Pig* and *Sooty* are in there, of course, but they're television. No, there are in fact only two film roles to which I would be happy to give that auspicious title. Vultan is one, but before I reveal the second, I must first ask you to step into my time machine while I whisk you off to a galaxy far, far away. Or, to be more exact, London in the mid-1970s.

Now, in my opinion, the 1970s were a bit of a dark decade. Some of the music was quite jolly, I suppose, but in general we were definitely lacking something. For a start, nobody had any bloody money, least of all the wonderful British film industry. That was on its knees at the time, feared lost. But even the countries that were making movies, like America, all seemed to be choosing very dark subject matter. Films like *Taxi Driver*, *Carrie*, *Deliverance*, *Mean Streets*, *Badlands*, *The Exorcist*, *The Godfather*, *French Connection*, *The Texas Chainsaw Massacre*, *Apocalypse Now*, *The Deer Hunter*. Not a happy ending in sight.

If you wanted to go to the cinema as a family, you were absolutely stuffed. 'Get the children ready, Doris, we're off to see *Deliverance*. Oh, and do remember to tell little Johnny to cover his eyes during the "Piggy" scene. You remember how upset he got during the shenanigans in *A Clockwork Orange*.'

Don't misunderstand me: the aforementioned films are all great works of art. Absolute dynamite, some of them. But they represent a decade that was teetering on the brink of moral, not to mention financial, bankruptcy, and people were crying out for change. Seven miserable years of *The Godfather*, of darkness and strikes and depression – and then, just when you were deciding whether to end it all using either the blue pills or the red ones – WWWWWHAM! Along comes the antidote. Everyone's heart and soul just opened up. This is no exaggeration, by the way. It was happening all over the world.

So what was it in the end that began to shine some light on this most dour of decades?

Well, for me and millions like me, it was a brand new science-fiction film that had been made just up the road from me at Elstree Studios. Costing only $11 million to make, it boasted Alec Guinness, Harrison Ford *and* Peter Cushing as its stars, and also featured two little-known American actors, Carrie Fisher and Mark Hamill. That film was, of course, *Star Wars*, an entertainment behemoth that revolutionized the film industry. I myself owe a great deal to that first film, and not just because of *The Phantom Menace*. You see, had *Star Wars* failed at the box office, films like *Flash Gordon* would never have been made. Can you imagine a world without Vultan? It's unthinkable!

I remember the day I first saw a billboard for *Star Wars*. It was November 1977 and I was on my way to film a TV play. I can't for the life of me remember what it was. I did an awful lot of TV in the 1970s, you see. I must have appeared in around forty or fifty series in all – anything from *I, Claudius* to *Space 1999* – and this took me all over the country. More often than not, I travelled by train (what a moribund industry that was!) and I was running to catch one at Waterloo station one day when all of a sudden something caught my eye. It was an absolutely gigantic billboard – at least thirty foot high.

'STAR WARS' it read. 'IT'S COMING!'

When I alighted at my destination, there it was again.

'STAR WARS – IT'S COMING!'

Being a man who would quite happily spend his entire life hopping round the universe – and beyond – I was intrigued. Even slightly agitated! Then, a few days later, I saw another billboard, this time at King's Cross. It was just as large as the one at Waterloo and had emblazoned on it in giant letters: 'A LONG TIME AGO IN A GALAXY FAR, FAR AWAY . . .' God! I was even more intrigued!

Apart from the now increasingly familiar *Star Wars* logo, which was in the corner of the poster, that's all it had written on it. By this time, I was beginning to behave like an expectant parent. I was galvanized and excited by the billboards. But what was the film about, exactly? Were the stars making war on each other? I wanted to know!

As the weeks went on, the film company began dripfeeding us little bits of information from time to time: a still image leaked to a newspaper or an interview with George Lucas or a cast member. The marketing campaign was like nothing we'd ever seen before.

Just after Christmas that year, I had to go up to Birmingham to narrate *Peter and the Wolf* with the Moscow Symphony Orchestra. The morning after the performance, I wandered out of my hotel and decided to meander down towards Station Street, which is where the old repertory theatre used to be. I hadn't been back since I had left so had no idea whether it was still there. The theatre was still there, I'm pleased to say, and is in use to this very day, but as I walked away from my old stomping ground, I heard a commotion coming from the next street. As I turned the corner to have a nosy, there before me was this enormous bloody cinema; and what do you think was showing there? *Star Wars*, of course! I'd been so busy preparing for *Peter and the Wolf* that I'd forgotten it was about to come out.

The entire street outside the cinema was swarming with children, parents and school teachers, but mainly children. There were hundreds of them and they were all going in to watch *Star Wars*. I looked at my watch. I had an hour till my train. *Oh, to hell with it*, I thought. *I'll get a later train. I'm going in. I must see it!*

The screen was absolutely enormous, the biggest I'd ever clapped eyes on. And the sound! It came at us from every direction. There were at least a thousand people in that cinema, and I counted no more than twenty adults. There was me, of course, although at that particular moment you could hardly have classed me as an adult. The atmosphere reminded me so much of those Saturday mornings in the Empire cinema, waiting impatiently for the projectionist to crank up the latest episode of *Flash Gordon*. There was an all-pervading air of excitement and expectation, driven on and on by the unremitting sound of excitable young voices. I fed on this like a lion feeds on meat.

As the lights dimmed, a few cheers rang out and then – WHAM! The sound was so huge that your bloody ears nearly came off. I feared this might terrify the youngsters – some of whom can't have been more than about five or six – but I was wrong. My word, I was wrong! They embraced the sound.

As John Williams's astonishing score began to boom out of the speakers, there was a giant collective 'WOOOOOO-OOOOH' from the kids. Honestly: in unison, every single one of these nippers just sat there with their mouths open and went, 'WOOOOOOOOOH.' They'd never heard anything like this before in their lives. Real music! It lit up their imaginations.

Not many people know this, but back in the 1960s I met

and very nearly worked with the great John Williams. I shan't be a tick with this tangent, I promise. You see, he'd written a musical about Thomas Becket and had asked to meet me with a view to my playing the king. He accompanied me on the piano while I sang one or two of the songs from the musical. I even remember a line from one of them. 'I know I'd rather be, a man who goes down in history as a man of wit, a man of chaaaaaaarm, a man of loooooove.'

The part never materialized, but perhaps that's just as well! Anyway, back in the cinema, the very first scene took my breath away. As I said, the screen in this cinema was huge, and so when the arc of the planet appeared, and that gigantic Imperial Cruiser hoved into view, I was completely dumbstruck. It went on and on and on and on until it filled the entire screen! I have never known such a beginning to a film. I was mesmerized! I felt so happy.

Everything about it was cutting edge, especially the special effects. When I first saw the two suns in the sky, I almost fell off my chair. They looked so real! But it was the characters that, to me, made *Star Wars* one of *the* films of the century, not to mention those superb actors who brought them all to life. Have you ever seen a film with so many strong characters in it? I'm sure I haven't. And the performances are all terrific. Alec Guinness in particular is outstanding as Obi-Wan Kenobi. I remember the bar scene where he has to protect Luke from an alien troublemaker. Alec showed wonderful finesse with the lightsaber. The Shakespearean actor shines through, you see, and when he's finished chopping off the alien's limbs he simply looks from left to right, with dangerous and frightening authority. OK, maybe nothing quite as scary as that, but he certainly means business! The point being that this lovable, gentle old monk suddenly becomes an incredibly dangerous warrior. It really is the most marvellous contrast.

There was one part of the film which made me howl with

laughter. You remember when Han, Luke, Leia and so on are trying to board the *Millennium Falcon* so they can make their escape from the planet? Well, as those white Stormtrooper fellows are chasing our heroes, they come across a hooded creature sporting a trunk. As they approach the rather bizarre alien, they stop, making a silent enquiry. 'Eek,' says the Elephant Man. Nothing more, nothing less: just – 'Eek.' Nodding enthusiastically, the Stormtroopers then continue their pursuit. Obviously, 'Eek' meant 'The rogues you are chasing went that-a-way. They're rebels, of course, and are about to board the *Millennium Falcon*. If you hurry, you might just catch them.' All this information conveyed by an 'Eek!'

Bloody Eek!

It wasn't until the end of the film, when the credits rolled, that I realized I actually knew at least half of the supporting cast. Peter Diamond, a fellow Yorkshireman who had been a stuntman on *Z Cars* and *The Three Musketeers*, played at least four roles in the film, including a Stormtrooper, a Tusken Raider, a Death Star Trooper and Garouf Lafoe. He also choreographed all the great stunts!

I spoke to Peter about *Star Wars* a year or so after it came out and he told me he'd had an absolutely marvellous time working on it. As well as acting and choreographing the stunts, he'd had to teach Guinness, Dave Prowse, Mark Hamill and all the other actors how to use a sword – or, should I say, what eventually became a lightsaber. He was on set for months on end – fabulous! He then went on to play a similar role on both *The Empire Strikes Back* and *Return of the Jedi*. Delightful man, Peter, and a master swordsman.

I was green with envy at not having been part of this wonderful new film – and I wasn't alone. The whole of the acting profession was frustrated. I'd never known anything quite like it. I had conversation after conversation after conversation with hundreds of fellow thespians, and we were all calling our agents and asking them exactly the same question: 'Why the hell didn't you get me an audition to appear in bloody *Star Wars*, you useless bastard!'

All the usual snobbery and so-called artistic integrity went flying out of the window faster than the *Millennium Falcon*. This was a phenomenon! Actors are just big children, you see. It doesn't matter if you're Alec Guinness, Brian Blessed, Carrie Fisher or Max von Sydow; underneath it all we are but children, and that is what *Star Wars* did – it brought out the child in us all.

Yours truly never got a look-in on the first three films. Sob sob sob! Not so much as an interview. We made *Flash Gordon* only a couple of years after *Star Wars* came out, and so I suppose that precluded me from taking part in the two sequels. Sci-fi character cross-contamination doesn't rub – more's the pity.

You know, while I said above that *Star Wars* envy was industry-wide, there was one actor I knew who was completely and utterly unaffected by all things *Star Wars*. I'm jumping forward a bit here, but you'll see why in a moment. It's a wonderful story.

Now, does the name Sebastian Shaw mean anything to you? It will to some, but probably not to the majority. Well, Sebastian Shaw was one of the most eminent British stage and film actors of the mid-twentieth century. He was with the Royal Shakespeare Company for eons, had studied drama with the great Charles Laughton and was an awfully good-looking chap. The ladies (and men) just flew at him.

In the late spring of 1983 I was in London's West End and in a rather chipper mood when all of a sudden I saw Sebastian and his wife sitting on a bench. Incidentally, Sebastian's wife was none other than Joan Ingpen, the lady who discovered Luciano Pavarotti!

'Hello, you two,' I said, 'what are you up to?'

Now, I'd known Sebastian since the mid-1960s and saw

him quite often back then. He looked as pleased to see me as I was him.

'Brian!' he cried. 'Just enjoying the good weather. How are you, dear boy?'

'I'm marvellous thanks,' I beamed. 'Just on my way to buy a ticket for *Return of the Jedi*!'

This seemed to mean something to Sebastian, which I have to say surprised me somewhat.

'Is that the new *Star Wars* film?' he asked.

'Yes, that's right,' I said. 'Although I have to confess, Sebastian, I wouldn't have put you down as a fan.'

'Ha! He's not,' piped up Joan. 'He can't stand all that nonsense. You're in the film though, aren't you dear?'

'Oh yes, yes I am,' said Sebastian vaguely.

I couldn't believe what I was hearing.

'You're in the new *Star Wars* film? *Return of the Jedi*?'

'Apparently!' said Sebastian.

I had to sit down. 'But I only saw you a couple of months ago. Why didn't you tell me?'

'Why on earth would I, dear boy? It's only a film. And besides, we were all sworn to secrecy so I wouldn't have been allowed to tell you. I assume it'll be OK now. What an exhausting experience though. Do you know what time they picked me up? Three a.m.! And I was in make-up for hours. Then they dressed me in some awfully elaborate black armour costume and made me lie on my back all day. I'm afraid I kept on nodding off.'

'Was this up at Elstree?'

'Yes, that's right. Elstree Studios.'

By this time I was an emotional wreck, flitting between extreme excitement and pure jealousy!

'But what part did you play?' I asked. I'm afraid my question seemed to confound Sebastian somewhat.

'Oh, goodness,' he said, looking perplexed. 'It was a strange name – Dark something or other?'

I was at a loss. 'It must be a new character,' I said. 'I can't think of anyone in *Star Wars* called Dark . . .'

Then all of a sudden it clicked.

'Surely you don't mean Darth Vader? You can't be.'

'That's it!' he said, sitting up with a jolt. 'Darth Vader! I knew it was something like that.'

I couldn't bloody believe it. 'Sebastian,' I said, 'you do realize every actor in the world would give his right arm to be the face of Darth Vader? In fact I'd have given my life. You're in *Star Wars*! *The Return of the Jedi*! The entire world cannot wait to see this film and you've got the role of Vader!'

Sebastian still wasn't impressed.

'Really, Brian?' he said. 'I'm glad I didn't know all this beforehand. Otherwise I would have been terrified!'

He had no idea that he had made history.

But how on earth did George Lucas find that face? To think he picked a star from the 1940s and 1950s. Amazing! And despite Sebastian not really knowing what day it was, he gives a really marvellous performance. Inspired casting!

Something very original had taken place, then, and by the time *Return of the Jedi* was ready to be released in the summer of 1983, the entire world was chomping at the bit. I was away from home filming a television programme when it came out, and so made Hildegard and Rosalind promise me they'd wait until I got back before they went to see it. 'Don't you dare go and see it without me,' I said – but by the time I got home, they'd been to see it *twice*! I'd have done exactly the bloody same, of course, so instead of giving them a ticking-off, I simply took my daughter to see it a third time. What an old softie I am.

Anyway, so the *Star Wars* trilogy literally zoomed into our cinemas and I became well and truly hooked. In fact, I would probably class myself as a bit of a *Star Wars* nerd. I don't dress up as a Wookiee or anything – I'm most probably half-Wookiee anyway – but I did watch the films an awful lot, and I studied them at length. You can imagine then, twelve or thirteen years later, the kind of state I got myself into when I read that George Lucas planned to bring the series back. Three new prequels, no less! Once again, my entire being was awash with intergalactic enthusiasms. I was floating on air! But if somebody had told me then that I'd actually go on to appear in one of the films I would most likely have run round Mars naked and mated with a Tano Giant on Jupiter!

The Phantom Menace was released almost sixteen years to the day after *Return of the Jedi*. A long sabbatical had been inevitable: for as well as George Lucas being completely burned out following making the original three films, technology simply couldn't keep up with his incredible imagination. I must admit that the possibility of Lucas one day picking up his lightsaber again just never occurred to me in the intervening years.

On first reading about his 'prequel plans', my initial thoughts were thus:

When is it being made?

When is it being released?

And,

How long will I have to wait until the next one?

It never occurred to me that I might get a part in the new film – I was still 'King of the Hawkmen', remember? 'Gordon's alive!' everyone shouted at me!

So when the casting process did crank into action, I simply sat on the sidelines, pointed and laughed. To quote the title of this book once again, it was ABSOLUTE PANDEMONIUM! Every actor and actress in the land headed for London. Fat ones, thin ones, tall ones, short ones, good ones, awful ones – London had them all flouncing around its streets. The entire city was swimming in Equity cards! And if their agents hadn't managed to get them an audition, they'd get on the phone themselves and try and get one. And if that didn't work, they'd bang on the doors of the production offices. These people would have climbed on rocket ships, mounted dinosaurs or ridden elephants to get at the casting directors. The sky was the limit and the world of entertainment rejoiced at the prospect of the new film. It was the same when they began making the Harry Potter films. Get yourself in on a nice successful franchise and you're made for life. You don't have to have a big role, and the chances are you won't be able to retire from the proceeds of the film itself. But the personal appearances and repeat fees and so on could provide you with a nice little income for life. All enquiries to my agent please . . .

Celia Imrie, one of our finest living actresses, was thrilled to bits to get a small part on the new film. Now, you've got to look hard to find her because you can't see her face, but when you hear a pilot say the word 'Affirmative' during *The Phantom Menace*, that's Celia! She was just thrilled to be in it. I remember her coming up to me shortly before she began filming. 'Everyone's jealous, Brian,' she squealed. 'Everyone wants to be in it!'

Anyway, so George Lucas and his team had the pick of Britain, and before the auditions themselves they held a series of interviews at various hotels throughout London. Not long after all this had started, I received a call from Derek Webster, my agent.

'You've got an interview with George Lucas for the new *Star Wars* film.'

'But that's impossible!'

'Why is it impossible?'

'Because I'm Vultan.'

'What on earth's that got to do with anything?'

I suddenly realized the ridiculousness of what I was saying.

'Sorry, Derek, forgive me. I was stuck in the early 1980s for a moment. Where and when, love?'

I tried my best not to think about the interview and where it might lead, and in a way it worked. I kept myself busy and whenever a thought about *Star Wars* came into my head, I redirected my attention onto something else.

When the day of the interview arrived, I was both quietly confident and pleasantly relaxed. I was aware that the odds were long, and so had managed to keep both my expectations – and my dreams – firmly in check. I knew I could act. There'd either be a role for me or there wouldn't.

When I arrived, the mood in the hotel was somewhat desperate. There were actors praying in every corner. Some of them were in tears, overcome by nervousness.

According to a friend, even Samuel A. Jackson had dropped a huge film so he could try and persuade George Lucas to cast him as one of the Jedi knights. He was one of the biggest actors in the film world at the time!

The interview went well. I saw George and the producer Rick McCallum, whom I'd met on a number of occasions, and I talked about things like space and the importance of the previous three films. I wasn't flattering, just honest. As I spoke, George Lucas grinned from ear to ear. I suppose I was entertaining him in a way, but he also appeared to be genuinely interested in what I had to say. I told him how I'd rolled about the floor at watching the 'Eek' creature, but also how I'd been impressed by the homages he'd paid in the films to many of the ancient religions.

The fact that I was a member of the British Interplanetary Society, the world's oldest space advocacy organization, deeply impressed him – and so we very quickly established a connection. I flatter myself, but I feel the upshot of this was that George subconsciously attached me to the film there and then. I was an ally, a fellow cosmic-romantic. Does that make sense?

The part I was being interviewed for was Sio Bibble, the governor of Naboo, who, despite being a Jedi, is a politician and quite a gentle character. It took George but a few minutes to realize that there was a potential miscasting on the cards.

'You're far too powerful for Sio Bibble, Brian,' he laughed. 'I need to have a think about this. I know there's something for you; something powerful and larger than life.'

'You mean I don't have to sleep with you, George?' I said, feigning disappointment. 'You're sure you don't want me to kill somebody?'

This had them both in fits.

'No to both!' George implored. 'Just give me a few days. I'll think of something. You're right for the film and that's all that matters.'

When the interview was over, George and I carried on our conversation. We talked about rocketry, and we talked about ion fields, and we talked about scientists Robert Zubrin and Matthew Golombek and about NASA. We talked about the speed of light. It was illuminating *and* stimulating. So, all in all, it went very well. I thought, *If nothing else, at least I can say I've had tea with George Lucas*. I found him extraordinary, you see, and I was grateful for the meeting. Even though he was in a position of immense power, he never abused this and there was always a great humility about him.

A few days later, I was safely back in Wiltshire, where I'd been filming *The History of Tom Jones*. Anyway, one morning, in between me throwing chickens at vicars on my daughter's wedding day and knocking out Peter Capaldi, I received a telephone call from my rather excitable-sounding agent.

'Brian! It's Derek. Look, George Lucas's people have been on. You've been offered a role in the new *Star Wars* movie!'

I did my level best to remain composed, but I don't mind telling you I was cock-a-hoop with excitement!

'That's marvellous, Derek. Who am I playing?'

After much rummaging of paper, he was ready with his reply.

'It says here you're to play somebody called – erm – Boss Nass? I assume it's pronounced as written. Anyway, they're going to fax over some of the dialogue straight to your hotel. It should be there by about four p.m., so make sure you're by the fax machine, OK? We've had orders that nobody else must see it.'

'Fine, love. I'll be there, four p.m.'

This was 1997, remember, and so fax machines – to me at least – were still classed as bleeding-edge technology. At about ten to four, I made myself known to the receptionist, told her I was expecting some top-secret astronomical information, and took my place by the appliance. Now, although fax machines were still regularly used back then, I'm afraid this one was obviously a bloody prototype or something. It actually had jaws on it, this thing, and used paper that was too thin even to wipe a gnat's bottom. It was almost translucent!

I'll tell you what, though: never judge a fax machine by its cover, because when George's classified copy began appearing just after 4 p.m., it came out like shit off a stick! The whole of reception was covered in dialogue from the new *Star Wars* movie – the most hotly anticipated film for years.

'How the hell do you stop this bloody thing?' I begged. 'It's printing too quickly!'

'Yeah, it does that,' replied the less-than-helpful receptionist.

In the end, some of my fellow actors came to my aid, but as opposed to simply handing the dialogue over, they began reading it.

'Get your grubby little maulers off my *Star Wars* script,' I protested. 'It's top secret!'

Anyhow, once I'd collected my copy and had shooed away my prying helpers, I raced to my room and began trying to get to grips with my new character. I picked up one of the pages and tried to focus my eyes on the almost invisible ink thereon. It said:

> BOSS NASS: Naboo biggen. Yousa bringen da
> Mackineeks . . . Dya busten uss-en omm. Yousa all
> bombad. Yousa all die'n, mesa tink weesong!

What in the name of old Ben Kenobi's bum was this supposed to be? I couldn't understand a bloody word! It was gobbledegook – like something Professor Stanley Unwin would write. After a further study, I thought it might actually have been some kind of strange Jamaican dialect, but then, when I had another look, it seemed different again. After five or six attempts to get my head round it, I came to the slightly unnerving conclusion that what had in fact been sent to me was just a load of old tosh.

Quick as a flash, I got on the phone to Derek.

'I can't understand a bloody word, love! I think the opening bowler of the West Indies cricket team has written the script.'

While Derek was off calling George's office, I went back to my room, picked up another page and gazed down at the print. This, I saw, was page one. It read:

> BOSS NASS – KING OF THE GUNGANS
>
> Rugor Nass, also known as Boss Nass, is a male
> Ankura Gungan. He is the Boss of all the Otolla
> Gungans, of Otoh Gunga, and of the Gungan High
> Council. He speaks the ancient Gungan dialect as is . . .

'Oh no!' I muttered to myself. 'You bloody idiot! Why didn't you read a bit more before picking up the phone? George's people will think you're a right tit!'

Boss Nass had his own language, then, just like Chewbacca and many of the other characters. It was too late to call Derek back, so I just cracked on.

A few days later, George's people posted me some designs for the Gungan people, as well as for my own character, Boss Nass. I couldn't believe it. Boss Nass was enormous, like some kind of giant amphibian. I was on the phone again.

'Is this *Star Wars* part a voice-over or an actual live role, Derek? I've just seen the designs for Boss Nass and as far as I can make out he's like a giant extra-terrestrial toad! It's far too elaborate for them to make a costume for me, so it must be a voice-over.'

Once again I'd jumped the gun. On the back of the designs were explanations as to how the characters would be brought to life. They were going to film me playing Boss Nass in front of a giant blue screen, before animating the character over my shape. Now it all made sense.

Although the blueprints for the characters confused me a little — because I was too daft to flip over the pages — I'm pleased to say I didn't make the same mistake with the designs for Naboo and, in particular, the underwater Gungan city of Otoh Gunga. These simply took my breath away. If you're not a fan of *Star Wars* it'll bore the flaming arse off you, so I won't go on, but from a broader point of view they signified to me that we were at the dawn of a new cinematic age. CGI technology was now well and truly upon us!

It only seemed like yesterday since we were gazing in wonder at all those marvellous Ray Harryhausen creations in films like *It Came from Beneath the Sea* and *One Million Years B.C.* Dinosaurs, wild animals and all manner of bizarre mythical creatures; each one painstakingly crafted from nothing but Plasticine and then filmed using techniques that required the patience of a thousand saints. I had received designs for costumes before, of course, and had even seen rough drawings of the Hawkmen's Sky City before filming *Flash Gordon* — but computer-generated designs of vast underwater cities and entire worlds? This was creative freedom gone mad. Fancy bread for the eyes! Harry and the geniuses who had pioneered stop-motion technology had been usurped. Computer whiz-kids now presided over the world of special effects and they had removed the boundaries of visual possibility. Movie-making, my dear reader, would never, ever be the same again.

So, eventually, after making a fool of myself with the producers and getting carried away by the possibilities of CGI, I was ready to take my place in front of George's big blue screen and help bring to life his reluctant hero.

The film was shot at Leavesden Film Studios in Hertfordshire, where they later made all the Harry Potter films. Before we began filming, I had dozens of meetings with George about how best to interpret Boss Nass. Normally, you either get a script (usually written in English) and a costume – or, if it's a voice-over, just a script. After that, you take direction and away you go. Easy! All I had for Boss Nass was a script I didn't understand and a blue screen. In fact, lots of blue screens. The difference, though, was in my director. I didn't *need* anything else. I had George Lucas's vision and expertise, not to mention his army of cinematic masterminds. For my part, I had a lively imagination and oodles of enthusiasm. What a combination! We literally bounced off each other with uncontrolled zeal.

At our first meeting, George told me how he saw Boss Nass.

'He's an eccentric, Brian. Everything about him is eccentric: his personality, his mannerisms – everything. And he's volatile. I think Boss Nass could explode at any moment!'

'You've come to the right place, George! I've been accused of being an eccentric on more than one occasion and I can explode with the best of them. You watch this.'

With that, I quite literally went head-over-heels, 24-carat, apo-bloody-plectic. Blessed went atomic. Nay, nuclear! I roared, I screamed, I BOOMED, I shook, I ranted, I raved, I stamped and I beat my chest like a million rabid Kongs. The entire room was in mayhem – a fiesta of extreme noise, hair and saliva.

'There you go!' I yelled. 'How's *that* for volatile?'

'Yes, Brian, but what about eccentric?' said George with a cheeky grin.

'You're joking, love! I'm pooped!'

What a creative yet ribald time we had. Acting's not like work, you know. Every role is a discovery.

Anyway, with the character now taking shape, it was time for me to assume my position in front of the blue screen. I'd worked in front of blue screens before, of course. Remember the Hawkman mobile in *Flash Gordon*? And I suppose I was expecting something quite similar.

Not on your life. As I walked into the gargantuan hangar at Leavesden, I got my first glimpse of a blue screen – *Star Wars* style. It must have been hundreds of feet tall and hundreds of feet wide, and filled the entire front end of the building. And there, right in the middle of the screen, was a raised platform, probably about twenty foot high.

'OK, Brian,' said George, pointing to the platform. 'This is going to be your home for the next few weeks. When Qui-Gon Jinn, Obi-Wan Kenobi and the Queen come to address you, you're either sitting on your throne or standing by a great tree. Either way, they have to look up at you. That's why we've built the platform.'

Every interior scene that involved me, and there were quite a few, would be filmed here, and so I quickly familiarized myself with my new surroundings. There were ladders leading up the side of the platform, and when I finally reached the summit of this new, mini blue mountain of mine, I discovered that George and his people had even kitted it out for me. There was a dip towards the rear and there they had placed a chair, a table and a small fridge. *Very nice*, I thought. *I just need a bookshelf, a few scatter cushions and a picture of Hildegard and we'll be about there.*

The following day, I was introduced to Ewan McGregor and Liam Neeson, two immensely clever actors, but, more importantly, two absolutely splendid fellows, and we got on famously. They were big fans of mine, I'm pleased to say. After that, I met little Natalie Portman. What a stunning creature she is, and so bright.

So there I was, atop Mount Blessed, surveying all that was mine. Subjects scurried to and fro, fetching, carrying and building, and the entire place was a hive of activity. Eventually, I brought my chair to the front of the elevation and sat there, like King Canute.

The only thing that was hard to cope with was the noise; when it came to filming a shot, it took twenty minutes to get everything quiet. This hangar must have been a quarter of a mile long and we only took up the first couple of hundred yards. I don't know exactly what was going on behind me – building sets, most probably – but it definitely wasn't a yoga class. There were horns going off, klaxons and all manner of ear-splitting heavy machinery. There was also some quite colourful language, which made me snigger occasionally.

Once we were ready to go, the assistant director would pick up his megaphone and shout, 'Brian's going to do a few lines. Can we have quiet please?' Then you'd hear somebody in the distance shouting exactly the same thing: 'Brian's going to do a few lines. Can we have quiet please?' On it went, all the way down the building. After about the tenth request, we eventually had hush.

'Remember what we said, Brian,' shouted George through his loud-hailer. 'You're a giant eccentric toad!'

'I didn't spend half my life with the Royal Shakespeare Company to end up as a toad! What a cheek!'

'OK, Brian. How about a salamander? Would that do?'

'Perfect! Ready when you are.'

George and his crew used to love my little impromptu outbursts. I'd try and do one before every take.

What was it I said a little earlier about roles in general? 'You take direction and away you go.' Well, in George's case it was different. When I asked for some direction, for the interiors at least, he was non-forthcoming.

'I'm not going to direct you, Brian. I've got untold cameras in place. We've talked about how Boss Nass *might* be, but to tell you the truth I'm still not really sure. That's why I'm relying on you. He's going to be your creation.'

'But what about the voice?' I asked.

'Once again, over to you. It has to sound like you, though, Brian. That's all I'll say. Don't try and be somebody else.'

I thought about this for a moment and then remembered that toads make clicking noises. I used to have an air-raid shelter full of them when I was a youngster, of course, and I remembered that the younger toads would always go *click, click, click*. When I tried this out on George, he creased up with laughter.

'That's fantastic, Brian! Do toads really do that?'

'They do indeed! I'm an expert on amphibians.'

'OK, well, you go for it!'

So that's what I did in between lines – I clicked – and later on I expanded this a bit by adding grunts and long groans. Poor old Liam Neeson and Ewan McGregor struggled to keep a straight face while I was delivering the clicks and belches.

One of the biggest scenes I had in the film is when the Queen and the Jedis all turn up in Naboo to try and persuade Boss Nass to help them take on the Empire. Before Boss Nass addresses them, they kneel before him to pay tribute. All the cast were on their knees then, but just before I delivered my first line, George shouted, 'Stop!' and then began to ascend Mount Blessed.

'You're trespassing,' I said.

When he got to the top, he walked down to my little home-from-home and beckoned me to join him.

'Have you seen their faces, Brian?' he said in a hushed

tone. 'I don't know what's wrong, but everybody seems to be a bit flat today. Could you do me a favour and make them all laugh? I can't go ahead with them like this and I'm not really a comedian.'

'Leave it to me,' I said. 'Just go back down, shout, "Action!" as if you were filming, and then leave the rest to me. And, by the way, if I ever catch you up here again without permission, I'll blast you into space, OK?'

'OK, I promise,' he said. 'I think I might quite like that, Brian.'

When George got down, he scurried off behind the cameras.

'OK, everyone – ACTION!'

After a few warm-up clicks, I set about them with a series of enormous hippo-like belches.

That did the trick. Five minutes of sweary nonsense and they were as right as ninepence. Once everyone had stopped laughing, George gave me double thumbs-up and we carried on.

Did you know that Keira Knightley plays the decoy queen in *The Phantom Menace*? Not many people do. It was only her second film, you see. Lovely girl!

The next delay in this scene came courtesy of Kenny Baker, who played R2-D2. Cast your mind back to the *Flash Gordon* chapter, dear reader, and to all the fun he and his diminutive mates caused then. Now he was at it again! Every time they went for a take, he went too far and ended up losing his way and falling into a hole. They did take after take, but it was no good. Good old Kenny. He got it right in the end.

Anyway, just before the final shot of the scene, George said to me, 'Brian, when the Queen asks you to help her, I want you to do something unusual. It's the climax of the scene, you see, the start of the final battle – so it has to be good.'

I thought about it for a second and then told him I was ready. After delivering my last line, which was, 'MIIIIIISA LIKE-A DIS!' I did the biggest cheek-quivering, mouth-trembling 'BWIBBLEY' thing you have ever seen (or heard) in your entire life.

'You goddamn mad bastard!' George said. 'That's perfect.'

It became the *pièce de résistance* of my pseudo alien-amphibian sound collection, but the animation they put over it was absolutely inspired. George phoned me as soon as they'd finished it and invited me over to have a look. As Boss shakes his huge wobbly chops from left to right, saliva begins flying all over the place. It was marvellous! According to George, it cost them a bloody fortune to do.

During breaks in filming, George and I would often go for walks together around the studios, just like I did with Katharine Hepburn on *The Trojan Women*. As we'd done at my initial interview, we'd talk about time travel and the moon landings and so on, as well as all our favourite films. We were both very big fans of the Howard Hawks film *The Thing from Another World*, and I remember George saying how impressed he'd been by how much Hawks had managed to squeeze in to the eighty-seven minutes. That must have influenced him a great deal, I think, as he always seems to maintain a good pace in his films.

A few weeks after I'd finished filming, my agent received a telephone call from George's office.

'Some of the sound hasn't quite worked out so we need to come over and record some additional dialogue. Is that OK?'

'Yes, of course,' said Derek on my behalf. 'We just need to arrange the time, date and location.'

'It's tomorrow. We're coming later today. Will that be alright?'

Fortunately, I was free.

'Yes, alright,' agreed Derek. 'What time and where?'

'That's the problem. We haven't been able to find a suitable sound studio that isn't already booked. Would you mind if we used one of your offices?'

'We only have one large room, and it's not likely to be suitable.'

'We could easily turn it into a temporary sound studio, if that's OK by you?'

Derek agreed to the temporary occupation and so the next morning, at about 11 a.m., he opened the door to what he assumed would be two men and a microphone. How wrong can you be? Standing in front of him was Rick McCallum, the producer, and an army of about twenty men. After exchanging a few good mornings, they marched into Derek's office and began the task of setting up shop. There was a huge articulated lorry parked outside and it was being unloaded into his office! Derek was astonished. Once they'd finished unloading, they started blocking out all the windows, then when they'd finished that they began covering all the walls and the ceiling with soundproofing. Five-inch foam! Two hours later, after testing for traffic, wind and heaven knows what else, they were ready to record.

'I just need these three lines and some more clicks,' said Rick.

Three minutes later, we were done.

'Great! That's it. Thanks, Brian. Thanks, Derek. We'll see you soon.'

Five minutes later, they were gone and the whole place was back to normal. It was *the* most bizarre experience my agent had ever had. Perfectionism in action! His whole office taken over for *Star Wars*.

About a month later, it happened again; except this time they had to film some of the end sequence. They weren't going to set up at Leavesden again, of course, but they did hire an entire studio in the West End. Unfortunately, Derek was away at the time and the temps he had in charge completely forgot to tell me that the most powerful man in the bloody film industry had asked me to be at this studio by 4 p.m. When I eventually found out, at about 6 p.m., my eyes were bloodshot with vexation! I won't tell you what I said to the temps. George and his team had been waiting all day. I called George at the studio and told him how sorry I was.

'Don't worry, Brian, these things happen. Get here when you can. We've a little surprise for you.'

When I eventually arrived at the studio, I got the shock of my life. There was George, his wife, his three children, producer Rick, lovely Robin the casting director, the lighting guys and the sound men. They even had a cake.

'Do you know what we're working on today, Brian?' said George. 'We're completing the last line of the film, and you have that last line.'

'You mean the cake and all the people are here for me?'

'You *and* the film, Brian!' he laughed. 'Once we're done here, that's it. It's the end of the film.'

Since 1977, I'd dreamed about appearing in a *Star Wars* film, and now here I was, about to deliver the last line in the new one – the most hotly anticipated film since *Return of the Jedi*!

Love it or hate it, *The Phantom Menace* became a cinematic giant, and the effect it had on all of our lives was extraordinary. When it finally came out it emptied the schools, and it emptied the factories, and it emptied the offices. Productivity all over the world nosedived! Half of us were bunking off school or work going to see the film, while the other half were queueing up for tickets. All told, it made over $1 billion at the box office. One billion! That's almost as much as I charge for a voice-over. Once again, all enquiries to my agent please . . .

After doing the final line, or to be accurate the final word, which is 'peace', I spent an hour with George, his family and the team.

'Well, thanks for everything, Brian,' George said. 'I'll see you at the premiere, right?'

'You will indeed. I can't wait.'

It then dawned on me once again what a privilege all this had been. I'd just finished working with the man responsible for creating one of the most fantastically original set of films ever made. He had fired more imaginations and, in so doing, had created more dreams and ambitions than anybody I'd ever known. He was an innovator and a hero – the father of modern science fiction. I was privileged to be able to call him a friend.

There was time for one last momentous exchange before I left.

'What are we, Brian?' George asked. 'What on earth are we doing here?'

I placed my hands on his shoulders and looked deep into his eyes. 'George, we are the children of stardust, yearning for the stars.'

He returned my gaze and smiled broadly. 'Do you know, Brian, I couldn't agree more. Let's keep it that way. See you on the other side of Orion on one of my ships.'

10

LIFE IS ALL THAT MATTERS

Now, what would you say if I were to tell you that this entire chapter is strewn with nothing but death? Death, death, death, death, death! You'd most probably utter a benediction ending with the word 'off'. Well, you can swear until you're blue in the face, love, because it is. This is BRIAN'S BLOODY DEATH CHAPTER!

What an awful way to finish a book, I can hear you say!

But this is me, remember. The Overlord of life itself! You didn't honestly think I'd finish my book on a downer, did you? Well, no, of course you didn't.

No, no: this is something very, very different.

It is a chronological compendium of anecdotes concerning my *relationship* with death, which has been up and down to say the least. You see, ever since I was a small child I've been in almost constant contact with the Grim Reaper – and I'll tell you, right now, I've got the measure of the bugger. It's taken me a while, but I know what he feeds off, and I also know what makes him tick and, you mark my words, once you're in that position, he's not half as scary as he thinks he is. It's all to do with attitude, my dear reader. As it says at the top of the page: LIFE IS ALL THAT MATTERS!

Allow me to put some meat on the bones.

Although there is no direct translation, the closest word the Tibetans have to the word death is *bardo*. Isn't that a much nicer word? *Bardo*, as in the delectable Brigitte. But, as I said, death and *bardo* are not quite the same. Translated, *bardo* means 'intermediate state', whereas the word death means 'state of being dead'. Tibetans are taught from a very early age that there is no such thing as a 'state of being dead', which is why they have no word for it. They are taught that all they will ever know during their time on this earth is life. Well, that certainly gets my vote. Can you describe what it was like before you were born? No, you can't. And can you describe what it's going to be like after you've pegged it? Once again, no you can't. You might have an opinion based on a religious belief, but regardless of how much you believe it, as long as you're on this earth that's all it will ever be, an opinion.

No, you take my word for it, LIFE is all there is and LIFE is all that matters. That's the message I want you to take from this chapter. From the entire book, even! You see, if we all spent the time we waste worrying about death actually concentrating on life, we'd all be a good deal happier. You mark my words.

Aren't I terribly wise?

So here we go, then, the last hoorah! Some of what you're about to read may pull on the old heartstrings a little – and death is never far away – but, to use a theatrical analogy, it only has a supporting role. LIFE takes the lead and it gives a rousing performance!

My earliest memories of life in South Yorkshire are literally festooned with death. Now, isn't 'festooned' a marvellous word? I once claimed in an interview that 'undulating' was my favourite word in the English language. Well, I'll tell you what, as of today it's 'FESTOONED'! Anyway, as children we not only embraced death, but we actually celebrated it. We found it fascinating. Money was hard to come by in those days and so toys were really quite scarce; which meant a lot of the time we had to improvise. It was then that death became our benefactor. There were dead dogs, cats, newts and frogs pretty much everywhere, and as opposed to simply stepping over these poor unfortunate creatures, we would often use some of them as toys. We couldn't afford to buy the lead soldiers in Booth's shop window. They were sixpence each! Also, you could do a lot more with a dead cat than you ever could with a lead soldier. For instance, with a dead cat you could pretend to be Tarzan. I used to lay one on a branch and pretend it was a leopard. Then I'd fire arrows at it using my home-made archery set. Great fun! I even used to act out scenes from *Jungle Book*. That was if I managed to find a deceased black cat, of course. It would be Bagheera the panther and I would be Mowgli. Granted, you had to have quite an imagination to make it work, but that's what kids are all about, imagination!

You'd often see me, and sometimes one or two of my pals, walking down Probert Avenue swinging a dead cat round by its tail; much to the disgust of the neighbours, of course. They all thought I was slightly peculiar. I remember once the Shepherd family threw a party for one of their children, and every child on the street had been invited, except me.

'We just don't know what he's going to do,' said Mrs Shepherd to my mother. 'He's so unpredictable.'

Mother wanted to stick up for me, but I'm afraid she didn't have a leg to stand on. I *was* unpredictable. I'd ruined dozens of parties over the years by bringing dead animals along or by telling the smaller children terrifying stories. I never meant any harm, by the way. I was simply a born raconteur with a departed menagerie!

Being barred from the Shepherds' party didn't upset me at all, but it did annoy me somewhat, and I'm afraid that often unfortunate emotion left me with a yearning for revenge. The only question was: should I seek my revenge before, during or after the party? During, of course. It had to be during.

The party was on a Saturday afternoon and once all the kiddies were congregated in the Shepherds' garden I shimmied up the drainpipe, climbed over the roof and jumped onto a tree, which was only inches away from the drainpipe. From there, I manoeuvred my way onto an adjacent tree, which brought me roughly into the middle of the garden. The vista was a gay one: hordes of happy children playing in the afternoon sun. There was jelly on a table below me, plus some sandwiches and a huge jug of lemonade. A perfect scene, really. Who could possibly ask for more?

Not wishing to leave without first dropping off my present, I held the dead cat out over the table, squeezed its stomach as hard as I could and watched with glee as the entrails and shit gushed from its arse. It went absolutely everywhere: over the jelly, over the sandwiches, over the parents, over the children. It was like something out of a Peter Greenaway film. Chaos!

Rapidly appreciating the enormity of what had just taken place, not to mention who was actually to blame, I dropped the cat (which landed on a parent), leapt through the trees, climbed back over the roof, shimmied back down the drainpipe and ran like the bloody wind.

Left in my wake was what can only be described as absolute pandemonium. The children were traumatized; the parents were traumatized. Apparently even the police were traumatized when they saw what I'd done.

Anyway, when the police eventually found me, I was dragged in front of them, the Shepherds and my parents. I was unrepentant, though.

'How would any of you feel to be the only child on the street not to be invited to a party?' I said. 'It's just not fair! As far as I'm concerned, they deserved all they got!'

Funnily enough, that didn't help my cause much, and I was told in no uncertain terms that if I was ever caught doing anything like that again, I'd be taken straight to the juvenile courts! Some people have no sense of humour, do they?

After that, I gave up on dead animals for a while and began to wreak havoc using live ones. Our neighbour Mrs Simmons was the first one to get it. She was having tea with my mother one day when all of a sudden a huge fat toad – which I had planted moments before – jumped out from behind a chair and landed on Mrs Simmons's foot. I take it you're familiar with the phrase 'I nearly had a heart attack'? Well, Mrs Simmons nearly did have a heart attack. In fact, after dropping her tea, she fainted. Poor Mrs Simmons refused to set foot in our house for weeks after that.

As I said, no sense of humour.

Believe it or not, we weren't totally lacking in respect for these animals, even the dearly departed ones. Yes, we used to play with the odd dead cat every now and then, but more often than not if we saw a dead animal we would take it away and bury it, and we did the same with the cats once we'd finished playing with them. We had our own cemetery at the back of a field and it was full of all kinds of deceased creatures. Each grave would be marked using a cross made out of twigs and once the animal was safely underground, a prayer would quite naturally break forth from our lips. Something like: 'Lighten our darkness, we beseech thee, O Lord; and by thy great mercy defend us from all perils and dangers of this night; for the love of thy only Son, our Saviour, Jesus Christ. Amen.'

I remember there was one dead cat we didn't bury, however. Instead of our usual burial ceremony, we decided to leave it on the railway embankment and over the coming weeks and months observed it in its various stages of decay. We found this absolutely fascinating!

So, as I said, as small children we had absolutely no problem with death. After all, we'd only been born a few years before. That fluid vale between life and death was not feared by us. Our knowledge of it was absolute. We found it peaceful and knew instinctively, with our big eyes and our cheeky wide smiles, that the vast majority of our elders, between say the ages of twenty-five and forty, had lost this knowledge. Of course, it would return to them in due course, but as children it was the very old to whom we were attracted. We couldn't resist them. They seemed so brave and full of fun.

Victorian in their attitude, they had inherited from their own parents strong convictions about the eternal soul and the resurrection of the body. The Victorians' outlook on death and on dying was so very different from our own. In those days, many more people died at an early age and so they were used to death. My grandparents on my father's side – who were of course both Victorians – would visit the family mausoleum and spend the day there, taking a picnic with them. More often than not, I'd go along for the ride.

I remember one fellow we used to meet, Mr Kenny Swallow, who was dying because of injuries he'd sustained during the First World War. He had gangrene in both legs yet he was one of the most cheerful people I have ever met in my life.

I asked him one day if he was dying, knowing full well that he was, and the moment I did, a great big smile enveloped his face.

'Aye, I'm dying alright, lad. But just because I'm dying it doesn't mean I have to die.'

And with that he got up, laid himself down on top of the nearest grave and burst into fits of laughter. I joined him on the grave and we lay there for about five minutes, laughing at what he'd said. This man had no fear of death, for the simple reason he had no interest in it. It didn't change his life at all.

I remember Pope Paul VI once saying that somebody, at the very start of our lives, should tell us that we're dying.

That way, we might be free to live life to the full. Fine words, eh? Well, alas, they're not that easy to follow these days.

So, I suppose you could say that my early relationship with death was based primarily around curiosity and mischief. But as the years passed, I began to find the rotten thing more and more unacceptable. I was growing up, wasn't I? Suddenly, it wasn't animals that were dying all around me, it was people; and instead of smiling at death, I wanted to kick the bugger into the middle of next week. I wanted to chin the bastard!

At about ten years of age, I was part of a delightful gang of boys. We'd been pals for years and were known as the Probert Avenue Kids. They were the ones I used to watch *Flash Gordon* with, remember? Well, we used to do absolutely everything together, me and my gang, and we lived the most idyllic life imaginable. Real *Swallows and Amazons* stuff! Then, one day, everything in our world went black. One of the members of our gang, young Tank, drowned in a nearby pond. We were all there at the time and tried to save him, but the banks of the pond were too steep and none of us could swim strongly enough. Tank was a big lad, you see, hence the name, and it would have taken at least one fully grown adult to get him out.

Now, I'm not going to dwell on this as I've already covered the story in my previous book, *The Dynamite Kid*. Suffice to say the experience forced us all to take swimming lessons, and six months later we swam the length and breadth of Brick Pond and laid Tank's ghost to rest.

Not long after this, another member of our gang, a lad called David Dunbar, lost his dad. He'd had a heart attack in his chair one day and had died almost instantly. I remember seeing David the next day.

'What's the matter?' I asked.

'Me dad's dead,' he said.

'What?'

'Me dad's dead. He was sitting in his chair last night and just died. He had a heart attack, so me mum says. She hasn't stopped crying since.'

Poor, poor David. He was such a nice lad.

'Never mind,' I said. 'Tomorrow's Saturday. I'll collect you on the way to the cinema and I'll also pay for your ticket. How's that?'

This cheered him up no end and life carried on as before. Life always carried on.

So, by now, my relationship with death had flipped 180 degrees. So much so that I even began obsessing about it, and about the effect it was having on the lives of those around me. I now looked on Mr Swallow as being callous and disrespectful. How could he joke about such a serious, solemn subject?

All of a sudden, death was my enemy, and I began noticing it everywhere. And just think about where I lived for a moment. I lived in South Yorkshire, and what do you have in South Yorkshire? You have tunnels; hundreds and hundreds of tunnels about a thousand feet below the ground. And what did you have in these tunnels, apart from coal? You had coal miners, coal hewers, seeping gas, dynamite, bending pit props, steel tubs breaking loose from their moorings and hurtling their way along rusting rails. These places were full of death. Teeming with it!

My Uncle Bernard was the first person close to me to be killed down the mines. He'd been found one day, his head crushed under a falling boulder. My father and his brothers said little, their faces expressionless, their demeanour almost taciturn. What was there to say, though? Whenever I asked a question, my father would look up for a moment. 'It happens, lad,' he said. 'It happens.'

After that, I had nightmares for weeks on end. Death came everywhere with me.

Of course, as a young child, I never thought it possible that my own father might be killed down the mines. He'd been gassed once, but although that had been a difficult time for everybody, he had never really been at death's door. But after the death of my Uncle Bernard, the paradigm shifted somewhat. All of a sudden it wasn't just possible that my father might be killed, it was likely. Or at least it was in my mind. Then, in 1951, when I was just fifteen years old, all my worst fears came perilously close to becoming a reality when, during a freak accident down the mine, my father was crushed by a falling boulder, just as my Uncle Bernard had been. Both his hips were shattered and he suffered all kinds of awful internal injuries. According to the doctors, he should have died there and then, but somehow he managed to remain conscious until he was found, and so his life was saved. Paradoxically – and this is why I am telling you this story – although my father didn't die, his accident brought me so close to death that I could actually touch it.

We arrived at Mexborough hospital to find my father pale and in terrible pain. Despite his physical injuries, the biggest danger to his life was shock. Several of his colleagues who had been involved in the same accident had died from shock overnight, and so it seemed almost inevitable that he would also succumb.

'Don't die, Dad,' I pleaded.

'I'm trying my best not to, lad. If I can get through the next night, Doctor says I'll be fine.'

And he did: he made it through the night and lived. A few weeks later, he was moved to Purbeck Rehabilitation Centre to convalesce, but even then it had already been made clear to us that his recovery was going to take many, many months. This meant he was unable to work, of course, and if he was unable to work, where would the money come from?

You already know what happened when he was gassed. The compensation pay simply wasn't enough to live on. Sure, we could get by for a few weeks, but this was going to be months. Maybe even a year. Despite the severity of the situation, I'm afraid I still wasn't prepared for what was about to befall me.

'Brian, lad,' said my father during a visit to Purbeck one day. 'I'm afraid we're going to have to take you out of school and put you to work, lad. Until I'm fit again, you're the man of the house, and I need you to look after your mother and young Alan for me. Can you do that, lad?'

'Of course I can, Dad,' I said. 'You leave it to me.'

What a performance that was. One of my best ever, in fact. Despite appearing keen and cooperative to my father, I was devastated. Absolutely flattened! You know how well I was doing at school; after such an inauspicious start, I was now the model pupil. I had a terrific relationship with the teachers, in particular Mr Jones and Mr Donaldson, and had just been made the school captain. That place was my life! To have it all taken away seemed so unfair. My final year at school – gone.

At first, my father's brothers had provided for us, but after a few weeks that simply wasn't sustainable. They all had families of their own, and with families come unexpected expenses. This meant that some weeks they were able to supplement my father's loss of income, and on other weeks they were not. This uncertainty was unbearable for my mother, and drove her to the verge of yet another nervous breakdown.

'Brian,' she said. 'You're eating us out of house and home. Look at you, lad. You must weigh at least thirteen stone. I need you to work, Brian!'

She had a point. So active was I – what with school, drama and all the sport I used to play – that I had the appetite of a medium-sized bull. No, I had to concede that there was indeed only one thing for it; I would have to go out and work. But what on earth would I do? I had no formal training. Would I be a butcher, a baker? Well, no, of course not. I became an undertaker's assistant.

The happiest child in school, with an unhealthy fear of death, had been removed from his seat of learning and given a job making coffins. Bleeding marvellous! You couldn't make it up, could you?

Percy Philipson was my boss – the genial Percy Philipson. I'm afraid I'm being sardonic, as Percy Philipson was in fact the most miserable man who has ever set foot on this earth. You'll pardon the pun, but having a boss who thought smiling was a sackable offence really was the final nail in the coffin for me. Depressed? I should say I was depressed. I'm naturally quite a happy person – excitable, even – but I'm afraid my situation felt almost intolerable.

Now, Mr Philipson was a self-made man, and he was also quite a wealthy man. This meant there was always quite a lot of resentment towards him in the town. People were jealous of his success and he used to thrive on this. He was very rough in character and was quick to temper, but as I got to know him I soon discovered that underneath he was, in fact, quite a kindly man. Dickensian, really.

He loathed me at first, and I him. I was appalling with wood, and this drove him to despair.

'Why do I have to get lumbered with an apprentice who can't work with wood?' he moaned. 'You're no use to me, lad. You're no use to me.'

But because of what had happened to me, I was in no mood to be shat upon, and so whenever the old sod started whinging, I always gave him both barrels back.

'I never asked to make bloody coffins. Why can't I work up in the shop?'

'You'll work wherever I tell you, lad. Now shut yer trap and try and get to grips with that sander!'

This kind of repartee went on all the time, and I actually think he rather enjoyed our little squabbles. He must have, I suppose, otherwise he'd have got rid of me.

My place of work was the basement underneath Mr Philipson's undertaker's shop. It was a large room with absolutely no natural light and it was there that he taught me how to make coffins.

'You're not bloody squeamish, are you, lad?' he asked on my first day. 'Because if you are, you may as well make yourself scarce. You'll be handling wood and dead bodies while you're here. Did you hear that, lad? Wood and dead bodies. Now, how do you think you'll cope with that?'

'I'll cope just fine,' I said, lying through my teeth. The thought of working with wood was bad enough, but dead bodies?

In actual fact, it was the best thing for somebody with a fear of death. Conditioning, I believe they call it. Within a week or two, I was as comfortable with death and dead human bodies as I had been with dead cats.

The local Co-operative was our main competitor, and they were, I suppose, a far more respectable organization; but our coffins were much better than theirs. You see, despite being a bit of a curmudgeon, old Percy Philipson was one of the best joiners in the country, and had received the MBE a few years earlier for that very reason. Once we got used to each other, I began to appreciate the fact that I was working for a master craftsman. He made it look so bloody easy! I would watch him demonstrate something to me, and I'd think, *That looks easy enough*. Then, when I tried to do it myself, I'd make a complete bloody hash of it. No, I had to admit it, this man was an artist. And his work rate was phenomenal. It took him one hour to build a coffin from scratch. One hour!

Anyway, after a few weeks' training, not to mention one or two cross words, Mr Philipson had succeeded in teaching me how to make the perfect coffin. I was now a self-sufficient undertaker's assistant! I could do the lot: I could wash the body with carbolic soap, massage it where rigor mortis had set in, use make-up if they'd started to go off a bit, bring the eyes out from their sockets (they were always the first to go), build a nice new coffin, line it with fabric and sawdust, dress the body and *voil*à! One perfectly prepared corpse, all ready for either the furnace or the hole in the ground. Entirely your choice, madam!

Although, after a while, I began getting used to this new vocation of mine, I still found my predicament terribly embarrassing; never more so than when my friends came to visit me on their way home from school. If Philipson was out, which he often was at that time, they'd pop down and see me occasionally, but I could tell by the looks on their faces that they found the situation awkward. 'Look what he's been reduced to.' That's how their expressions translated. They couldn't leave fast enough, and after the third or fourth visit they stopped coming. I was relieved in a way. I still saw them all socially, but it always had to be on neutral ground.

Now, the one thing Mr Philipson did that got right on my bloody tits was he used to slap me across the back of the head whenever he passed me in the workshop. I don't mind taking a punch, so long as it's to my front, but a slap on the back of my head used to leave me reeling! Every time he did it, I'd say to him, 'Don't do that, Philipson. Don't do that again.' To him it was an extension of our badinage, of course. He found it funny when I told him to bugger off, and he also found it funny slapping me across the back of the head. I, on the other hand, did not.

'You do that again and I'll bloody well crack you one, OK?' I hasten to add that he was about six foot tall and sixteen stone.

He accepted my warning as well as Peter O'Toole accepted stage direction.

'Ha! Your gob's almost as big as your head, lad. Don't you

threaten me! I was Chief Petty Officer on HMS *Cleopatra*. I'll kick your arse into the middle of next week.'

This encounter was, in fact, just a rehearsal for what was to come. I'll get to that in a moment.

We had what was known as a 'cold room' for the bodies, which was really just a room with a bit of ice in it. So ineffective was the 'not very cold room' that Mr Philipson eventually had to have a morgue fitted in there, which was basically just a big fridge with lots of shelves in it. This was quite an exciting time at Philipson's Undertakers. Until then, we'd had dead bodies going off all over the place, and the stench – not to mention some of the noises decomposing bodies make – almost drove us to distraction.

Although my friends from school no longer visited me at work, members of my gang used to pop in all the time.

Sometimes I'd have four or five bodies waiting to go into the morgue. They had to be embalmed first – which was something Mr Philipson usually did – and so while I waited for him to get back, I'd line them up outside the morgue door. This gave me an idea one day. Do you remember me telling you about my talent for terrifying children? Well, what better way to terrify a child – or in this case some young adults – than by using a selection of stiffs! The bodies were still full of gas, which meant that even the slightest pressure on the stomach would result in anything from a fart to one of them actually sitting upright.

My pals were due to visit me about 4 p.m. and Mr Philipson usually came back about 5 p.m. This meant I had a full hour to try and terrify them. It took me about three hours to prepare but in that time I managed to set up, underneath the sheets, a lever that, when manipulated, would apply enough pressure to make the bodies break wind or, better still, move.

I kept the lights low so as to create the right effect and when my gang duly arrived they naturally took great interest in my collection of covered corpses.

'What have you got there, Brian?' asked one of them.

'Two pensioners, a middle-aged man and a middle-aged woman,' I said, doing my best to sound like Colin Clive.

'How long have they been dead?'

'Long enough,' I said.

'Can we have a look at them?'

By this time, they were shaking like Oliver Reed passing a pub.

'Of course you can,' I said eerily. 'Lean over them while I pull back the sheets.' As they did so, I pushed down the lever and let nature take its course. I have to say, I was delighted with the results. I got two almighty farts from the pensioners, a groan from the middle-aged woman and a nice 'jolt' from the middle-aged man. Bingo!

Have you ever seen a group of fifteen-year-old boys lose complete control of themselves? It really is quite something. One of them, who shall remain nameless, actually pissed his pants! He couldn't get out, you see. In fact, none of them could, because after they'd arrived I'd very quietly locked the door. So for my two farts, a groan and a jolt, I'd received about a thousand screams, lots of running round and a small yellow puddle. Not a bad return! It took me about ten minutes to persuade them that the bodies had just been letting out wind.

'You bastard, Brian,' they said. 'You big horrible bastard!'

Fortunately, they didn't stop visiting me at work, but from then on they were always very cautious when entering the workshop.

My only fault as an undertaker's assistant was that I was forever buggering up the measurements for the coffins. This happened quite regularly, I'm afraid, and used to have poor old Mr Philipson reaching for the bottle. If truth be known, as opposed to measuring the bodies with a tape measure like I was supposed to, I actually used to challenge myself to be able to guess them. I didn't have a bad success rate – probably about three out of four – but because I *had* a tape measure it should have been four out of four. There was really no excuse. It wasn't really a problem when I made the coffins too big for the body; it was when I made them too small that difficulties began to occur. Many was the time Mr Philipson would walk into the workshop only to find me with my knee on some poor corpse's chest, desperately trying to lever him or her into their new home.

'What the bloody hell are you doing, lad? You shouldn't be treating a body like that. Have some respect!'

'Well, they can't feel anything, can they? What's the problem?'

Now, the richest person in Goldthorpe at the time – even richer than Mr Philipson – was a Mr Yardley. He was a tall gentleman, about six foot three, and one day he arrived in my workshop. Dead as a doornail, of course. He was in his seventies, which back then wasn't bad, so he'd had a good innings. Anyway, after getting rid of his wind and massaging away a bit of rigor mortis, I lined him up outside the morgue so Mr Philipson could embalm him. After he'd finished, I started washing Mr Yardley with carbolic soap, but when I was about halfway through, he started turning this awful greenish colour. I stared at the lump of soap, which was also green, and wondered if the colour had somehow washed off on him.

'Mr Philipson,' I said. 'Mr Yardley's turning green!'

'What on earth are you talking about, lad? If this is one of your bloody jokes I'll—' As soon as he saw the body, he stopped. 'Oh my God, lad, I've used the wrong embalming fluid! What are we going to do? They want his coffin open before the funeral.'

Apparently, Yardley had died of yellow jaundice, and if you died from yellow jaundice you had to be embalmed with a different kind of fluid. Mr Philipson had obviously forgotten the cause of death and had carried on as normal.

Anyway, Mr Philipson and I now had a bona fide crisis

on our hands. For a start, when the family discovered what had happened they'd be furious! Turning the richest corpse in the town green was probably not going to be good for business, either, especially as they wanted his casket open prior to the funeral. He looked like the Green Mekon from the *Dan Dare* comic. Mr Yardley had ended up as a Treen!

'What are we going to do, lad?' said Mr Philipson. 'Think, lad, think!'

'I've got it!' I said. 'My make-up bag.'

'Your WHAT?'

The look on Philipson's face was a picture.

'My make-up bag I use at the theatre. I can use that.'

'Really, lad?' said Mr Philipson. 'Do you think it'll work?'

'Well, he's only light green, isn't he? I reckon I can get him back to normal.'

'Off you go then, lad.'

It really was our only hope. If it didn't work, nobody would ever use Philipson's again, which would mean I'd be out of a job. I didn't want that to happen. My parents were relying on me and, in addition, although I'd much rather have been at school, I actually kind of enjoyed my job there.

Fortunately, after a generous application of Number 9, Number 5 and some lipstick, Mr Yardley began looking like a normal corpse again. Or at least his face and neck did. As long as his family didn't look underneath his clothes – and let's face it, why on earth would they? – we should be OK.

'You've done me and this company a big favour today, lad,' said Mr Philipson. 'Thank you!'

You could have knocked me down with a feather. A 'thank you' from Mr Philipson! As well as being a welcome gesture, it also helped soften the blow a little when he realized I'd made Mr Yardley's coffin about a foot and a half too long.

'It's about eight foot long, lad! Think of all that wood you could have saved.'

At the funeral service at the church, people, on seeing the size of the coffin, commented: 'It looks as though he's taken his money with him!'

Anyway, although the Grim Reaper and I were now back on speaking terms, I still wasn't completely impervious to the more distressing aspects of my job. I don't care if you're the Dalai Lama or God himself, seeing the body of a child is one of the most distressing things a human eye can witness. Unfortunately, child mortality was quite high in those days, and so it was something I just had to try and get used to. This worked to a point, I suppose, but I'm afraid that no amount of dead bodies could have prepared me for what I saw at work one morning.

I arrived at the usual time of 8 a.m. As I started to head down to the basement, Mr Philipson stopped me.

'There's a new customer downstairs, lad. He's already been embalmed.'

Nothing out of the ordinary there, of course. We had one or two arrivals every day, sometimes more during winter! So down the stairs I went. I turned on the lights, hung up my coat, opened the morgue and pulled back the sheet covering our new arrival. And there, lying perfectly still on the slab, was Barry Patterson, one of my oldest friends. Tears welled up in my eyes. He had had such a promising future. Barry was such a bright lad and attended the local grammar school. He was a keen cyclist in his spare time and I later learned he had been knocked down by a car. You didn't see many cars on the roads back then, and because of that there weren't many accidents. How on earth could it have happened? Lost in thought, all of a sudden I heard a voice.

'What's up with you, lad? You're not crying, are you?' It was Philipson, of course.

'He was a friend of mine, that's all.'

'Ha! A bit soft-hearted are you, lad? Pathetic. Get on with the coffin. He's no different to anyone else.'

He never saw the first, or indeed the second punch I threw; both of which landed precisely where they'd been aimed, on his left and then his right cheek.

'You horrible old BASTARD!' I roared, before getting my head down and letting go a plethora of body punches. 'You really are a horrible old BASTARD!'

Although taken by surprise, Philipson was quick to retaliate and caught me with an elbow to the nose (that hurt!), followed by an upper cut to the chin. By now, the fight was well and truly on. We laid into each other like a couple of rabid Tasmanian devils, except I was fifteen and about five foot seven at the time, and he was fifty-five and about six foot three. God only knows what it must have looked like. There was blood on the walls and bits of lip flying through the air. It really was a proper warts-and-all scrap!

'He was my friend!' I roared. Philipson didn't answer me. He was too busy dodging my fists, not to mention my feet. I have never been so angry in all my life.

The whole thing actually reminded me of the end of *On the Waterfront*, when Marlon Brando fights Lee J. Cobb. Brando is by far the smaller of the two, and so has to use a lot of inside punches, and that was pretty much what happened with Philipson and me. I just kept my head down and tried to land as many inside punches as possible. Bang!

Anyway, after about five minutes, Philipson's wife came rushing in and eventually managed to separate us.

'What on earth is going on?' she shouted. 'Look at you both; you're absolutely covered in blood!'

She was actually a lovely woman, Mrs Philipson. She was a real lady. Being chastised by her made me feel very small indeed.

'I'm very sorry, Mrs Philipson,' I began. 'It was my fault. I reacted stupidly to something—'

But before I could finish, Mr Philipson interrupted me.

'It's not his fault, love. It was my fault. That boy lying on that slab is a friend of his, and I mocked him for getting upset. It was the wrong thing to do, lad, and I'm sorry.'

With that, we shook hands and began clearing up the workshop. It was like an old-fashioned butcher's shop, all blood and sawdust. But despite making my peace with Mr Philipson, I'm afraid I had to leave Philipson's Undertakers. Seeing Barry lying there had all been a bit much for me. After all, I was just a fifteen-year-old boy, not even a man. Mr Philipson took the news well and even paid me until the end of the month, which meant I had three weeks' money in hand; more than enough time to find another job. I did insist that he allow me to make Barry's coffin, although I'm afraid I couldn't bring myself to prepare the body. That would have been too much. I'll tell you what, though: when Barry Patterson was laid to rest, it was in one of the finest coffins that has ever been made. I spent over a day working on it, AND I measured his body beforehand! It was the very least I could do for him. My old pal Barry.

I'm afraid not even I can turn that story into a comedy. That said, out of pain comes strength, and when I left Mr Philipson's service, I did so not only with two very sore ears, but also with a greater appreciation of life and a much-diminished obsession with death. It was there that I learned to accept death for what it is and to embrace life for as long as it's here. I have good old Barry to thank for that. Seeing him reorganized my priorities – into the right bloody order, this time – and I'm pleased to say they've been steadfast ever since.

Fortunately, there was a very long gap before I experienced death close up again. The first time I ever experienced death as a professional actor was when I was working on *Z Cars*. As you know, one of the main characters in the early shows was the desk sergeant – Sergeant Twentyman – who was played by a lovely, lovely chap called Leonard Williams. Leonard was born in 1917 so would have been about forty-five at the time and he was without doubt the joker of the cast. He made absolutely everybody laugh, and pretty much all of the time.

Anyway, not long after *Z Cars* started there was a party held for the cast and crew. I forget what the occasion was, but I remember I'd been persuaded by Leonard to attend. Normally I pooh-poohed these events, as I'm sure you're now aware, but for some reason on this occasion Leonard had insisted.

'We'll have a laff, Brian,' he said, grinning from ear to ear. 'I promise you, whatever else happens, we'll have a right good laff!'

My God, he was right.

I remember there were lots and lots of actors at this party and about an hour in I was introduced to one called Glyn Houston. Now, Glyn was already a very popular character actor and was appearing in *Z Cars* as a guest. I got on very well with him. We seemed to have a mutual interest in the metaphysical and I found what he had to say very, very interesting.

Anyway, both Leonard and I had a reputation for being enormous piss-takers on *Z Cars*. The longer this conversation with Glyn went on, the more serious he became. He really started opening up about what he believed in and I have to say I was fascinated. His knowledge on the subject – or subjects – was phenomenal! Unfortunately, after earwigging on some of our conversation, Leonard got it into his head that I must have been taking the piss out of Glyn and so decided to try and infiltrate our tête-à-tête. Glyn was just getting on to Buddha, I think, when all of a sudden I saw Leonard's face slowly rise up from behind Glyn's shoulder.

'You're taking the piss, Blessed,' he mouthed silently to

me, while sporting an absolutely enormous grin. His jollity was so infectious!

I did my best to concentrate on nothing but Glyn's face, but I'm afraid it was futile.

Leonard's head soon appeared again.

'You're taking the piss, Blessed!'

By this time, Leonard's face was contorted with laughter and his eyes were literally streaming with tears. He genuinely thought I *was* taking the mickey. There was Glyn pouring his heart out about Buddha and all the time Leonard's mouthing foul oaths at me and dying with laughter.

He'd disappear for a few minutes and then, just when I thought it was safe, he'd appear again behind Glyn's face.

'Oi, Blessed, you're taking the piss!'

After about the sixth time of this happening, I suddenly had this overwhelming compulsion to laugh with Leonard. It really was the strangest experience, almost as if it would be my very last chance to do so. I knew it was the wrong thing to do and under normal circumstances I would never have dreamed of hurting Glyn's feelings – or anyone else's for that matter – but I just had to make Leonard believe that I *was* taking the piss. So the next time Leonard appeared over Glyn's shoulder, I broke down and started laughing. I wept! I laughed and I cried and I cried and I laughed. Poor old Glyn went absolutely apoplectic! I couldn't control it.

'How DARE you!' he boomed. 'You ignorant pig!'

And, with that, he stormed out of the party. I tried calling after him, but he wasn't having any of it. Leonard was on the floor by this time, howling uncontrollably.

'I knew it!' he cried. 'I knew you were taking the piss. That was brilliant, Brian! Thank you thank you thank you!'

Anyway, the next morning I turned up to the read-through as usual and, once everyone had arrived, David Rose, the producer, stood up.

'I'm afraid I have some terrible news for you all,' he said.

'Leonard Williams died last night. He died of thrombosis in his flat. I'm very sorry.'

We were all ill with grief. There were literally thousands of people associated with *Z Cars* over the years, but I promise you none of them was as loved as Leonard Williams. He was just a dear, dear man.

After being told the news, I sat in a corner for a while and tried to get my head around what had happened. All of a sudden, I remembered the previous night. That's *why I chose Leonard over Glyn*, I thought. That's *why I laughed at the expense of Glyn Houston's feelings*. It was indeed my last chance to laugh with Leonard! It would never happen again. I loved Leonard so much I just had to do it, and as much as I admire Glyn and felt bad about it at the time, I'm very glad I did.

Isn't that funny, though? You often hear stories of people experiencing a kind of sixth sense, but it's only when it happens to you that you're able truly to appreciate its significance.

I've met Glyn Houston twice since then, both times at Television Centre, and each time I've tried to explain to him what happened that night – but I'm afraid the moment he looks at me, all I see is Leonard's face mouthing, 'You're taking the piss, Blessed!' and so immediately I begin to laugh. It's as if I become momentarily possessed by the ghost of Leonard Williams. Sorry Glyn!

I think the strangest story I have to offer regarding death concerns a television series I made back in 1987 called *My Family and Other Animals*, which was of course based on the marvellous book by the late Gerald Durrell and tells the story of his early life on Corfu. It's as light as a feather really and features all kinds of endearing characters; not to mention animals, of course. It was real 'Sunday evening seven o'clock' type stuff. Compulsive viewing!

All kinds of people were in it: Hannah Gordon and Anthony Calf, for instance, and the producer was a chap called Joe Waters. It was all filmed on Corfu and I played the part of Spiro, a local taxi driver who had kind of looked after the Durrells while they were there. He was a real character, Spiro, and so it was wonderful playing him. Everything was so idyllic. Here we were, filming a new adaptation of a well-loved and joyous book, and on such a beautiful island! We were all very, very lucky. And there were animals absolutely everywhere, which of course made yours truly feel even luckier still.

Oh yes, and we also had lots of death. That's right. Death! The entire bloody production was chock-a-block with it!

Joe Waters really did have a horrible time on the show. In fact, everything that could have gone wrong did go wrong. Two days into filming, one of the extras dropped dead. Just like that. Halfway through a scene . . . *thud*! It was unfortunate, but these things happen.

'Don't worry, Joe,' I told him. 'People die all the time. Just think yourself lucky it wasn't live, love!'

'You're not helping, Brian! You're not bloody helping!' he responded.

Now, you wouldn't believe it, but on Corfu there's hardly ever any bloody wind, and so for the sake of one or two scenes poor old Joe had to bring in a bloody wind machine. There was only one on Corfu at the time, which was owned by a man based in the southern part of the island, and so at enormous expense Joe hired this man, together with his big bloody wind machine.

While Joe was hiring wind machines and burying unfortunate extras and so on, there were all kinds of things going on on set. Animals had been escaping all over the place, and millions and millions of insects, which had been bought especially for the production, were all put in a freezer by mistake so had been frozen to bloody death. It was carnage, love! Millions were dying! We were only supposed to be making a series about toads and froggies and things.

To take everybody's minds off this series of unfortunate events, I took some members of the cast up Mount Pantokrator, which at 900 metres is the highest mountain on Corfu. It was a blisteringly hot day, and although I thought we'd taken plenty of water with us, they were all so bloody slow that by the time we were just over halfway up, they were all dying of dehydration. I almost killed half the cast! In the end, I made them drink goat's piss. I did! Mountain goats were pissing into these little pools on the rocks and so I said to them, 'If you want a bloody drink, love, it's either piss, piss or piss!' They all drank it, though. I made them.

By the time we reached the top, they were almost vomiting. Fortunately, there was a monastery at the top of Mount Pantokrator, and so as soon as we arrived our bottles were replenished, and we were able to make it safely back down to the town.

So, what's the tally so far? One dead extra, several million dead insects, a plethora of dehydrated actors and actresses and some escaped animals. We can do better than that, though.

On the next day of filming, one of the crew was bitten by a scorpion, and another was hit on the head by a camera. Both lived, but were hospitalized.

By the way, just across from us in Athens at this time, Ken Branagh and Emma Thompson were making *Fortunes of War*, and nothing – be it a human, centipede or duck-billed platypus – came to any harm whatsoever. *Fortunes of War*! Here we were making something even lighter than *Dumbo* and there was more bloodshed than the Hundred Years' War! Typical bloody Branagh.

Anyway, after enjoying about a week's grace, during which only one goat was killed after being run over by a local, this chap turned up with his wind machine. Later that day, while I was standing talking to a member of the crew, the director of the series, Peter Barber-Fleming, walked slowly out of the production offices shaking his head.

'Brian,' he said. 'All our worst nightmares have come true. Please don't go in there.'

'But what on earth has happened, Peter?' I asked.

Inside the offices were three big rooms, and the man with the wind machine had asked if he could store his apparatus in the middle one, as there was nobody else based there. After putting it down, he decided it would be a good idea to take the guard off and test it, after which he tripped over a piece of furniture, fell straight in and it took his bloody head off.

The fun doesn't stop there, though. After he lost his head, he carried on walking straight into the next room, where one of the accounts ladies was going about her business. Can you imagine that? One minute you're trying to do a bloody sum, and the next minute you're coming face to face with a man who's been murdered by his own wind machine.

All this happened about three days before the press were due to arrive to cover some of the filming and start building their stories for when the show hit the TV screens.

Sure enough, a few days later about ten journalists turned up. Poor old Joe was in a permanent state of nervousness, trying to make sure the journalists didn't get wind – pardon the pun – of any of our little catastrophes.

Unbelievably, everything seemed to go without a hitch, and after two or three days of interviews and photo sessions our good friends from the press were all ready to depart. They just had to attend one last bit of filming before they went, which took place next to the harbour. All the actors and crew were in place.

'Places, everybody, please. Lights, camera, action!'

And what happened next? Another extra dropped dead. One minute he was having a coffee, and the next he was fuck-offee. Gone! Right in front of the press. To be fair to them, they were all over the poor chap trying to revive him, but apparently his heart had given way. Joe Waters, who had been a few hundred yards away at the time, suddenly came running onto the set with his arms in the air.

'What the hell's happened now?' he yelled.

'You've lost another one, Joe,' I said, in full earshot of the press. 'Another one bites the dust, my old son.'

So there you have it: one of the most gentle screen adaptations ever committed to celluloid was in actual fact a gigantic death-fest! Not unlike this chapter.

Here we are, then, at the precipice of my concluding anecdote. The final pages of the final chapter of *Absolute Pandemonium*. If you've enjoyed reading this just half as much as I've enjoyed writing it, I think we'll all walk away with smiles on our faces. If you're not smiling, balls to you!

Now, some of you will have seen the programme *Have I Got News for You* and some of you won't. For those of you who haven't seen it, it's basically a satirical quiz show featuring Paul Merton and Ian Hislop. They're the team captains and in addition to a guest on each team, they also have a guest presenter each week. This was my role. Now, before I go on, I'd just like to say a few words about the uniqueness of this kind of role; for me, anyway. You see, when I'm on television or on a stage or on film, I'm always acting. I've done the odd interview, of course, but have never been able to relax and be myself. If you're being asked personal questions, you're going to be on your guard, aren't you? No, it's impossible to simply be yourself. So that's exactly why I was attracted to this offer of presenting *Have I Got News for You*. They asked me to be myself.

Why not? I thought. *Like it or loathe it, it'll be a new experience, and new experiences are what I'm all about.*

Remember what I said? Just go for it! And so I followed my own advice.

When the episode aired, I had my critics, of course, but on the whole people seemed to like the real me − or at least liked being entertained by me − and I myself had an absolutely marvellous time. I can be a bit of a loose cannon at times, so to put me in front of a studio audience with two of the country's funniest and cleverest men was always going to be a gamble. If it had been live, I'd never have got as far as the car park! But Ian, Paul and I seemed to gel, and we ended up delivering what I believe are two of the programme's best ever episodes. I can hear some of you now saying, 'Oh well, you would say that, wouldn't you?' Well, of course I would! Get off your high horse!

Because the first show went so well, I was invited back for second helpings. *Very brave of them*, I thought. *Well, if they're good enough to invite me back, I'll do my very best.*

'Just be yourself again, Brian,' they said. 'Don't change a thing, just be you, OK?'

Now, about a week before we were due to film this second episode, Margaret Thatcher shuffled off this mortal coil. This was one of the biggest news stories in years, of course, and was immensely divisive. This increased tenfold, however, when details of her funeral were released. It was going to cost the taxpayers millions, apparently, and half the country was in uproar about it. I couldn't give two hoots either way, as long as it wasn't my funeral.

I had a meeting with the production people a day or two before filming and they complained to me that the story was in danger of casting a shadow over the show. *Have I Got News for You* has a glorious tradition of being able to find the funny side of *any* kind of news story.

'We need you to brighten it up a bit, Brian,' they said. 'This Thatcher funeral's becoming far too depressing. You can do anything you like, just don't make it serious.'

Talk about a red rag to a bull! I can do anything, you say? Well, I had a couple of days to mull it over, but in the end I decided I'd just wing it. If I thought about it too much, it wouldn't be funny. No, I put my trust in my sense of humour and ability to shock.

As well as Paul and Ian, they had a comedian on the show and the former Mayor of London, Ken Livingstone. I thought, *If you're worried about it becoming depressing, what the hell have you got him on for? As far as I can tell, Livingstone's slightly left of Lenin!*

Anyway, we had a good start to the show – lots of banter between Ian, Paul and me, and almost all of it taking the piss out of me – then eventually we got on to Mrs Thatcher. They had to include it, of course; they just didn't want the controversy regarding her funeral to become some kind of whinge-athon. First of all, I had to read out some reactions to her death from public figures. *Right*, I thought, *here we go*.

The first one was a quote from Gerry Adams: 'Mrs Thatcher did great harm to the British people.'

To which I replied, 'But not as much as all those bombs, eh Gerry?'

Lots of 'ooooooohs' from the audience.

Just to spice it up a bit, I made a fist at the camera and shouted, 'Anytime, Gerry, yer bastard! I'll get you straight in the gizzard!'

That seemed to go down quite well.

The next one was a quote from a fifty-eight-year-old unemployed factory worker who said something like, 'I've been waiting thirty years for that witch to die. Tonight I'm going to have one drink for every year I've been out of work.'

I looked at the screen with incredulity.

'You mean you haven't worked for thirty years? PULL YOUR FINGER OUT, YOU LAZY BASTARD, OR I'LL BLOODY CHIN YER!'

That too went down well. I went totally overboard. Full of righteous indignation!

And now for the funeral. *Right*, I thought, *here goes nothing*. I'm paraphrasing now, but in a fit of pique I came out with the following:

'How can you spend forty million on a funeral? I used to make coffins! You should have asked me.

'After washing her down with carbolic soap, I'd have massaged her body to get rid of the rigor mortis. Then I'd push down on her belly to get rid of any flatulence. Dead bodies are prone to farting, you know, so you've got to get rid of the gas. After that, I'd have pummelled her into the coffin, covered her in glycerine and rose-water to make her comfortable and sweet, poured sawdust round her body, nailed a robe around her made of good old-fashioned roofing felt, screwed the lid down, painted the coffin blue, taken it by horse and cart to Westminster Abbey, and delivered the sermon – and all for fifty quid. That's quite a saving!'

Obviously as I'm saying all this people are actually picturing it, and although I say so myself, the thought of a large bearded man washing Mrs Thatcher's body with carbolic soap, making her fart and then delivering her to Westminster Abbey on a horse and cart is potentially quite an amusing scenario, if also a little controversial! Anyway, we all had a marvellous time and the show was a tremendous success.

A short while later, I had to go to 10 Downing Street to attend a function. I was standing outside, waiting to be allowed in, when all of a sudden I saw the bloody Prime Minister walking towards me.

Oh God, I thought, *Maggie Thatcher's flatulence! What the hell's he going to say? Poor old George Osborne was in tears at the funeral. Imagine what he'd have been like if I'd been doing the service?*

David Cameron was the first to speak.

'On behalf of Her Majesty's Government, Brian,' he said,

'I would like to thank you for turning an extremely depressing day into an extraordinarily happy one.'

Flaming hell, I thought. *I've got away with it!*

'Really?' I said. 'I was half expecting to get a ticking off!'

'No, Brian, it was exactly what everyone needed. It broke the ice.'

'Well, I'm very glad I could be of service.'

'Before we go in, Brian,' asked the PM, 'please say it. Please, Brian, just one more time.'

'Oh alright, love,' I said. 'Just once more.'

I'll tell you what, dear reader, let's all shout it together, shall we – just for old time's sake?

After three then? One, two, three . . .

'GORDON'S ALIVE!'

That's the way to finish a bloody book.

POSTSCRIPT

THE WHITE DRAGON: MAY 2015

Dedicated to the people of Nepal

I started my book three-quarters of the way up Everest and that's where I'm going to end it.

As I was putting the finishing touches to this manuscript, the breaking news of the terrible earthquake in Nepal appeared in the world's headlines. Thousands had been killed in sacred Kathmandu, and the whole Kathmandu valley decimated. The impact of this destructive earthquake, which charted on the Richter scale at 7.8, stretched far beyond Nepal, deep into Tibet and India. A horrible tragedy, beyond comprehension. It has rendered the Nepalese nation confused and terrified, seemingly totally helpless to defend themselves.

But these wonderful people are born survivors. As I write, they are slowly beginning to put their world back in order. They have tremendous courage and I know they will succeed. Thank God the rest of the planet has come to their aid. The rescue teams are performing heroically.

A short distance up the Khumbu valley, beyond Teng-boche Monastery, is Everest Base Camp. In the midst of the earthquake, this was destroyed on a massive scale; something that has never happened before. I am patron of the climber Ellis J. Stewart, who was rescued at the top of the Khumbu icefall at 19,000 feet. A brave lad! But thirteen climbers were killed. In their memory, I would like to convey the nature of the Khumbu glacier without the additional problem of a huge earthquake. This giant glacier has been described as a white dragon.

In 1993, I ascended the menacing place five times – which of course meant that I had to descend it five times also. It is not an experience that I would recommend to the faint-hearted. There are thousands of 'icefalls' throughout the great mountain ranges of the world, but none compares in notoriety to that of the Khumbu. It guards the approach to the Western Cwm and South Col of Everest and is one of the most formidable defences. Higher up the mountain, problems of altitude, short-wave ultraviolet rays, weather and technical difficulties can be met by human skill, but the icefall presents the mountaineer with a sinister game of Russian roulette. It brings into play a term that all mountaineers dread – 'objective danger'. It is a term that implies the kind of peril over which humans, however cautious, however experienced, can exert little control.

The Khumbu icefall is a frozen cascade of ice on a gigantic scale, like a massive waterfall squeezed between the shoulders of Everest and Nuptse. Moving over a steep underlying bed of rock, the surface of the glacier is criss-crossed with open-mouthed crevasses and fallen blocks of ice, some as big as small skyscrapers. Its reliable-looking snow bridges have a nasty habit of disappearing suddenly into the depths. But if you wish to climb Everest by the South Col route, then there is no escaping it. Should you try and climb around its sides, you will almost certainly be killed by enormous avalanches from the walls of Nuptse and Everest's West Ridge. No: there is no way around it! This immense staircase is the only way to the Western Cwm.

The first time I gazed at this terrifying obstacle, it so stirred my imagination that I half-expected the snow and ice to melt and transform itself into a foaming, raging, roaring torrent of water, many times greater than the Niagara Falls. Fortunately, the icefall's colossal strength has been restrained by 'Old King Cold'. But only restrained. It may look totally immobilized, but you can actually hear it, if you try, breathing and moving like a great white dragon. Its frustrations pierce the frosty air. The silence is broken by moaning and groaning as its body quivers with the tons of ice that crush its black innards. With dark passion, it grinds remorselessly downwards in a desire to crush all in its path. At night, when you are alone in your tent at Base Camp, the noises it emits play havoc with your nerves and frequently make sleep impossible.

In morbid curiosity one night I unzipped the flap on my tent, plunged my head into the freezing air and peered in the direction of 'The Dragon'. Under a full moon, the lunar-kissed peaks shone out like vast white giants. What stars! Stars of an autumn night on Mount Everest. The Milky Way, with its gracious curve, enfolded the mountain in its dense tapestry of glowing lights – blue, gold, green, white, yellow and red. Orion and his outriders twinkled in the blanket of the night with their dazzling brightness. Rejoicing and cascading meteorites lent their brief fiery sparks to the heavenly scene, and Everest slept.

Not so 'The Dragon'. With eyes wide with insomnia, it glared hungrily at the tiny figures in the tents at Base Camp. In the ghostly moonlight, the scales of the monster took on a new aspect. The great blocks of ice were transformed into hundreds of ruined castles, their twisted towers and subterranean dungeons reverberating with the wailing voices of all the mortals who had perished there.

I am afraid that the icefall's stunning beauty was wasted on me, for as the ghosts of the night dissolved with the appearance of the dawn, they were replaced by the demons of the day. As the blazing semi-tropical sun poured down through the thin air, the labyrinth of ice turned into a furnace of remorseless heat as it reflected the sun's rays. You are attacked by heat from above and below. There is no respite from this torture, and climbers who, due to unforeseen circumstances, have been forced to descend the glacier in the midday sun emerge at the bottom like over-cooked loaves, their faces red like fire, greatly relieved they have survived the ordeal. They sink in the snow by their tents at Base Camp, and with burned throats and chapped lips they whisper thanks to the Goddess Mother of the Earth for sparing their lives.

The awesome power of the icefall commands respect. Every time the Sherpas prepare to ascend it, they perform a simple ceremony to Everest, which includes burning juniper, throwing rice and chanting the sacred mantra 'Om Mani Padme Hum' ('Hail, Jewel in the Lotus Flower'). Whether the climbers are agnostics, atheists or believers, they join with the Sherpas and sing out the mantra with all their might. The moving sound of the ceremony blends with the roar of the avalanches and the groans of the icefall and the whole scene takes on the epic grandeur of a Wagnerian opera.

Well, dear reader, do you still want to climb Everest? Of course you do!

To cut a long story short, in the autumn (post-monsoon period) of 1993, having ascended the Khumbu glacier and become fully acclimatized, I ascended the next obstacle – the Valley of Silence – to 22,000 feet. I experienced terrible avalanche conditions from Nuptse on my right and the West Ridge of Everest on my left. You can ask the great climbers Steve Bell and Graham Hoyland for confirmation of this! It was absolutely terrifying; at that time the worst conditions ever experienced on Everest. Two days later, I ascended halfway up the Lhotse face at 24,000 feet. I did not use oxygen on this climb; I have never used oxygen. After that, I climbed across the Lhotse face, past the Geneva spur and finally reached the South Col at 26,000 feet. After a night there, I moved up the south-east ridge above the balcony at roughly 27,400 feet.

I could feel the short-wave ultraviolet rays and cosmic rays beginning to affect me; I could almost taste them. I felt a crackle in the air. The radiation seemed to penetrate my lungs. All this while I had Dojie, my faithful Sherpa, by my side. The Sherpas named me 'Barjee', which means 'grandfather'.

Those who seek adventure at these tremendous heights face frightful altitude problems. The brain has a well-known intolerance for lack of oxygen, leaving you at risk of mountain sickness with acute pulmonary and cerebral oedema. My blood now had the consistency of glue. On Everest, I had witnessed several deaths and permanent damage to body and brain as a result of anoxia. I was not using oxygen, remember. By using oxygen, you reduce the height of Everest by several thousand feet. But I feel wearing a mask cuts you off from being at one with the mountain.

This was 9 October 1993: my birthday. I was fifty-seven years old and the oldest man at that time to reach so high. I continued upwards surrounded by steep slopes. Dojie confessed to having cramps and I massaged his arms. Then he massaged mine. There was little wind and I could see the south summit in front of us at 28,750 feet. We were now above 28,000 feet. Reinhold Messner said at this point that he became a lung and nothing more. I felt the same at 28,400 feet by my altitude watch. We were deep in the troposphere and near the frontier of the stratosphere. It is here that you experience the great white veil between life and death. It is sweet, intoxicating! It is at this point that Everest is at its most dangerous. I wanted to sit down and sleep a little. Had Dojie and I done so, we would never have woken up. He produced a flask of tea (God knows from where) and gave me a long drink. Again I remembered what Messner had said to me: 'Brian, we go up Everest to live – not to die.'

Dojie looked at me and said, 'We go home, Barjee.'

I looked at the summit – so close. We might have reached it, but we would not have made it back. The saying goes in the mountains, 'God give me the strength to reach the summit and God give me the strength to stop and turn around.'

Slowly, over the next three days, we reached Base Camp, Namche Bazaar, Lukla and Kathmandu. Five days later, I was back home with my lovely wife and daughter, and our legions of rescued animals.

But to return to the tragedy in Nepal. The Nepalese people love us. Scottish, Irish, Welsh, English: they are devoted to us all. In history, they have fought and died by our side. On the world's greatest mountain, they will sacrifice their lives to protect us. One word can describe the Himalayas: Sherpa.

Dear reader, over the next weeks, months, years, please help the Nepalese people as much as you can. They need us!

ACKNOWLEDGEMENTS

This book is a celebration. Working on it has rekindled wonderful memories of people, places and events from my life, and my enjoyment has been all the greater for having the privilege of meeting and working with the remarkable fellow Yorkshireman James Hogg, a terrific and talented lad.

I have written five books, all in the accepted literary style, but this book's style is different, a new experience for me. I suppose you could describe it as a 'series of conversations, conducted in my log cabin' with James sitting opposite me at my round table. Over the weeks it has been enormous fun to see his face contort with laughter, tears and amusement. We have had a wonderful time together, punctuated each lunchtime by that traditional Yorkshire dish, fish and chips: yummy!

On completing the book, I made a trip to London to meet my publishers at the renowned Pan Macmillan. It was an astonishing, epic experience. In the past when I met my publishers, there would be four or five people in attendance, but not on this occasion. 'Wham, bam, Alakazam': I was gobsmacked. It seemed like there were over a hundred people, cheering and posing for photos and 'selfies' galore! The crowd virtually spilt out of the main reception and onto the street. I was ecstatic with happiness as members of the various departments embraced me like a long-lost prodigal son! Of course I roared 'Gordon's alive!' and wanted to buy everyone a drink.

I am sure, over the next few months, as we work together to edit, sell and promote the book, that I will get to know all of their names by heart!

In the meantime, this book has been a tremendous team effort. I have already mentioned the redoubtable James Hogg, and I would also like to pay special tribute to Ingrid Connell, my editorial director, for her wonderful guidance, kindness and wisdom.

Now for the Roll of Honour: I owe an immense debt of gratitude to Tim Bates, authors' agent at Pollinger; Zennor Compton and Laura Carr in editorial at Pan Macmillan; Philippa McEwan and Dusty Miller in publicity; Fergus Edmondson in marketing; and Stuart Wilson in art – heroes and heroines all! Not forgetting the agents at A.I.M., Nicola Mansfield and Derek Webster; their tolerance of my appalling spelling amazes me.

You must understand that I still live in the nineteenth century, and I am nonplussed by computers, laptops, iPhones and email. I was brought up on 'Press Button A' and 'Press Button B' for your money back! Thank goodness, then, for my friend, agent and egghead Stephen Gittins, a true 'Sir Galahad' if ever there was one. Many thanks also to Steve Knight for gathering together so many photographs for me.

As I write this, I can see my two white pigeons outside; surely they will come in handy if my new-found friends at Pan Macmillan require additional pages?

Pan Macmillan, I thank you for your wonderful inspiration. 'GO FOR IT, AND DON'T LET THE BASTARDS GRIND YOU DOWN!'

PICTURE ACKNOWLEDGEMENTS

All photographs are from the author's own collection,
with the exception of the following:

Page v © Steve Knight
Page 3 top © *South Yorkshire Times*
Page 4 bottom © Ochs / Moviepix / Getty Images
Page 5 © Donald Cooper / Rex Shutterstock
Page 6 bottom and page 9 top © BBC
Page 7 bottom © Advertising Archives
Page 8 all photos by Franco Vitale © Fòrum
Page 10 top and bottom © ITV / Rex Shutterstock
Page 11 bottom © Phillip Jackson / *Daily Mail* / Rex Shutterstock
Page 12 top © Moviestore Collection / Rex Shutterstock
Page 12 bottom left © Universal / Everett Collection / Rex Shutterstock
Page 13 middle © Stephen Macmillan
Page 14 bottom © Yui Mok / PA Archive / PA Images
Page 15 top © Steve Bell

INDEX